BECAUSE THE
TIME ɪs NEAR

JOHN MACARTHUR
Explains the Book of Revelation

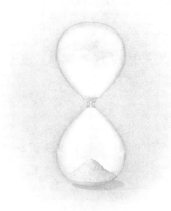

BECAUSE THE TIME IS NEAR

MOODY PUBLISHERS

CHICAGO

All Scripture quotations, unless otherwise indicated, are taken from the *New American Standard Bible*®, Copyright ©1960, 1962, 1963, 1968, 1971, 1972, 1973, 1975, 1977, 1995 by The Lockman Foundation. Used by permission. (www.Lockman.org)
Scripture quotations marked KJV are taken from the King James Version.
Scripture quotations marked NKJV are taken from the *New King James Version*. Copyright © 1982 by Thomas Nelson, Inc. Used by permission. All rights reserved.

Cover design: John Hamilton | johnhamiltondesign.com
Cover image: Matthias Kulka | corbis
Interior Design: Smartt Guys
Editor: Jim Vincent

ISBN: 0-8024-0728-5
ISBN-13: 978-0-8024-0728-3

Library of Congress Cataloging-in-Publication Data

MacArthur, John, 1939-
 Because the time is near : John MacArthur explains the book of Revelation.
 p. cm.
 Includes bibliographical references (p.   ).
 ISBN 978-0-8024-0728-3
 1. Bible. N.T. Revelation—Commentaries. I. Title.

BS2825.53.M33 2007
228'.077—dc22

2006101908

We hope you enjoy this book from Moody Publishers. Our goal is to provide high-quality, thought-provoking books and products that connect truth to your real needs and challenges. For more information on other books and products written and produced from a biblical perspective, go to www.moodypublishers.com or write to:

Moody Publishers
820 N. LaSalle Boulevard
Chicago, IL 60610

1 3 5 7 9 10 8 6 4 2

Printed in the United States of America

Contents

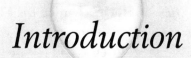

Introduction

The late British prime minister Winston Churchill once described the former Soviet Union as "a riddle wrapped in a mystery inside an enigma." Many Christians view the book of Revelation in much the same way. Bewildered by its mystifying symbolism and striking imagery, many believers and church leaders avoid serious study of the book. Such shortsightedness deprives believers of the blessings the book promises to those who diligently read it (1:3; 22:7).

Those who ignore Revelation miss out on a rich treasure of divine truth. Revelation takes a high view of God's inspired Word. It claims divine inspiration for itself (1:2), and 278 of its 404 verses allude to the Old Testament Scriptures. Revelation reveals God the Father in all His glory and majesty, describing Him as:

- holy (4:8)
- true (6:10)
- omnipotent (4:11)
- wise (7:12)

- sovereign (4:11)
- eternal (4:10)

Revelation also details the depths of man's sinfulness. Despite experiencing the final outpouring of God's devastating judgment on unbelieving humanity, people will nevertheless harden their hearts and refuse to repent. Scripture contains no clearer summary of redemption than Revelation 1:5: "Jesus Christ . . . loves us and released us from our sins by His blood."

Some who study Revelation primarily seek evidence to support their own views regarding the end times. However, Revelation teaches much more than prophecy. While the book is a rich source of truth about the end times, Revelation also portrays Christ's ultimate victory over Satan, depicts the final political setup of the world, and describes the career of the final Antichrist. It also discusses the rapture of the church (3:10) and the seven-year time of tribulation. It explains the three and one-half years of the great tribulation (7:14), the second coming of Christ, the climactic battle of Armageddon, the thousand-year earthly kingdom of Jesus Christ, the final great white throne judgment, the final state of the unbelievers in hell (the lake of fire), and the redeemed in the new heaven and new earth.

But the book of Revelation is preeminently "the "Revelation of Jesus Christ" (1:1). It describes Jesus by many titles. (See next page.)

Revelation also affirms the full deity of Jesus Christ. He possesses the attributes of God, including sovereignty (1:5), eternity (1:17–18), and the right to judge who lives and who dies (1:18; 2:23). He also receives worship (5:13) and rules from God's throne (22:1, 3). Revelation affirms His equality of essence with God the Father by applying Old Testament passages that describe God to Jesus Christ.

THE EQUALITY OF GOD THE FATHER AND JESUS CHRIST

GOD THE FATHER IN THE OT	CHRIST IN REVELATION
Deuteronomy 10:17	19:16
Proverbs 3:12	3:19
Daniel 7:9	1:14
Isaiah 44:6	1:17; 22:12–13

THE NAMES OF JESUS IN REVELATION
....

- *The faithful witness (1:5)*
- *The firstborn of the dead (1:5)*
- *The ruler of the kings of the earth (1:5)*
- *The Alpha and the Omega (1:8; 21:6)*
- *The first and the last (1:17)*
- *The living One (1:18)*
- *The One who holds the seven stars in His right hand, the One who walks among the seven golden lampstands (2:1)*
- *The One who has the sharp two-edged sword (2:12)*
- *The Son of God (2:18)*
- *The One "who has eyes like a flame of fire, and ... feet ... like burnished bronze" (2:18)*
- *The One "who has the seven Spirits of God and the seven stars" (3:1)*
- *The One "who is holy, who is true" (3:7)*
- *The holder of "the key of David, who opens and no one will shut, and who shuts and no one opens" (3:7)*
- *The Amen, the faithful and true Witness (3:14)*
- *The Beginning of the creation of God (3:14)*
- *The Lion that is from the tribe of Judah (5:5)*
- *The Root of David (5:5)*
- *The Lamb of God (5:6; 6:1; 7:9–10; 8:1 and others)*
- *The "Lord, holy and true" (6:10)*
- *The One who "is called Faithful and True" (19:11)*
- *The Word of God (19:13)*
- *King of kings, and Lord of lords (19:16)*
- *Christ (Messiah), ruling on earth with His glorified saints (20:6)*
- *The root and the descendant of David, the bright morning star (22:16)*

Far from being a mysterious, incomprehensible book, Revelation's purpose is to reveal truth. The very title in the first verse, "The Revelation of Jesus Christ," introduces this fact. Even the Greek word translated "Revelation" can be translated "an uncovering" or "a disclosure." It is used in the New Testament to speak of revealing spiritual truth (Romans 16:25),

the revealing of the sons of God (Romans 8:19), and of Christ's manifestation at both His first (Luke 2:32) and second (2 Thessalonians 1:7; 1 Peter
1:7) comings. In each case, the word describes something or someone formerly hidden, but now made visible.

Revelation unveils truths about Jesus Christ, clarifying features of
prophecy only hinted at in other Bible books. This clarity is sometimes
obscured by a rejection of literal interpretation in favor of an allegorical
or spiritual approach. Such approaches attempt to place Revelation's
account in the past or present rather than the future. But once the plain
meaning of the text is denied, readers are left to their own imagination,
leaving the truths of this book lost in a maze of human inventions. As we
will see through our study, a literal approach provides the most accurate
handling of this inspired portion of Scripture.

THE AUTHOR

Four times in Revelation the author identifies himself as John (1:1, 4, 9;
22:8). Until the third century, the early church unanimously affirmed this
John as the son of Zebedee, one of the twelve apostles and author of the
Gospel According to John and the epistles of John.

Writing early in the second century (ca. A.D. 135), Justin Martyr
declared, "There was a certain man with us, whose name was John, one of
the apostles of Christ, who prophesied, by a revelation that was made to
him, that those who believed in our Christ would dwell a thousand years
in Jerusalem; and that thereafter the general, and, in short, the eternal resurrection and judgment of all men would likewise take place."[1] Since
Justin lived in Ephesus, one of the seven churches mentioned in
Revelation, his testimony is especially significant.

Dating from about the same time as Justin (ca. A.D. 100–150) is the
gnostic writing known as the Apocryphon of John. It cites Revelation
1:19, attributing it to John the brother of James and son of Zebedee.[2]

Another second-century affirmation that the apostle John penned
Revelation comes from Irenaeus. He introduced a string of quotations
from Revelation with the statement, "John also, the Lord's disciple, when

beholding the sacerdotal and glorious advent of His kingdom, says in the Apocalypse."[3] Irenaeus's words are valuable because he was a native of Smyrna, another of the seven churches John addressed in Revelation. Interestingly, as a boy Irenaeus had been a disciple of Polycarp, who in turn had been a disciple of the apostle John.

Also writing in the second century, Clement of Alexandria noted that it was John the apostle who had been in exile on Patmos.[4] Obviously, it was the John who had been exiled to Patmos who penned Revelation (1:9).

Other early testimony to the apostle John's authorship of Revelation comes from Tertullian (Against Marcion, 3.24), Origen (De Principiis, 1.2.10; 1.2.7), Hippolytus (Treatise on Christ and Antichrist, 36), and Victorinus, author of a third-century commentary on Revelation (in his comments on Revelation 10:3).

Such strong, early, and consistent testimony to the apostle John's authorship affirms the book's internal claims and clearly confirms his hand in its writing.

DATE

Two main alternatives have been proposed for the date of Revelation: during either the reign of Nero (ca. A.D. 68) or of Domitian (ca. A.D. 96). The earlier date is held primarily by some who adopt the preterist interpretation of Revelation. It is based largely on attempts to relegate its prophetic fulfillment entirely to the period before the destruction of Jerusalem in A.D. 70. Those who hold to the early date see in Jerusalem's destruction the prophesied second coming of Jesus Christ in its first phase. However, external evidence for this earlier date is almost nonexistent.

On the other hand, the view that the apostle John penned Revelation near the end of Domitian's reign was widely held in the early church. The second-century church father Irenaeus wrote, "We will not, however, incur the risk of pronouncing positively as to the name of Antichrist; for if it were necessary that his name should be distinctly revealed in this present time, it would have been announced by him who beheld the apocalyptic vision [the book of Revelation]. For that was seen not very long time since, but almost in our day, towards the end of Domitian's reign."[5] The church fathers Clement of Alexandria, Origen, Victorinus, Eusebius, and Jerome also affirm that Revelation was written during Domitian's reign The testimony of the early church that Revelation was written during Domitian's reign is difficult to explain if it had been written at an earlier date.

Revelation was written during a time when the church was undergoing persecution. John had been exiled to Patmos, at least one believer had already suffered martyrdom (2:13), and more persecution loomed on the horizon (2:10). The condition of the seven churches to whom John addressed Revelation also argues for the later date. As seen in Ephesians, Colossians, and 1 and 2 Timothy, those churches were spiritually healthy as of the mid-sixties, when Paul last served in that region. Yet by the time Revelation was written, those churches had suffered serious spiritual decline. Such a decline would have taken longer than the brief period between the end of Paul's ministry in Asia Minor and the end of Nero's reign.

A final reason for preferring the late (A.D. 95–96) date for Revelation is the timing of John's arrival in Asia Minor. According to tradition, John did not leave Palestine for Asia Minor until the time of the Jewish revolt against Rome (A.D. 66–70). Placing the writing of Revelation during Nero's reign would not allow sufficient time for John's ministry to have reached the point where the Romans would have felt the need to exile him.

The weight of the evidence clearly favors a date for the writing of Revelation in the midnineties, near the end of Domitian's reign. This is critically important, because it eliminates the possibility that the prophecies in Revelation were fulfilled in the destruction of Jerusalem in A.D. 70.

INTERPRETATION

Four main perspectives have been taken to interpret Revelation. The *preterist approach* views Revelation not as future prophecy, but as a historical record of events in the first-century Roman Empire. The preterist view ignores the book's own claims to be a prophecy (1:3; 22:7, 10, 18–19). The second coming of Christ described in chapter 19 has obviously not yet occurred. The preterist view requires that one see the words about Christ's second coming as fulfilled in the destruction of the temple in A.D. 70, even though He did not appear on that occasion.

The *historicist approach* portrays Revelation as a record of the sweep of church history from apostolic times to the present. Historicist interpreters often resort to allegorizing the text in order to find in it the various historical events they believe it depicts. This subjective approach has given rise to a complexity of conflicting interpretations of the actual historical events in Revelation.

The *idealist approach* views Revelation as the timeless struggle between good and evil that is played out in every age. According to this view Revelation is neither historical record nor predictive prophecy. If carried to its logical conclusion, this view disconnects Revelation from any reality with actual historical events. The book is reduced to a collection of myths designed to convey spiritual truth.

THE FOUR MAIN VIEWS ON REVELATION

INTERPRETIVE SCHOOL	BASIC APPROACH TO REVELATION
Preterist	Believe that the events of Revelation were fulfilled beginning in A.D. 70 with the destruction of Jerusalem by the Romans.
Historicist	View the book of Revelation as an overview of church history, describing various times of persecution and tribulation.
Idealist	Interpret Revelation symbolically, as a nonliteral depiction of the battle between God and the satanic forces of evil.
Futurist	Understand Revelation 4–22 as a prophetic account of actual future events, specifically focused on the end of this age. This view is the natural result of a straightforward reading of the book.

The *futurist approach* sees chapters 4–22 as predictions of people and events yet to come in the future. Only this approach allows Revelation to be interpreted following the same literal method used throughout the rest of Scripture. The other three approaches are frequently forced to resort to allegorizing or spiritualizing the text to sustain their interpretations. The futurist approach provides justice to Revelation's claim as prophecy.

Other approaches leave the meaning of Revelation to human opinion. The futurist approach takes the book's meaning as God gave it. In studying Revelation, we will take this straightforward view, accepting what the words say.

As noted on page 332, the book of Revelation deserves immediate proclamation because the end is near. As the angel told John in the final chapter of Revelation, "Do not seal up the words of the prophecy of this book, for the time is near." (22:10). And so we study Christ's future return—a return Jesus Himself says is imminent (22: 7, 12, 20).

PART

I

"The Things Which You Have Seen" (1:1–20)

REVELATION AS A TIMELINE OF FUTURE EVENTS

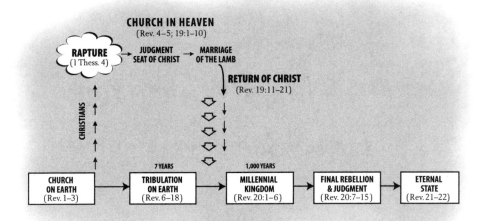

Adapted from Paul Benware, *Understanding End Times Prophecy* (Chicago, Moody, 2006), 201

I

The Prologue of
CHRIST'S
Revelation
(1:1–8)

Many people are fascinated with the future. They faithfully read their horoscopes, seek out tarot-card readers, have their palms read, or consult psychics. All such attempts to discern the future, however, are in vain. God is the only One who knows and declares the future (Isaiah 44:7; 45:21; 46:9–10). Only in Scripture can truth about the future be found. The Old and New Testament writings provide glimpses of the future. The book of Revelation provides the most detailed look into the future in all of Scripture, unveiling the future history of the world, with the return of Christ and His glorious kingdom.

John begins his Revelation in 1:1–8 with two major sections. First, he presents the specific characteristics of this unique book. Second, he provides a preview of the second coming of Christ.

THE PROCLAMATION OF REVELATION'S
SPECIFIC CHRACTERISTICS (1:1–6)

Many people are confused by the book of Revelation, viewing it as a bizarre mystery. However, far from hiding the truth, the book of Revelation reveals it. It tells how everything ends. Just as the creation account was written in clear detail, God has given a detailed record of the ending. Verses 1–6 provide eleven specific characteristics that reveal the uniqueness of Revelation.

1. Its Essential Nature
The Revelation (1:1a)

The Greek word for "revelation" appears eighteen times in the New Testament. In Luke 2:32, Simeon praised God for the infant Jesus, describing Him as "a Light of revelation to the Gentiles, and the glory of Your people Israel." Simeon exulted that the Messiah had been made visible to men. Paul spoke in Romans 8:19 of the transformation of believers in glory as "the revealing of the sons of God." Both Paul (1 Corinthians 1:7) and Peter (1 Peter 1:7) used the word to refer to the revelation of Christ at His second coming.

Revelation shares several significant divine truths. It warns the church of the danger of sin and instructs it about the need for holiness. It reveals the strength Christ and that believers have to overcome Satan. It reveals the glory and majesty of God and depicts the reverent worship that constantly attends His throne. The book of Revelation reveals the end of human history, including the final political setup of the world, the career of Antichrist, and the final battle of Armageddon. It reveals the coming glory of Christ's earthly reign during the millennial kingdom, the great white throne judgment, and depicts the eternal joy of the new heaven and the new earth. It reveals the ultimate victory of Jesus Christ over all human and demonic opposition.

Yet overarching all those features, Revelation communicates the majesty and glory of the Lord Jesus Christ. It describes in detail the events associated with His second coming, revealing His glory that will blaze forth as unmistakably as lightning flashing in a dark sky (Matthew 24:27).

2. Its Central Theme
of Jesus Christ (1:1b)

While all Scripture is revelation from God (2 Timothy 3:16), the book of Revelation is *of* Jesus Christ. While this book is certainly revelation *from* Christ (22:16), it is also the revelation *about* Him.

Even a cursory glance through the book of Revelation reveals that Jesus Christ is its main theme. He is "the faithful witness" (1:5); "the first-born of the dead" (1:5); "the ruler of the kings of the earth" (1:5); "the Alpha and the Omega" (1:8; 21:6); the one "who is and who was and who is to come" (1:8); and "the Almighty" (1:8). Eight references can be found in just the first chapter! (See additional references in 1:17, 18.) The book of Revelation reveals the majesty and glory of the Lord Jesus Christ in song, poetry, symbolism, and prophecy. In it the heavens are opened and its readers see, as did Stephen (Acts 7:56), visions of the risen, glorified Son of God.

3. Its Divine Source
which God gave Him (1:1c)

The book of Revelation is the Father's gift to the Son in a deep and marvelous sense. As a reward for His perfect, humble, faithful, holy service, the Father promised to exalt the Son:

> **Christ Jesus, . . . humbled Himself by becoming obedient to the point of death, even death on a cross. For this reason also God highly exalted Him, and bestowed on Him the name which is above every name, so that at the name of Jesus every knee will bow, of those who are in heaven and on earth and under the earth, and that every tongue will confess that Jesus Christ is Lord, to the glory of God the Father. (Philippians 2:5, 8–11)**

Christ's exaltation, promised in the last three verses of that passage, is described in detail throughout Revelation. The book of Revelation chronicles the Son's inheritance from the Father, ending in the showing of the full glory of Christ.

4. Its Human Recipients
to show to His bond-servants (1:1d)

To further exalt and glorify His Son, the Father has graciously granted to a special group of people the privilege of understanding this book. John describes those people as Christ's "bond-servants," from a Greek word literally meaning "slave." The bond-servant was a special type of slave, one who served out of love and devotion to his master (cf. Exodus 21:5–6). This is why unbelievers find the book of Revelation such a mystery. It was not intended for them. It was given by the Father to the Son to show to those who willingly serve Him. Those who refuse to acknowledge Jesus Christ as Lord cannot expect to understand this book. "A natural man," explains Paul, "does not accept the things of the Spirit of God, for they are foolishness to him; and he cannot understand them, because they are spiritually appraised" (1 Corinthians 2:14). The unbelieving skeptic finds Revelation as nothing but confusion. Yet for willing bond-servants of Jesus Christ, this book unveils prophetic truth about the future of the world.

5. Its Prophetic Character
the things which must soon take place; (1:1e)

Revelation's emphasis on future events sets it apart from all other New Testament books. The first four books of the New Testament are about the past, especially the life, death, and resurrection of Jesus Christ; the next twenty-two are about the present, especially the life of the church. Revelation, though it contains some information about the past (Revelation 1) and the present (Revelation 2–3), focuses on the future.

A dual emphasis can be found in Revelation. One emphasis is the portrayal of Christ in His future glory with the blessedness of the saints. The second emphasis is the judgment of unbelievers to eternal punishment. The profound and compelling truths in the book of Revelation result in both sorrow and joy.

Believers are not to try to set the "times or epochs which the Father has fixed by His own authority" (Acts 1:7). Instead, they are to follow the Lord's warning to "be on the alert, for you do not know which day your Lord is coming" (Matthew 24:42). The knowledge that the events depicted in the book of Revelation are soon to take place should motivate Christians to live holy, obedient lives (2 Peter 3:14).

6. *Its Supernatural Delivery*
and He sent and communicated it by His angel (1:1*f*)

Revelation is unique in the New Testament because it is the only book sent and communicated by angels. As Jesus declared, "I, Jesus, have sent My angel to testify to you these things for the churches" (22:16). Angels were involved in the giving of the book of Revelation to John, just as they were in the giving of the Law to Moses (Acts 7:53; Galatians 3:19; Hebrew 2:2). Not only were angels involved in transmitting the book of Revelation to John, but they also play a prominent role in the scenes it portrays. Angels appear in every chapter of Revelation except 4 and 13. The words "angel" or "angels" are used seventy-one times in the book of Revelation—more than in any other book in the Bible. In fact, one out of every four uses in Scripture of those words is in the book of Revelation. This book thus serves as an important source of information on the ministry of angels.

7. *Its Human Author*
to His bond-servant John, who testified to the word of God and to the testimony of Jesus Christ, even to all that he saw. (1:1*g*–2)

The human agent to whom the angelic messengers communicated the book of Revelation is here identified as "His bond-servant John." This was

John the apostle, the son of Zebedee and brother of James. John wrote the book of Revelation while in exile on the island of Patmos (1:9).

The enormity of the visions John received on that barren island staggered him. Throughout his gospel, John never directly referred to himself. Yet here he bookends his vision with the statement, "I, John" (1:9; 22:8)— an exclamation that expressed his amazement that he was receiving such overwhelming visions.

As he had loyally testified to the first coming of Christ (John 19:35; 21:24; 1 John 1:2; 4:14), so John faithfully proclaimed all that he saw concerning His second coming. The word of God expressed in the book of Revelation is the testimony about the coming glory of Christ given to His church and recorded by His faithful witness, John.

8. Its Promised Blessing
Blessed is he who reads and those who hear the words of the prophecy, and heed the things which are written in it; (1:3a)

The book of Revelation begins and ends with promises of blessing to those who read and obey it. In total, the book contains seven promises of blessing. (See "The Seven Beatitudes of Revelation.")

Reading, hearing, and obeying the truths taught in the book of Revelation are to be a way of life for believers. Revelation is God's final word to man, marking the completion of the canon of Scripture (22:18–19), and its scope encompasses the entire future of redemptive history (1:19). It is imperative that believers follow the truths it contains.

9. Its Compelling Urgency
for the time is near. (1:3b)

This phrase restates the truth taught in verse one. The Greek word for *time* here does not refer to time on a clock or calendar, but to seasons or eras. The next great era of God's redemptive history is near. The imminent return of Christ has always been the church's hope. Jesus commanded His followers to watch expectantly for His return (Luke 12:35–40). The apostles Paul, Peter, James, and John all wrote that the day of His return is near. (See, for example, Romans 13:12, 1 Peter 4:7; James 5:7–9; 1 John 2:18.)

THE SEVEN BEATITUDES OF REVELATION

1. *Blessed is he*

who reads and those who hear the words of the prophecy, and heed the things which are written in it. (1:3a)

2. *"Blessed are the dead*

who die in the Lord from now on!" "Yes," says the Spirit, "so that they may rest from their labors, for their deeds follow with them." (14:13)

3. *"Behold, I am coming like a thief. Blessed is the one*

who stays awake and keeps his clothes, so that he will not walk about naked and men will not see his shame." (16:15)

4. *"Blessed are those*

who are invited to the marriage supper of the Lamb." (19:9)

5. *Blessed and holy is the one*

who has a part in the first resurrection. (20:6)

6. *"Blessed is he*

who heeds the words of the prophecy of this book." (22:7)

7. *Blessed are those*

who wash their robes, so that they may have the right to the tree of life, and may enter by the gates into the city. (22:14)

Despite the skepticism of the scoffers, who demand, "Where is the promise of His coming? For ever since the fathers fell asleep, all continues just as it was from the beginning of creation" (2 Peter 3:4), the Lord Jesus Christ will return. And His return is near.

10. Its Trinitarian Benediction

John to the seven churches that are in Asia: Grace to you and peace, from Him who is and who was and who is to come, and from the seven Spirits who are before His throne, and from Jesus Christ, the faithful witness, the firstborn of the dead, and the ruler of the kings of the earth. (1:4–5a)

Ancient letters named their writers at the beginning. John identifies himself as the author and names the seven churches in 1:11 as the recipients. "Grace to you and peace" was a standard greeting in New Testament letters, used here by John with an added Trinitarian conclusion.

The phrase "Him who is and who was and who is to come" identifies the first Person of the Trinity, God the Father, described here in humanlike terms. The eternal Father God is the source of all the blessings of salvation, all grace, and all peace.

"The seven Spirits before His throne" refers to the Holy Spirit. The number seven depicts Him in His fullness (5:6; Isaiah 11:2; Zechariah 4:1–10). Grace and peace also flow from "Jesus Christ." It is only fitting that John mentions Christ last, and gives a fuller description of Him, since He is the theme of Revelation.

Jesus is labeled as a "faithful witness," One who always speaks and represents the truth. Next, He is "the firstborn of the dead." Of all who have ever been or ever will be resurrected, He is the premier one. Third, He is "the ruler of the kings of the earth." He is Lord, who according to the Father's plan and the Spirit's work, grants believers His royal blessing of grace and peace.

11. Its Exalted Doxology

To Him who loves us and released us from our sins by His blood—and He has made us to be a kingdom, priests to His God and Father—to Him be the glory and the dominion forever and ever. Amen. (1:5b–6)

The work of Christ on behalf of believers caused John to burst forth in inspired praise to Him. In the present, Christ loves believers with an unbreakable love (Romans 8:35–39). The greatest expression of that love came when He released us from our sins by His blood—a reference to the atonement provided by His sacrificial death on the cross on our behalf.

John concludes his doxology with the only proper response in light of the magnitude of the blessings Christ has given believers: "To Him be the glory and the dominion forever and ever. Amen." This is to be the response of all who read Revelation with this future glory in mind.

THE PREVIEW OF
CHRIST'S SECOND COMING (1:7–8)

The book of Revelation is the ultimate action thriller. Anyone who loves a great novel will certainly love this book. It contains drama, suspense, mystery, and horror. It tells of rebellion, unprecedented economic collapse, and the ultimate war of human history. Revelation is a book of astounding drama and horror, but also of hope and joy. It culminates with a happy ending, as sin and death are banished forever (21:4; 22:3).

In verses 7–8, John provides his readers with a preview of what will come later in the Revelation. In doing so, he reveals the theme of the book as the second coming of Christ. Five truths about His second coming are communicated for our understanding:

1. The Necessity of the Second Coming
Behold, He is coming (1:7a)

Verse 7 begins the first great prophetic oracle of Revelation. "Behold" is intended to arouse the mind and heart to consider what follows. This is the first of its twenty-five uses in Revelation—a book filled with startling truths that demand careful attention.

The "Coming One" was a title for Christ. This Greek word (*Erchomai*) is used nine times in Revelation to refer to Jesus Christ; seven times by our Lord in reference to Himself. Thus, the theme of the book of Revelation is the Coming One, the Lord Jesus Christ.

Despite the scoffers who deny the second coming (2 Peter 3:3–4), the

Bible repeatedly affirms that Jesus will return. That truth appears in more than five hundred verses throughout the Bible. It has been estimated that one out of every twenty-five verses in the New Testament refers to the second coming. Jesus repeatedly spoke of His return (Matthew 16:27; 24–25; 26:64; Mark 8:38; Luke 9:26) and warned believers to be ready for it (Mathew 24:42, 44; 25:13; Luke 12:40; 21:34–36). The return of the Lord Jesus Christ to this earth is a central theme in Scripture.

The hope that Christ will one day return and take believers to heaven to live forever in His presence provides hope and comfort for those who know Him (John 14:1–3; 1 Thessalonians 4:17–18).

2. The Glory of the Second Coming
with the clouds, (1:7*b*)

Clouds in Scripture frequently symbolize God's presence. A cloud was used as the visible manifestation of God's presence with Israel in the wilderness (Exodus 13:21–22; 16:10; Numbers 10:34). At Mount Sinai, "a thick cloud upon the mountain" symbolized God's presence (Exodus 19:16). When the Lord communicated with Moses at the Tent of Meeting, "the pillar of cloud would descend and stand at the entrance of the tent; and the Lord would speak with Moses" (Exodus 33:9). Both the tabernacle (Exodus 40:34–38) and the temple (1 Kings 8:10–12) were filled with a cloud symbolizing God's glory at their dedications. Jesus ascended to heaven on a cloud (Acts 1:9). Believers will ascend with clouds at the rapture (1 Thessalonians 4:17), and Christ will return with clouds (cf. Daniel 7:13; Matthew 24:30).

The clouds picture Christ's descent from heaven. More significant, they symbolize the brilliant light that accompanies God's presence. The appearance of the Christ and the brilliance of innumerable angels and the redeemed who accompany Him will be both an indescribable and terrifying event.

3. The Scope of the Second Coming
and every eye will see Him, even those who pierced Him; and all the tribes of the earth will mourn over Him. (1:7c)

During the incarnation, Christ's glory was hidden. Only Peter, James, and John caught a glimpse of it at the transfiguration. At His second coming, *every* eye will see Him. His glory will be obvious to all humanity.

John divides those who will see the second coming into two groups. "Those who pierced Him" does not refer to the Roman soldiers involved in Christ's crucifixion but to the unbelieving Jews who instigated His death. In Zechariah 12:10 God says, "I will pour out on the house of David and on the inhabitants of Jerusalem, the Spirit of grace and of supplication, so that they will look on Me whom they have pierced; and they will mourn for Him, as one mourns for an only son, and they will weep bitterly over Him like the bitter weeping over a firstborn." Peter affirmed that the Jewish people were responsible for Christ's execution, boldly declaring

> Men of Israel, listen to these words: Jesus the Nazarene, a man attested to you by God with miracles and wonders and signs which God performed through Him in your midst, just as you yourselves know—this Man, delivered over by the predetermined plan and foreknowledge of God, you nailed to a cross by the hands of godless men and put Him to death. (Acts 2:22–23; cf. 3:14–15)

Israel's mourning, noted in Zechariah 12:10, will be that of genuine repentance. Many Jews will be saved during the tribulation, both the 144,000 and their converts. But for many others, the second coming will be the time of their salvation. It will be "in that day [that] a fountain will be opened for the house of David and for the inhabitants of Jerusalem, for sin and for impurity" (Zechariah 13:1).

John describes the second group as "all the tribes of the earth," a reference to the unbelieving Gentile nations. Like the Jewish people, they will also mourn over Christ. Some of that mourning may relate to the repentance of those who are saved at that time (7:9–10, 14). But unlike the Jewish nation, the Gentiles' mourning will not generally result from genuine repentance. "Mourn" is from *koptō*, which literally means "to cut." The word became associated with mourning due to the pagans' practice of cutting themselves when in extreme grief or despair. First Kings 18:28 records that the frenzied, panicked prophets of Baal "cut themselves according to their custom with swords and lances until the blood gushed out on them" in a desperate attempt to get their god's attention. The Israelites were strictly forbidden to engage in such pagan rituals (Leviticus 19:28; Deuteronomy 14:1).

The Gentiles' mourning will mostly be prompted by terror, not repentance. They will mourn not for the Christ they rejected, but over their doom. (9:21).

4. The Response to the Second Coming
So it is to be. Amen. (1:7*d*)

Experiencing the response of both believers and unbelievers to Christ's second coming, John includes his own response. Using the strongest words of affirmation both in Greek and Hebrew, John pleads for the Lord Jesus Christ to return before noting words from Christ's own voice.

5. The Certainty of the Second Coming
I am the Alpha and the Omega," says the Lord God, "who is and who was and who is to come, the Almighty" (1:8).

In this verse the Lord God puts His signature on the prophecy of the second coming recorded in the previous verse. He calls Himself "the Alpha and the Omega," emphasizing His perfect knowledge. Alpha and Omega are the first and final letters in the Greek alphabet. Second, as the one "who is and who was and who is to come," God is forever present; He is not confined by time or space. His promise that He will come settles the issue. Third, "the Almighty" affirms His perfect power. Nothing can stop Him from carrying out His will.

These terms also imply that He is the creator and consummation of all history. He is *the Beginning and the End* (cf. 22:13).

It has been noted that:

- Jesus came the first time in humiliation. He will return in exaltation.
- He came the first time to serve. He will return to be served.
- He came the first time as the suffering servant. He will return as the conquering king.

The challenge the book of Revelation makes to every person is to be ready for His return.

Only those "who have loved His appearing" (2 Timothy 4:8), who love Him and acknowledge Him as the rightful king, will enjoy the blessings of His kingdom.

2

The Preview of
CHRIST'S
Return
(1:9–20)

In the early second century, Pliny called Christianity a "depraved and extravagant superstition" and complained that "the contagion of this superstition [Christianity] has spread not only in the cities, but in the villages and rural districts as well."[1] The Roman historian Tacitus, a contemporary of Pliny, described Christians as "a class hated for their abominations"[2]

Politically, Romans viewed Christians as disloyal because they refused to acknowledge Caesar as the supreme authority. Religiously, Christians were denounced as atheists because they rejected the Roman gods and worshiped an invisible God instead of idols. Socially, Christians were often despised, since many came from the lower classes of society (cf. 1 Corinthians 1:26). The Christian teaching that all people are equal (Galatians 3:28; Colossians 3:11) threatened to undermine the cultural structure of the affluent Romans and intiated concerns of a slave revolt.

In that superstitious age many Romans feared that natural disasters resulted from the neglect of the pagan gods. The third-century church leader Tertullian noted, "If the Tiber reaches the walls, if the Nile does not rise to the fields, if the sky doesn't move or the earth does, if there is famine, if there is plague, the cry is at once, 'Christians to the lion!'"[3] .

During the first few decades after the death of Christ, the Roman government considered Christianity as a sect of Judaism (Acts 18:12–16). Eventually, Christianity was recognized by the Romans as a religion distinct from Judaism. That identified Christians as worshipers of an illegal religion (Judaism being a *religio licita*, or legal religion). Yet there was no official persecution by the Roman authorities until the time of Nero. Seeking to divert public suspicion that he had caused the great fire in Rome (July 19, A.D. 64), Nero blamed the Christians for it. As a result, many Christians were executed at Rome, soon followed by empire-wide persecution.

Thirty years later, Domitian instigated an official persecution of Christians. It extended to the province of Asia (modern Turkey) during the time the apostle John had been exiled to the island of Patmos. The persecuted believers John wrote to in Revelation desperately needed encouragement. The other apostles were dead, and John had been banished to Patmos.

John's readers took comfort in the fact that Christ will one day return in glory to defeat His enemies. Yet the vision of Jesus Christ that begins the book does not describe Jesus in His future glory, but depicts Him in the present as the glorified Lord of the church. In spite of all disappointment, the Lord had not abandoned His people or His promises. This powerful vision of Christ's present ministry to them must have provided great hope to the wondering and suffering churches to whom John wrote.

The Setting of the Vision (1:9–11)

I, John, your brother and fellow partaker in the tribulation and kingdom and perseverance which are in Jesus, was on the island called Patmos because of the word of God and the testimony of Jesus. I was in the Spirit on the Lord's day, and I heard behind me a loud voice like the sound of a trumpet, saying, "Write in a book what you see, and send it to the seven churches: to Ephesus and to Smyrna and to Pergamum and to Thyatira and to Sardis and to Philadelphia and to Laodicea." (1:9–11)

This is the third time in the first nine verses that John refers to himself by name (1:1, 4). John was astounded that despite his unworthiness, he had the incomparable privilege of receiving this monumental vision.

John was an apostle, a member of the inner circle of the Twelve with Peter and James, and the writer of a gospel and three epistles. Yet he humbly identified himself simply as "your brother." He did not write to impress, but as an eyewitness to the revelation of Christ that begins to unfold with this vision.

John also humbly identified with his readers by describing himself as their "fellow partaker." Like them, John was suffering severe persecution for the cause of Christ, having been exiled as a common criminal. He could identify with other suffering believers. John was also part of the same kingdom as his readers—the redeemed community of those following the risen Christ. Finally, John identified with his readers in the area of perseverance. The Greek word for "perseverance" in verse 9 literally meant "to remain under," that is, to patiently endure difficulties without giving up.

When he received this vision, John was in exile on the island called Patmos, a barren, volcanic island in the Aegean Sea. At its extremities it is about ten miles long and six miles wide, located forty miles offshore from modern-day Turkey. According to the Roman historian Tacitus, exile to such islands was a common form of punishment in the first century. At about the same time that John was banished to Patmos, Emperor Domitian exiled his own niece, Flavia Domitilla, to another island.[4] John's conditions would have been harsh. Exhausting labor under the watchful eye of a Roman guard, insufficient food and clothing, and having to sleep on the bare ground would have taken their toll on a ninety-year-old man. It was on that bleak, barren island, under those brutal conditions, that John received the most extensive revelation of the future ever given.

John received his vision while he was "in the Spirit." His experience transcended the bounds of normal human understanding. In that state, God supernaturally revealed things to him. Though rare, such encounters occurred with other leaders in the Bible, such as Ezekiel (Ezekiel 2:2; 3:12, 14), Peter (Acts 10:9ff.), and Paul (Acts 22:17–21; 2 Corinthians 12:1ff.).

John received his vision on "the Lord's day." Some argue that this refers to the time of future judgment called the day of the Lord, but it is best understood as a reference to Sunday. The Greek phrase translated "the Lord's day" is different from the one translated "the day of the Lord" (1 Corinthians 5:5; 1 Thessalonians 5:2; 2 Thessalonians 2:2; 2 Peter 3:10) and appears only here in the New Testament. Further, the vision John received had nothing to do with the future day of the Lord. It was a vision of Christ's current ministry in the church. Finally, in the second century the phrase was widely used to refer to Sunday.[5] The phrase "the Lord's day" became the customary way of referring to Sunday because Christ's resurrection took place on that day.

John received his commission to record the vision in dramatic fashion (1:10b). The loud voice was the voice of the Lord Jesus Christ (1:12–13, 17–18), sounding to John "like the sound of a trumpet." Throughout Revelation, a loud voice or sound indicates the seriousness of what is about to be revealed.

The sovereign, powerful voice from heaven commanded John, "Write in a book what you see." This is the first of twelve commands in the book of Revelation for John to write what he saw. On one other occasion he was forbidden to write (10:4).

After writing the vision, John was to send it to the seven churches. As noted earlier, these cities were located in the Roman province of Asia (modern Turkey). These seven churches were chosen because they were located in the key cities of the seven postal districts into which Asia was divided. They were the central points for the sharing of information.

The seven cities appear in the order that a messenger, traveling on the great circular road that linked them, would visit. After landing at Miletus, the messenger or messengers bearing the book of Revelation would have traveled north to Ephesus (the city nearest to Miletus), then in a clockwise circle to Smyrna, Pergamum, Thyatira, Sardis, Philadelphia, and Laodicea. Copies of Revelation would have been distributed to each church. (See the map "Patmos and the Seven Churches of Asia" on page 44.)

THE UNFOLDING OF THE VISION (1:12–16, 20)

After describing his circumstances, John related the unfolding of the vision. This revealing look at the present work of Christ discloses seven aspects of the Lord's ongoing ministry to His church.

1. Christ Empowers His Church
Then I turned to see the voice that was speaking with me. And having turned I saw seven golden lampstands; and in the middle of the lampstands I saw one like a son of man, . . . the seven lampstands are the seven churches. (1:12–13a, 20b)

John began with his back to the voice, so he "turned to see the voice that was speaking with" him. As he did, he first saw seven golden lampstands, identified in verse 20 as the seven churches. These were like the common portable oil lamps placed on lampstands that were used to light rooms at night. They symbolize churches as the lights of the world (Philippians 2:15). They are golden because gold was the most precious metal. The church is God's most beautiful entity on earth. "Seven" is the number of completeness (Exodus 25:31–40; Zechariah 4:2). Here, the seven churches symbolize the churches in general. These were actual churches in real places, but are symbolic of the kinds of churches that exist through all of church history.

In the middle of the lampstands John saw "one like a son of man" (cf. Daniel 7:13)—the glorified Lord. Jesus promised His continued presence with His church. In Matthew 28:20 He said, "I am with you always, even to the end of the age."

2. Christ Intercedes for His Church
clothed in a robe reaching to the feet, and girded across His chest with a golden sash. (1:13b).

The first thing John noted was that Christ was "clothed in a robe reaching to the feet" (cf. Isaiah 6:1). Such robes were worn by royalty (e.g.,

Judges 8:26; 1 Samuel 18:4) and prophets (1 Samuel 28:14). In the Greek Old Testament, the word translated "robe" was most frequently used to describe the robe worn by the high priest. While Christ is biblically presented as prophet and king, the robe here pictures Christ in His role as the Great High Priest of His people. The picture of Christ "girded across His chest with a golden sash" reinforces that interpretation, since the high priest in the Old Testament wore such a sash (Exodus 28:4; Leviticus 16:4).

As our High Priest, Christ once offered the perfect and complete sacrifice for our sins and now permanently, faithfully intercedes for us (Romans 8:33–34). He has an unequaled capacity to sympathize with us in all our sorrows and temptations (Hebrews 2:18; 4:15). The knowledge that their High Priest was moving sympathetically in their midst to care for His own provided great comfort and hope to the persecuted churches.

3. Christ Purifies His Church
His head and His hair were white like white wool, like snow; and His eyes were like a flame of fire. His feet were like burnished bronze, when it has been made to glow in a furnace, (1:14–15a)

John describes Christ Himself in verses 14–15; he begins by depicting Christ's work of chastening and purifying His church. This resonates with the New Testament teachings that clearly set forth the holy standard that Christ has established for His church. "Therefore you are to be perfect as your heavenly Father is perfect" (Matthew 5:48).

John's description of Christ's "head and . . . hair as white like white wool, like snow" is a clear reference to Daniel 7:9, where similar language describes the Ancient of Days (God the Father). The parallel descriptions affirm Christ's deity. He possesses the same attribute of holy knowledge and wisdom as the Father. "White" includes the idea of "bright" or "brilliant." It symbolizes Christ's eternal, holy truthfulness.

John also notes that His eyes were "like a flame of fire" (cf. 2:18; 19:12). His searching gaze penetrates to the very depths of His church, revealing with piercing clarity the reality of everything there is to know.

That Christ's feet were "like burnished bronze, when it has been made to glow in a furnace," is a clear reference to judgment on sinners in the church. Kings in ancient times sat on elevated thrones, so those being judged would always be beneath the king's feet. The feet of a king came to symbolize his authority. The red-hot, glowing feet of Christ picture Him moving through His church to exercise His holy scrutiny.

4. Christ Speaks Authoritatively to His Church
and His voice was like the sound of many waters. (1:15*b*)

When Christ spoke again, it was no longer with the trumpetlike sound of verse 10. His voice was now "like the sound of many waters," a familiar analogy to the surf crashing on the rocky shores of Patmos in a storm. The voice of the eternal God was similarly described in Ezekiel 43:2, showing another parallel affirming Christ's deity.

When Christ speaks, the church must listen. At the transfiguration God said, "This is My beloved Son, . . . listen to Him!" (Matthew 17:5). "God, after He spoke long ago to the fathers in the prophets in many portions and in many ways," wrote the author of Hebrews, "in these last days has spoken to us in His Son" (Hebrews 1:1–2). Christ speaks to His church directly through the Holy Spirit-inspired Scriptures.

5. Christ Controls His Church
In His right hand He held seven stars . . . the seven stars are the angels of the seven churches, (1:16*a*, 20*a*)

As the head of His church (Ephesians 4:15; 5:23; Colossians 1:18), Christ exercises authority in His church. In John's vision, Christ is holding seven stars in His right hand, identified in verse 20 as "the angels of the seven churches," which symbolized those authorities. That He held them in His right hand does not picture safety and protection, but control.

The Greek word translated here as "angels" is the common word for angels, leading some interpreters to conclude that angelic beings are in view in this passage. But the New Testament nowhere teaches that angels are involved in the leadership of the church. Angels do not sin and have no need to repent, as the messengers, along with the congregations they represented, are exhorted to do (2:4–5, 14, 20; 3:1–3, 15, 17, 19). Dr. Robert L. Thomas notes a further difficulty with this view: "It presumes that Christ is sending a message to heavenly beings through John, an earthly agent, so that it may reach earthly churches through angelic representatives."[6]

It is better understood as "messengers," as in Luke 7:24; 9:52; and James 2:25. Some suggest that these messengers were representatives from each of the seven churches who came to visit John on Patmos and took the book of Revelation back with them. But since Christ is said to hold them in His right hand, they were more likely leading elders and pastors, one from each of the seven churches.

These seven men demonstrate the function of spiritual leaders in the church. They are to be instruments through which Christ mediates His rule. That is why the standards for leadership in the New Testament are so high. To be assigned as an intermediary through which the Lord Jesus Christ controls His church is to be called to a serious responsibility (cf. 1 Timothy 3:1–7; Titus 1:5–9).

6. Christ Protects His Church
and out of His mouth came a sharp two-edged sword; (1:16b)

Christ's presence also provides protection for His church. The "sharp two-edged sword" that came "out of His mouth" is used to defend the church against external threats. Here, though, it speaks primarily of judgment against enemies from inside the church (2:12, 16; Acts 20:30). Those who attack Christ's church, sow lies, create discord, or otherwise harm His people will be personally dealt with by the Lord of the church. His word is potent (Hebrews 4:12–13), and will be used against the enemies of His people (cf. 2 Thessalonians 2:8), so that all the power of the forces of darkness will be unable to prevent the Lord Jesus Christ from building His church.

7. Christ Reflects His Glory through His Church
and His face was like the sun shining in its strength. (1:16c)

John's vision of the glorified Lord of the church culminated in this description of the radiant glory evident on His face. John borrowed this phrase from Judges 5:31, where it describes those who love the Lord (Matthew 13:43). The glory of God through Christ shines in and through His church, reflecting His glory to the world (2 Corinthians 4:6). The ultimate result is that He is glorified (Ephesians 3:21).

THE EFFECTS OF THE VISION (1:17–19)

The overwhelming vision John witnessed transformed him. His initial response was devastating fear, which the Lord removed by assurance and then by giving John a sense of duty.

1. Fear
When I saw Him, I fell at His feet like a dead man. (1:17a)

In a manner similar to his experience at the transfiguration of Jesus more than six decades earlier (Matthew 17:6), John was again overwhelmed with fear upon encountering Christ's glory. Such fear was standard for those few who experienced such unusual heavenly visions (Isaiah 6:5; Ezekiel 1:28; 3:23; Daniel 10:8–9).

In stark contrast to the boastful claims of many in our own day who claim to have seen God, the reaction of those in Scripture who genuinely saw God was one of fear. Those brought face-to-face with the glory of Christ are terrified, realizing their sinful unworthiness to be in His holy presence.

2. Assurance
And He placed His right hand on me, saying, "Do not be afraid; I am the first and the last, and the living One; and I was dead, and behold, I am alive forevermore, and I have the keys of death and of Hades." (1:17b–18)

As He had done at the transfiguration (Matthew 17:7), Jesus placed His right hand on John and comforted him. This is a touch of comfort and reassurance. There is comfort for Christians overwhelmed by the majesty of Christ in the assurance of His gracious love and forgiveness. Jesus' comforting words, "Do not be afraid," reveal His compassionate assurance to the terrified apostle.

The comfort Jesus offered was based on His person and His authority. First, He identified Himself as "I am," the covenant name of God (Exodus 3:14). Jesus next identified Himself as "the first and the last" (see also 2:8; 22:13), a title used of God in the Old Testament (Isaiah 44:6; 48:12). Third, Jesus claimed to be "the living One" (cf. John 1:4; 14:6). God is the eternal, uncreated, self-existent One. Jesus' application of these titles to Himself are powerful proofs of His deity.

Christ's seemingly paradoxical declaration "I was dead, and behold, I am alive forevermore" provides further grounds for assurance. The Greek text literally reads, "I became dead." The living One, the eternal God who could never die, became man and did die (1 Peter 3:18).

"Behold" introduces a statement of amazement and wonder: "I am alive forevermore." Christ lives forever in a union of glorified humanity and deity, "according to the power of an indestructible life" (Hebrews 7:16). "Christ, having been raised from the dead," wrote Paul, "is never to die again; death no longer is master over Him" (Romans 6:9).

Jesus also "holds the keys of death and of Hades." Those terms are essentially synonymous, with *death* being the condition and *Hades* the place. "Hades" is the New Testament equivalent of the Old Testament term "Sheol" and refers to the place of the dead. "Keys" denote access and authority. Jesus Christ has the authority to decide who dies and who lives. John, like all the redeemed, had nothing to fear, since Christ had already delivered him from death and Hades by His own death.

Knowing that Christ has authority over death provides assurance, since believers need no longer fear it. Jesus declared, "I am the resurrection and the life; he who believes in Me will live even if he dies. . . . because I live, you will live also" (John 11:25; 14:19). The knowledge that Christ "loves us and released us from our sins by His blood"

(Revelation 1:5) provides the assurance that is the balance to the reverential fear that His glory and majesty evoke.

3. Duty

Therefore write the things which you have seen, and the things which are, and the things which will take place after these things. (1:19)

Finally, John was provided a reminder of his duty. Christ's earlier command to write is now expanded, as John is told to record three features. First, "the things which you have seen," the vision John had just seen and recorded in verses 10–16. Next, "the things which are," a reference to the letters to the seven churches in chapters 2 and 3. Finally, John was to write "the things which will take place after these things," the prophecies of future events unfolded in chapters 4–22. This threefold command provides an outline for the book of Revelation, encompassing the past, present, and future.

Like John, all Christians have a duty to pass on the truths they learn from the visions recorded in this book. Those visions at first may seem startling, even disturbing. But they, like all Scripture, are "inspired by God and profitable for teaching, for reproof, for correction, for training in righteousness; so that the man of God may be adequate, equipped for every good work" (2 Timothy 3:16–17). As believers study the glory of Christ reflected in Revelation, "we all . . . [will be] transformed into the same image from glory to glory, just as from the Lord, the Spirit" (2 Corinthians 3:18).

PART

2

"The Things Which Are"

(2:1–3:22)

MAP 1

PATMOS AND THE SEVEN CHURCHES OF ASIA

3

The Letter to the
BELIEVERS
at Ephesus
(2:1–7)

Francis Schaeffer once observed that "the meaning of the word *Christian* has been reduced to practically nothing. . . . Because the word *Christian* as a symbol has been made to mean so little, it has come to mean everything and nothing."[1] The term *Christian* in contemporary usage can mean anyone who claims any kind of allegiance to Jesus Christ.

Though our culture may confuse the definition of a Christian, the Bible is clear. Christians are those who are united to God through Jesus Christ (2 Thessalonians 2:13). They have exercised saving faith in Jesus (John 3:15–18; Acts 4:12; 1 John 5:1) and repented of their sins (Romans 2:4; 2 Peter 3:9). God has forgiven their sins (Acts 10:43), made them His children (Romans 8:16–17), and transformed them into new creatures (2 Corinthians 5:17) indwelt by the Holy Spirit (John 14:17).

While love for the Lord Jesus Christ will always be present in true Christians, it can fluctuate in its intensity. Christians will not always love Christ with all their heart, soul, mind, and strength. There is no better biblical illustration of the seriousness of allowing love for Christ to weaken than this letter to the Ephesian church.

The seven churches addressed in chapters 2 and 3 were actual existing churches when John wrote. They also represent the types of churches that have existed throughout the church's history. For example, five of the seven churches were confronted for tolerating sin in their midst, a problem still seen today.

The Ephesian church was not only first on the postal route. It was also the most prominent of the seven churches. It was the church that founded the other six (Acts 19:10) and the recipient of Paul's letter to the Ephesians. The contents of this first letter form the pattern for the other six. It contains seven distinct features: the correspondent, the church, the city, the commendation, the concern, the command, and the counsel.

THE CORRESPONDENT

The One who holds the seven stars in His right hand, the One who walks among the seven golden lampstands, (2:1b)

Though the writer is not named, the description makes it obvious who He is. He is the One depicted as the glorious Lord of the church in 1:9–20, the exalted Jesus Christ. These two phrases are taken from the description of Christ in John's vision (1:13, 16). In fact, Christ identifies Himself to each of the first five churches by using phrases from that vision. This reinforces the truth of His authorship through John.

The comment that Christ "holds the seven stars in His right hand" indicates that these churches are His servants. The "stars" refer to the leaders of each local congregation (1:20). Christ further describes Himself as "the One who walks among the seven golden lampstands." As its sovereign ruler, He has the authority to examine and address the church.

THE CHURCH

the church in Ephesus (2:1a)

Perhaps no church in history had as rich a heritage as the one at Ephesus. Priscilla and Aquila first introduced the gospel to that city (Acts 18:18–19).

Soon they were joined by the powerful preacher Apollos (Acts 18:24–26). Together, the three laid the groundwork for Paul's ministry in Ephesus.

The apostle Paul first stopped briefly in Ephesus near the end of his second missionary journey (Acts 18:19–21), but his real ministry there took place on his third missionary journey. Arriving in Ephesus, he first encountered some followers of John the Baptist (Acts 19:1–7). After preaching to them, he baptized them in the name of the Lord Jesus Christ (Acts 19:5). That began Paul's work of building the church at Ephesus for the next three years (Acts 20:31).

Later, on his way to Jerusalem near the end of his third missionary journey, Paul taught the elders of the Ephesian church the essential principles of church leadership (Acts 20:17–38), a message he later expanded in his pastoral epistles. Paul's protégé Timothy served as pastor of the church at Ephesus (1 Timothy 1:3). Onesiphorus (2 Timothy 1:16, 18) and Tychicus (2 Timothy 4:12), two more of Paul's fellow laborers, also served at Ephesus. Finally, according to the testimony of the early church, the apostle John spent the last decades of his life at Ephesus, from which he likely wrote his three epistles in which he calls himself "the elder" (cf. 2 John 1; 3 John 1). He was likely leading the Ephesian church when he was arrested and exiled to Patmos.

Paul's ministry profoundly affected not only the city of Ephesus, but also the entire province of Asia (Acts 19:10). During this time, the rest of the seven churches were founded. Shocked at realizing the futility of trusting in pagan practices, "many also of those who had believed kept coming, confessing and disclosing their practices. And many of those who practiced magic brought their books together and began burning them in the sight of everyone; and they counted up the price of them and found it fifty thousand pieces of silver" (verses 18–19). That staggering sum, equivalent to 50,000 days of workers' wages, reveals the magnitude of Ephesus's involvement in the magic arts.

The striking conversions of large numbers of Ephesians threatened the economy of the city's craftsmen. Ephesus was the center of the worship of the goddess Artemis, whose ornate temple was one of the Seven Wonders of the Ancient World. At the instigation of a silversmith named

Demetrius, the craftsmen began a riot that threw Ephesus into chaos (Acts 19:23–41).

Four decades later the apostle Paul was gone, as were many of the first generation of believers converted under his ministry. A new situation called for another inspired letter to the Ephesians, this one penned by the apostle John.

THE CITY

Ephesus (2:1a)

Although not the province's capital, Ephesus was the most important city in Asia Minor, and the Roman governor resided there. Its population in New Testament times has been estimated at 250,000 to 500,000 people. The city's theater, visible today, held an estimated 25,000 people. Ephesus was a self-governing city with no Roman troops stationed there. The city hosted athletic events rivaling the Olympic games.

Ephesus was the primary harbor in the province of Asia. The city was located on the Cayster River, about three miles from where it flowed into the sea. Those disembarking at the harbor traveled along a magnificent, wide, column-lined road called the Arcadian Way that led to the city's center. In John's day, silt deposited by the Cayster River was slowly filling up the harbor, forcing the city to fight to keep a channel open. That battle would ultimately be lost, with today's ruins some six miles inland from the sea.

Ephesus was also strategically located at the junction of four of the most important Roman roads in Asia Minor. That, along with its harbor, prompted the geographer Strabo (a contemporary of Christ) to describe Ephesus as the market of Asia.

But Ephesus was most famous as the center of the worship of the goddess Artemis, also called Diana (Acts 19:27, 35). The temple of Artemis was Ephesus's most prominent landmark, and it served as one of the most important banks in the Mediterranean world. The temple also provided sanctuary for criminals. Further, the sale of items used in the worship of Artemis provided an important source of income for the city (Acts 19:24). Every spring a month-long festival was held in honor of the goddess, complete with athletic, dramatic, and musical events. Meanwhile, the grounds surrounding the temple were a cacophony of priests, prostitutes, bankers, criminals, musicians, dancers, and frenzied, hysterical worshipers. The philosopher Heraclitus was called the weeping philosopher because no one, he declared, could live in Ephesus and not weep over its immorality.[2] Huddled in the midst of such pagan idolatry that characterized Ephesus was a faithful group of Christians. It was to them that Christ addressed this first of the seven letters.

THE COMMENDATION

I know your deeds and your toil and perseverance, and that you cannot tolerate evil men, and you put to the test those who call themselves apostles, and they are not, and you found them to be false; and you have perseverance and have endured for My name's sake, and have not grown weary. . . . Yet this you do have, that you hate the deeds of the Nicolaitans, which I also hate. (2:2–3, 6)

Before rebuking them for their failings, Christ commended the Ephesians for their positive actions. Specifically, Christ first commended the Ephesian believers for their "toil." The Greek word denotes labor to the point of exhaustion. The Ephesians were diligent workers for the cause of Christ. In the midst of the pagan darkness that surrounded them, they were aggressively evangelizing the lost, edifying the saints, and caring for those in need.

"Perseverance" denotes patience in trying circumstances. This commendation indicates that despite their difficult circumstances, the Ephesian believers remained faithful to their Lord.

Another praiseworthy aspect of the Ephesian believers was that they refused to "tolerate evil men." They held to a high, holy standard of behavior and were sensitive to sin. Nor was the Ephesian church lacking in spiritual discernment, since it "put to the test those who call themselves apostles, and

they are not, and . . . found them to be false." The Ephesians never forgot the
admonition Paul had addressed to their leaders so many years earlier to "be
on guard for yourselves and all the flock" against "savage wolves [trying to
ravage] the flock" (see Acts 20:28–31). Through all the difficulties the
Ephesians faced over forty years, through all their hard labor and patient
enduring of trials, and their refusal to tolerate evil, they maintained their perseverance. They endured, Jesus declared, for the highest of motives: "for My
name's sake." And they had done so without having grown weary. They
remained faithful to the Lord, loyal to His Word and to the work to which
He had called them.

Verse 6 adds a final commendation: "Yet this you do have, that you
hate the deeds of the Nicolaitans, which I also hate." The Nicolaitans,
mentioned also in 2:12–15, cannot be clearly identified. The few references to this heresy in the writings of the church fathers link it to Nicolas,
one of the seven men appointed to oversee the distribution of food in
Acts 6. Some argued that Nicolas was a false believer who rebelled, but
retained influence in the church because of his credentials. Others suggested that the Nicolaitans misrepresented his teaching. Whatever its origin, Nicolaitanism led people into immorality and wickedness. Revelation
2:12–15 links it with Balaam's false teaching that led Israel into sin.

Unlike the church at Pergamum, the Ephesian church did not tolerate the Nicolaitans but hated their heretical teachings. For that the Lord
commended them. Hatred was an appropriate attitude and exactly the
opposite reaction to the tolerance of the Pergamum church (2:14–15).

THE CONCERN

But I have this against you, that you have left your first love. (2:4)

Despite the positive highlights of the Ephesian church, Christ had spotted
a fatal flaw. Though they maintained their doctrinal purity and served
Christ, that service had turned mechanical. Forty years after being marked
by love (Ephesians 1:15; 3:17–19; 6:23), the affection had cooled. The current generation was maintaining the church's teachings, but it had left its

first love. They had sunk to the place where they were carrying out their Christian responsibilities with diminishing love for their Lord and others.

The grave danger of that situation is illustrated by the disaster that ensued when Israel's love for God cooled (Jeremiah 2:2–13; Ezekiel 16:8–15). God eventually brought judgment against His people when their love disappeared. As it had in Israel, the honeymoon had ended at Ephesus. The loss of a vital love relationship with the Lord Jesus Christ opened the doors to spiritual apathy and indifference to others. Despite its outwardly robust appearance, a deadly spiritual cancer was growing at the heart of the Ephesian church.

THE COMMAND

Therefore remember from where you have fallen, and repent and do the deeds you did at first; or else I am coming to you and will remove your lampstand out of its place—unless you repent. (2:5)

The Great Physician issued a prescription to the Ephesians that would cure their spiritual malaise. First, they needed to literally "keep on remembering" from where they had fallen. Forgetfulness is frequently the initial cause of spiritual decline, and the Ephesians needed to recognize the seriousness of such a lapse. Second, they needed to repent in an intentional turning from their sins, because to fail to love God fully is sin (Mark 12:30). Finally, they needed to demonstrate the genuineness of their repentance and return to their original deeds. They needed to recapture the richness of Bible study, devotion to prayer, and passion for worship that had once characterized them.

Underscoring the seriousness of the situation, Christ warned the Ephesians to take the necessary steps to recover their first love for Him. He demanded that they change or be chastened: "I am coming to you and will remove your lampstand out of its place—unless you repent." The coming He refers to is not His second coming, but His coming to them in local judgment on that church. Failure to obey the warning would cause Him to remove their lampstand (symbolic of the church; 1:20) out of its place. Tragically, Christ threatened divine judgment that would bring an end to the Ephesian church.

THE COUNSEL

He who has an ear, let him hear what the Spirit says to the churches. To him who overcomes, I will grant to eat of the tree of life which is in the Paradise of God. (2:7)

The letter closes with an exhortation and a promise. Christ's exhortation "He who has an ear, let him hear what the Spirit says to the churches" closes each of the seven letters. It emphasizes the serious responsibility believers have to obey God's voice in Scripture. The use of the plural noun "churches" signifies the universal nature of this invitation each time that it appears. This call cannot be limited just to a group of overcomers in a single church. It must apply to all churches. Every church needs to hear every message.

The promise, as are those associated with the other six letters (2:11, 17, 26; 3:5, 12, 21), is addressed to "him who overcomes." The term does not refer to those who have attained to a higher level of the Christian life, but to all Christians. The apostle John defines it that way in his first epistle: "For whatever is born of God overcomes the world; and this is the victory that has overcome the world—our faith. Who is the one who overcomes the world, but he who believes that Jesus is the Son of God?" (1 John 5:4–5). All true believers are overcomers, who have by God's grace and power overcome the power of the evil world system.

Christ promises the overcomers at Ephesus that they will "eat of the tree of life which is in the Paradise of God." The tree of life is first referred to in Genesis 2:9, where it stands in the garden of Eden. That earthly tree was lost due to sin. Adam was forbidden to eat from it (Genesis 3:22). However, the heavenly tree of life (Revelation 22:2, 14, 19) will last throughout eternity. The tree of life symbolizes eternal life. The "Paradise of God" is heaven (Luke 23:43; 2 Corinthians 12:4).

The example of the Ephesian church warns that right beliefs and outward service cannot make up for a cold heart. Believers must carefully follow Solomon's counsel: "Watch over your heart with all diligence, for from it flow the springs of life" (Proverbs 4:23).

The Letters to the
BELIEVERS
at Smyrna and Pergamum
(2:8–17)

Throughout its history, the more the church has been persecuted, the greater its purity and strength. For decades, churches in the former Soviet Union and Eastern Europe were oppressed by their atheistic communist governments. Believers continue to be persecuted in several nations today. People are forbidden to openly proclaim their faith. Many are imprisoned and some martyred. In the Soviet Union, for instance, Bibles were scarce. Yet not only did those churches survive, they prospered. When Communism fell, a powerful, pure church was revealed, characterized by genuine faith and deep zeal for God.

SMYRNA: THE SUFFERING CHURCH

Scripture links persecution and spiritual strength. James wrote that "the testing of your faith produces endurance" that leads to being spiritually "complete, lacking in nothing" (James 1:2–4). Peter encouraged suffering Christians with the truth that "after you have suffered for a little while, the God of all grace . . . will Himself perfect, confirm, strengthen and

establish you" (1 Peter 5:10). The church at Smyrna displayed the power
and purity that results from enduring persecution. Persecution had purified it from sin and affirmed the reality of its members' faith. Hypocrites
do not stay to face persecution, because false believers do not desire pain.
Trials and persecution strengthen and refine genuine saving faith, but
destroy false faith.

Though they suffered physically and economically, the Christians at
Smyrna clung to their spiritual riches. Interestingly, the church at Smyrna
is one of only two churches (along with Philadelphia) that received no
condemnation in its letter from Christ.

The Bible teaches that persecution and trials are an inevitable and
essential part of the Christian life (Acts 14:22; 2 Timothy 3:12). The
example of the church at Smyrna instructs all churches on how to properly respond when trials come.

The Correspondent
The first and the last, who was dead, and has come to life, says this
(2:8b)

As customary in ancient letters, Jesus identifies Himself at the beginning
of the letter instead of at the end. The depiction of the writer as "The first
and the last, who was dead, and has come to life" identifies Him as the
exalted Christ described in 1:12–20. "The first and the last" is an Old
Testament title for God (Isaiah 44:6; 48:12). Its application here affirms
His equality of nature with God. He is the eternal, infinite God, who
already existed when all things were created, and who will continue to
exist after they are destroyed.

Yet, amazingly, the eternal God became man and was dead and has
come to life. First Peter 3:18 reveals Christ was "Put to death in the flesh,
but made alive in the spirit." He died in His human body as the perfect
sacrifice for sin, but now has come to life and lives forever "according to
the power of an indestructible life" (Hebrews 7:16; cf. Romans 6:9).

This designation of Christ was to comfort the persecuted believers at
Smyrna. Knowing that they were undergoing difficult times, Christ

reminded them that He transcends this world and empowers them to do the same. Should they die at the hands of their persecutors, beside them is the One who conquered death (John 11:25–26; Hebrews 2:14).

The Church
the church in Smyrna (2:8a)

Scripture does not record the founding of the church at Smyrna, nor is the city mentioned in Acts. All that we know is revealed in this letter. Most likely, the church began during Paul's Ephesian ministry (Acts 19:10) by Paul or one of those he reached. At the end of the first century, life was difficult and dangerous in Smyrna. The city served as a hotbed of emperor worship. Under Domitian it became a capital offense to refuse to offer the yearly sacrifice to the emperor. Not surprisingly, many Christians faced execution. The most famous of Smyrna's martyrs was Polycarp, executed half a century after John's time.

The Greek word translated "Smyrna" was used in the Greek translation of the Old Testament to translate the Hebrew word for "myrrh," a substance used as a perfume for the living (Matthew 2:11) and the dead (John 19:39). Its association with death perfectly pictures the suffering church at Smyrna. Like myrrh, produced by crushing a fragrant plant, the church at Smyrna, crushed by persecution, gave off a fragrant aroma of faithfulness to God.

The City
Smyrna (2:8a)

Smyrna was an ancient city whose origins are lost in history. It may have been settled as early as 3000 B.C., but the first Greek settlement dates from about 1000 B.C. About 600 B.C. Smyrna was destroyed by the Lydians and lay in ruins for more than three centuries until two of Alexander the Great's successors rebuilt the city in 290 B.C. It was that rebuilt city that was the Smyrna noted in Revelation.

Smyrna's citizens were so loyal to Rome that they built a temple in

195 B.C. where Rome was worshiped. A century later the Roman general Sulla's ill-clad army faced bitter winter weather. When the Roman soldiers' plight was announced in a general assembly of Smyrna's citizens, they reportedly took off their own clothes to send to them. Rome rewarded Smyrna's loyalty by choosing it above all other applicants as the site of a new temple dedicated to the Emperor Tiberius (A.D. 26). When an earthquake destroyed the city late in the second century, Emperor Marcus Aurelius rebuilt it.

The city was said to be the most beautiful city in Asia. It was located on a gulf of the Aegean Sea and had an excellent harbor. Smyrna also profited from its location at the western end of the road that ran through the rich Hermus River valley. In addition to the natural beauty of its surroundings, the city itself was well designed. It stretched from the bay up the slopes of the Pagos, a large hill covered with temples and other public buildings. The streets were well laid out, with the outlying ones lined with groves of trees. Smyrna's most famous street, the "Street of Gold," curved around the slopes of the Pagos. At one end was the temple of Cybele, and at the other the temple of Zeus. In between were the temples of Apollo, Asklepios, and Aphrodite.

Smyrna was a noted center of science and medicine. It was also one of several cities that claimed to be the birthplace of the poet Homer. While the harbor of Ephesus eventually silted up and the city went out of existence, Smyrna survived numerous earthquakes and fires and exists today as the Turkish city of Izmir.

The Commendation
I know your tribulation and your poverty (but you are rich), and the blasphemy by those who say they are Jews and are not, but are a synagogue of Satan. (2:9)

Nothing escapes the vision of the glorious Lord of the Smyrna church, who knows every detail about His churches. He began His commendation by assuring the believers there that He understood their tribulation. "Tribulation" literally means "pressure," and it is the common New

Testament word for persecution or tribulation. The church at Smyrna was facing intense pressure because of their faithfulness to Jesus Christ for three reasons.

First, Smyrna had been fanatically devoted to Rome. The city was a leading center for the cult of emperor worship. The citizens of Smyrna willingly offered the worship that Emperor Domitian was now demanding of his subjects everywhere. Though the Christians willingly submitted to the emperor's civil authority (cf. Romans 13:1–7), they refused to offer sacrifices to him. They were then branded rebels and faced the wrath of the Roman government.

Second, Christians refused to participate in pagan religion in general. Smyrna's residents worshiped an eclectic mix of gods. The total rejection of the pagan idols by those in the church, along with their worship of an invisible God, caused them to be denounced as atheists. Much of Smyrna's social life revolved around pagan worship, and Christians were viewed as antisocial for refusing to participate.

Finally, the believers at Smyrna faced "blasphemy by those who say they are Jews and are not, but are a synagogue of [the ultimate blasphemer,] Satan." That shocking statement affirmed that those Jews who hated and rejected Jesus Christ were just as much Satan's followers as idol worshipers (John 8:44). Jesus' use of the strong term "blasphemy" indicates the slander's intensity and severity.

Unbelieving Jews commonly accused Christians of cannibalism (based on a misunderstanding of the Lord's Supper), immorality (based on a perversion of the holy kiss with which believers greeted each other), breaking up homes (when one spouse became a Christian and the other did not, it often caused conflict), atheism (because, as already noted, Christians rejected the pagan pantheon of deities), and political disloyalty and rebellion (because Christians refused to offer the required sacrifices to the emperor). Hoping to destroy the Christian faith, some of Smyrna's wealthy, influential Jews reported these blasphemous, false allegations to the Romans.

Sadly, the hostility of Smyrna's Jewish population to Christianity was nothing new. The book of Acts frequently records such Satan-inspired opposition.[1] In Smyrna, as had happened before, the hostile Jewish population spread negative opinions against Christians.

The statement that the Jews who persecuted the Smyrna church "say they are Jews and are not" has caused some to question whether they were racially Jewish. Surely they were physical descendants of Abraham, but not true Jews by Paul's definition: "He is not a Jew who is one outwardly, nor is circumcision that which is outward in the flesh. But he is a Jew who is one inwardly; and circumcision is that which is of the heart, by the Spirit, not by the letter; and his praise is not from men, but from God" (Romans 2:28–29). Though these were Jews by race, they were not spiritually.

Not only was the Lord aware of the persecution the Smyrna church faced, but also of its poverty. The Greek word here for "poverty" commonly describes beggars, who live not by their own labor, but by the alms of others.[2] Many of the believers at Smyrna were slaves. Most were destitute. Those few who had owned possessions had undoubtedly lost them in the persecution.

The church at Smyrna had every human reason to collapse. Instead, it remained faithful to Christ, never leaving its first love like Ephesus. For that reason, Jesus said to them, "You are rich." They had what really mattered —salvation, holiness, grace, peace, fellowship, a sympathetic Savior and Comforter. The church at Smyrna was the rich church spiritually, in contrast to the church at Laodicea, which was economically rich but spiritually poor (3:17).

The Command
Do not fear what you are about to suffer. Behold, the devil is about to cast some of you into prison, so that you will be tested, and you will have tribulation for ten days. (2:10a)

After commending them for faithfully enduring persecution, Jesus warned the believers that more was coming. First, He commanded them not to fear what they were about to suffer. He would give them strength to endure it. As He told His disciples in John 16:33, "In the world you have tribulation, but take courage; I have overcome the world."

Specifically, the Lord predicted that the Devil was about to cast some of them into prison. God's purpose in permitting imprisonment was so they would be tested. By successfully enduring the trial, they would prove the reality of their faith, be strengthened (2 Corinthians 12:9–10), and prove once again that Satan cannot destroy genuine saving faith.

God, who alone sovereignly controls all the circumstances of life, would not permit Satan to torment the Smyrna church for long. Jesus promised that they would have tribulation for only ten days. Though some see the ten days as symbolically representing everything from ten periods of persecution under the Romans, to an undetermined period of time, to a time of ten years, there is no exegetical reason to interpret them as anything other than ten actual days. Satan's major assault on that local church would be intense, but brief.

The Counsel

Be faithful until death, and I will give you the crown of life. He who has an ear, let him hear what the Spirit says to the churches. He who overcomes will not be hurt by the second death. (2:10b–11)

As previously noted, Christ has no reprimand for the faithful church at Smyrna. He closes the letter with some final words of encouraging counsel. Those who prove the genuineness of their faith by remaining faithful to the Lord until death will receive as their reward the crown of life. The "crown" (reward, culmination, outcome) of genuine saving faith is eternal life, and perseverance proves the genuineness of their faith as they endure suffering. The Scriptures teach that true Christians will persevere.

As noted in chapter 3, the phrase "He who has an ear, let him hear what the Spirit says to the churches" closes each of the seven letters. It stresses the vital significance of what God says in Scripture, and emphasizes believers' responsibility to heed it. The promise to "he who overcomes" is for all Christians, promising that they will not be hurt by the second death. Though persecuted believers may suffer the first, physical death, they will never experience the second death of hell (Revelation 20:14; 21:8). To stress the point, the text used the strongest negative the

Greek language can express for the word translated "not."

The persecuted, suffering, yet faithful church at Smyrna stands for all time as an example of those who "have heard the word in an honest and good heart, and hold it fast, and bear fruit with perseverance" (Luke 8:15). Because they loyally confessed Him before men, Jesus will confess them before the Father (Matthew 10:32).

PERGAMUM: THE WORLDLY CHURCH

The Bible does not hesitate to condemn worldliness as a serious sin. Worldliness is any preoccupation with the physical system of life that places anything on earth before the things of eternity. Since believers are not part of the world system (John 15:19), they must not act as though they were. Paul wrote, "Do not be conformed to this world, but be transformed by the renewing of your mind, so that you may prove what the will of God is, that which is good and acceptable and perfect" (Romans 12:2). First John 2:15–17 makes the believer's duty to avoid worldliness unmistakably clear:

> **Do not love the world nor the things in the world. If anyone loves the world, the love of the Father is not in him. For all that is in the world, the lust of the flesh and the lust of the eyes and the boastful pride of life, is not from the Father, but is from the world. The world is passing away, and also its lusts; but the one who does the will of God lives forever.**

The church at Pergamum, like many of today's churches, failed to follow the biblical warnings against worldliness. It had drifted into compromise and was in danger of becoming intertwined with the world.

The Correspondent
The One who has the sharp two-edged sword says this: (2:12*b*)

The holder of "the sharp two-edged sword" is the risen Christ (1:16). He communicates this letter through the apostle John. In this letter, like with

Ephesus and Smyrna, Christ identifies Himself using one of the descriptive phrases from John's vision in 1:12–17.

The sharp two-edged sword refers to the Word of God. Hebrews 4:12 says, "The word of God is living and active and sharper than any two-edged sword." The apostle Paul also uses the metaphor of a sword to describe the Word (Ephesians 6:17). The two edges of the sword depict the Word's power in exposing the innermost thoughts of the human heart. The Word never wields a dull edge.

This description pictures Christ as judge and executioner. Describing His appearance at the second coming, John writes that "from His mouth comes a sharp sword, so that with it He may strike down the nations, and He will rule them with a rod of iron; and He treads the wine press of the fierce wrath of God, the Almighty" (19:15). This is not a positive introduction, but a threatening one. It is the first negative introduction of Christ because the Pergamum church faced serious judgment. Disaster loomed on the horizon for this worldly church; it was and is but a short step from compromising with the world to forsaking God altogether and facing His wrath.

The Church
the church in Pergamum (2:12a)

The book of Acts does not record the founding of the church at Pergamum. According to Acts 16:7–8, Paul passed through Mysia (the region in which Pergamum was located) on his second missionary journey, but there is no record that the apostle either preached the gospel or founded a church there at that time. Most likely, the church at Pergamum was founded during Paul's ministry in Ephesus, when the gospel spread from there throughout the province of Asia (Acts 19:10). Because the church was surrounded by the pagan culture, it was continually exposed to temptation, in addition to severe persecution when standing against emperor worship.

The City
Pergamum (2:12a)

Pergamum was about a hundred miles north of Ephesus, with Smyrna located about halfway in between. Pergamum was not a port city but located about fifteen miles inland from the Aegean Sea. However, as the area's ancient capital, Pergamum was considered Asia's greatest city. The Roman writer Pliny called it "by far the most distinguished city in Asia."[3] By the time John penned Revelation, Pergamum had been Asia's capital for almost 250 years (since 133 B.C). Pergamum survives today as the Turkish city of Bergama.

Much of Pergamum was built on a large, conical hill towering a thousand feet above the plain. In the nineteenth century famed archaeologist Sir William Ramsay commented, "Beyond all other sites in Asia Minor it gives the traveler the impression of a royal city, the home of authority: the rocky hill on which it stands is so huge, and dominates the broad plain of the Caicus [River valley] so proudly and boldly."[4] Pergamum's huge library (200,000 handwritten volumes) was second only to that of Alexandria. So impressive was Pergamum's library that Mark Antony later sent it to his lover, Queen Cleopatra of Egypt. According to legend, parchment was invented by the Pergamenes to provide writing material for their library. Seeking to build a library rivaling the one in Alexandria, a third-century B.C. Pergamene king attempted to bring the librarian of the Alexandrian library to his city. Unfortunately, the Egyptian ruler got wind of the plan, refused to allow the librarian to leave, and prohibited the further export of papyrus to Pergamum. Out of necessity, the Pergamenes developed parchment, made of treated animal skins, for use as writing material. Though parchment was actually known from a thousand years earlier in Egypt, the Pergamenes were responsible for its widespread use in the ancient world. The word *parchment* may even derive from a form of the word Pergamum.

Because of its library, Pergamum was an important center of culture and learning. It also was a center of worship for four of the main gods of the Greco-Roman world, including temples dedicated to Athena,

Asklepios, Dionysos, and Zeus. Overshadowing the worship of all those deities was Pergamum's devotion to the cult of emperor worship. Pergamum built the first temple devoted to emperor worship in Asia (29 B.C.) in honor of Emperor Augustus. Later, the city would build two more such temples, honoring the emperors Trajan and Septimus Severus. The city became the center of emperor worship in the province, and Christians were in danger of harm from the emperor worship cult. In other cities Christians were primarily in danger on the one day per year they were required to offer sacrifices to the emperor. In Pergamum they were in danger every day.

The Commendation

I know where you dwell, where Satan's throne is; and you hold fast My name, and did not deny My faith even in the days of Antipas, My witness, My faithful one, who was killed among you, where Satan dwells. (2:13)

Despite the difficult circumstances, the believers at Pergamum courageously maintained their faith in Christ. He commended them for continuing to hold fast His name, even though they lived "where Satan's throne is," where Satan dwells. Many suggestions have been offered as to the identification of Satan's throne. Some identify it with the altar of Zeus in Pergamum, an altar 120 by 112 feet in size located within a colonnaded court that included a podium almost eighteen feet high.[5] Such an impressive structure could easily merit the designation "Satan's throne."

Others connect Satan's throne with the worship of the god Asklepios, prevalent in Pergamum. Asklepios was the god of healing, and people came from across the ancient world to be healed at his shrine. Asklepios was depicted as a snake, and nonpoisonous snakes roamed freely in his temple. Suppliants seeking healing either slept or lay down on the temple's floor, hoping to be touched by one of the snakes to be healed. Such symbolism would undoubtedly remind Christians of Satan (Revelation 12:9). During the reign of Emperor Diocletian, some Christian stonecutters were executed for refusing to carve an image of Asklepios.[6]

Others point out that, as noted above, Pergamum was the leading center of emperor worship in the province of Asia. Emperor worship certainly posed the greatest threat to the Christians in Pergamum. It was for their refusal to worship the emperor, not the pagan gods, that Christians faced execution. Satan's throne could easily be understood as a reference to the might of Rome under the "god of this world" (2 Corinthians 4:4), speaking against the true God by the emperor-worship cult.

For any or all of those reasons, Pergamum could understandably be called the city where Satan's throne is. In the midst of those difficult and trying circumstances, the believers continued to dwell in Pergamum. In other words, they "hung in there." Despite the persecution they endured, the believers at Pergamum continued to hold fast the name of Christ and did not deny the faith.

The church at Pergamum maintained its faithfulness even in the days of Antipas, whom Christ described as "My witness, My faithful one, who was killed among you." Nothing certain is known about Antipas apart from this text. He was probably one of the leaders of the Pergamum church. According to tradition, he was roasted to death inside a brass bull during the persecution by Emperor Domitian. Here was a man who paid the ultimate price for his refusal to compromise. Because of his faithfulness, the risen Lord commended Antipas with a title used elsewhere to refer to Himself: "My witness" (Revelation 1:5; 3:14). Antipas's faithfulness and courage were a rebuke to those at Pergamum who were tempted to compromise with the world.

The Concern
But I have a few things against you, because you have there some who hold the teaching of Balaam, who kept teaching Balak to put a stumbling block before the sons of Israel, to eat things sacrificed to idols and to commit acts of immorality. So you also have some who in the same way hold the teaching of the Nicolaitans. (2:14–15)

The church at Pergamum remained loyal to Christ and His truth. Yet all was not well. After commending the believers there, Christ informed them, "I have a few things against you." His concern was that they had some who held to false teaching. While the majority of the believers at Pergamum were faithful to the truth, there were some who followed wrong doctrines. While many in the Christian realm today make light of doctrine and theology as unimportant, that is not the perspective of Christ. Tragically, the rest of the church was tolerating the heretics' error instead of confronting them. Like many churches today, the church at Pergamum failed to obey the biblical mandate to practice church discipline (Matthew 18:15–18).

Specifically, Christ was concerned with two heresies. The first was associated with an Old Testament character. The second was associated with a New Testament person. First, some were following the teaching of Balaam. The story of Balaam, an Old Testament prophet for hire, is found in Numbers 22–25. Fearful of the Israelites because of what they had done to the Amorites, Balak hired Balaam to curse them. After trying unsuccessfully three times to curse Israel, Balaam came up with another plan. Since he was unable to curse the Israelites, he decided to corrupt them by teaching Balak to tempt them to eat things sacrificed to idols and to commit acts of immorality. He plotted to use Moabite women to lure the Israelites into the behavior of the godless world around them involving sexual immorality and idolatry (Numbers 25; 31:16). That blasphemous union with Satan and false gods would destroy their spiritual power. Balaam's plan succeeded. However, God intervened and brought judgment upon Israel, executing 24,000 people (25:9), including many of the leaders (25:4–5). The drastic action halted the Israelites' slide into immorality and idolatry.

Like the Israelites who were seduced by Balaam's false teaching, some in the church at Pergamum followed the ways of their surrounding culture (Jude 10–11). Peter rebuked the Balaamites in 2 Peter 2:15–16: "Forsaking the right way, they have gone astray, having followed the way of Balaam, the son of Beor, who loved the wages of unrighteousness; but he received a rebuke for his own transgression, for a mute donkey, speaking with a voice of a man, restrained the madness of the prophet." As God severely judged Israel for such living, Christ threatens to do the same here (see 2 Corinthians 6:14–17). Despite the graphic example of Israel, some in Pergamum persisted in following Balaam's teaching. They believed one could attend pagan feasts, and still join the church to worship Jesus Christ. However, James wrote that "friendship with the world is hostility toward God" (James 4:4; see also 1 Peter 2:11). The issue of whether Christians could participate in idolatrous feasts had been settled decades earlier at the Jerusalem Council, which issued a mandate for believers to "abstain from things sacrificed to idols and from blood and from things strangled and from fornication" (Acts 15:29).

The second heresy tolerated at Pergamum involved a New Testament figure named Nicolas. The context indicates that the teaching of the Nicolaitans led to the same wicked behavior as that of the followers of Balaam. As discussed earlier, Nicolas was one of the seven men chosen to oversee the distribution of food in Acts 6. Whether he rebelled (as some of the early church fathers believed) or his followers twisted his teachings is not known. Abusing Christian liberty, the Nicolaitans also taught that Christians could participate in pagan sexual practices. (As noted earlier, the believers at Ephesus fully rejected this fasle teaching.)

The majority of the believers at Pergamum did not participate in the errors of these two groups. They remained loyal to Christ and the Christian faith. Yet by tolerating the groups and refusing to exercise church discipline, they shared in their guilt and incurred the Lord's judgment.

The Command
Therefore repent; or else I am coming to you quickly, and I will make war against them with the sword of My mouth. (2:16)

The only remedy for sinful behavior is to repent. "Repent" is from a Greek word used to describe a change of mind that results in a change of behavior. While tolerance is celebrated in our culture, tolerating heretical teaching or sinful behavior in the church is sin. Christ warns them, "I am coming to you quickly, and I will make war against them with the sword of My mouth." The entire church faced Christ's judgment: the heretics for practicing sin, and the rest of the church for tolerating it.

The church cannot tolerate evil. Paul wrote to the Corinthians, who were proudly tolerating a man guilty of incest, "Your boasting is not good. Do you not know that a little leaven leavens the whole lump of dough? Clean out the old leaven so that you may be a new lump, just as you are in fact unleavened" (1 Corinthians 5:6–7). The goal of the church is not to provide an environment where unbelievers can just feel comfortable. It is to be a place where they can hear the truth and be convicted of their sins so they can be saved (Romans 10:13–17). Gently (2 Timothy 2:24–26), lovingly, graciously, yet firmly, unbelievers need to be confronted with the reality of their sin and God's gracious provision through Jesus Christ. Sin will never be suppressed by compromising with it.

The Counsel
He who has an ear, let him hear what the Spirit says to the churches. To him who overcomes, to him I will give some of the hidden manna, and I will give him a white stone, and a new name written on the stone which no one knows but he who receives it. (2:17)

Christ concludes His letter with words of encouragement. As noted earlier, the phrase "he who has an ear, let him hear what the Spirit says to the churches" stresses the vital importance of Christ's words and responsibility of believers to hear and obey them. The promises are addressed to him "who overcomes," a phrase encompassing all believers (1 John 5:4–5). Christ promises three things to the faithful members of the church at Pergamum.

First, He promises to give them some of the hidden manna. Manna was a honey-flavored bread God used to feed the Israelites during their years of wandering in the wilderness (Exodus 16). According to Exodus 16:33, the Israelites were to remember God's provision by keeping a jar of manna inside the ark of the covenant during their travels. The hidden manna represents Jesus Christ, the Bread of Life who came down from heaven (John 6:48–51). He provides spiritual sustenance for those who put their faith in Him. The hidden manna symbolizes all the blessings and benefits of knowing Christ (Ephesians 1:3).

There has been much speculation about what the white stone symbolizes. Some link it with the Urim and Thummim on the breastplate of the high priest (Exodus 28:15, 30). Those stones were used to determine God's will and represented the right of the high priest to request guidance from God for the leader who could not approach God directly. Somehow, God caused those stones to disclose His will. According to this view, by this white stone God promises the overcomers knowledge of His will. Others identify the white stone as a diamond, the most precious of stones, symbolizing God's gift of eternal life to believers. It seems best, however, to understand the white stone in light of the Roman custom of awarding white stones to the victors in athletic contests. A white stone, inscribed with the athlete's name, served as his ticket to a special awards banquet. In this view, Christ promises the overcomers entrance to the eternal victory celebration in heaven.

There will be a new name written on the stone no one knows but the person who receives it. As the phrase indicates, we cannot know what that new name is until we receive it (Deuteronomy 29:29). The Greek word here translated "new" does not mean new in contrast to old, but new in the sense of a different quality. The new name will serve as each believer's admission pass into eternal glory. It will uniquely reflect God's special love for every one of His true children.

The Pergamum church faced the same choice that every church faces today. It could repent and receive all the blessings of eternal life in the glory of heaven. Or it could refuse to repent and face the terrifying reality of having the Christ declare war on it. Maintaining the path of compromise ultimately leads to judgment.

The Letters to the
BELIEVERS
at Thyatira and Sardis
(2:18–3:6)

Christ has called His church to be holy and maintain purity by dealing with sin in its midst. In fact, the very first instruction He gave to the church was about confronting sin (Matthew 18:15–17). The practice of church discipline has a twofold purpose: to call sinning believers back to righteous behavior, and to remove from the church those who stubbornly cling to their sin. In either case, the purity of the church is upheld.

Despite this clear biblical teaching, churches throughout history have tolerated sin, following a pattern like the Thyatiran church, with members engaging in both spiritual and physical adultery. Through the efforts of an unnamed false teacher, those sins had become pervasive in the church at Thyatira. The letter is a sobering one, and marks a new phase in the letters to the seven churches. There is a progressive worsening in the character of these seven churches, as they depict becoming more and more influenced by evil. That downward spiral reached its lowest point at Laodicea.

THYATIRA: THE CHURCH THAT TOLERATED SIN

The letter to the church at Thyatira is the longest of the seven, though addressed to the church in the smallest of the seven cities. It has an important message for the church today: False teaching and sin are not to be allowed, even under the banner of toleration and unity. A church may appear on the surface to have an effective ministry and be growing numerically, but unconfronted immorality and false teaching will bring eventual judgment upon the church.

The Correspondent
The Son of God, who has eyes like a flame of fire, and His feet are like burnished bronze, says this: (2:18*b*)

The title "Son of God" and the two descriptive phrases drawn from the vision of the risen Christ in 1:12–17 identify the writer as the Lord Jesus Christ. The phrases chosen here focus on His role as divine Judge.

"Son of God" emphasizes Christ's deity, stressing that He is of one essence with the Father. This is a significant wording change. In the vision recorded in chapter 1, Christ was described as the Son of Man (1:13). The title "Son of Man" views Christ in His ability to sympathize with the needs, trials, and temptations of His church. Here, however, Jesus is identified as "Son of God," the only time this phrase appears in Revelation. The emphasis is on His deity, because His approach to the church at Thyatira is as divine judge.

As the divine Son of God, Jesus Christ has eyes "like a flame of fire." His piercing vision sees all. Revelation 19:12 describes Jesus Christ in His second coming glory with eyes that "are a flame of fire." A church may feel satisfied with itself, have a good reputation in the community, or even with other churches. However, Christ's eyes see things as they truly are.

The description of His feet as being "like burnished bronze" is similar to Revelation 19:15, where it says Christ "treads the wine press of the fierce wrath of God, the Almighty." That Christ's feet glowed brilliantly "like burnished bronze" depicts His purity and holiness as He tramples out impurity.

This terrifying description of the Lord Jesus must have created shock when this letter was read to the church at Thyatira. It came as a sobering realization that Christ will judge ongoing, unrepented sin.

The Church
the church in Thyatira (2:18a)

As with the churches at Smyrna and Pergamum, the Bible does not record the founding of the church at Thyatira. In Acts 16:14 Lydia, from the city of Thyatira, was converted under Paul's ministry at Philippi. Verse 15 records that members of her household also came to faith in Christ and were baptized. It is possible that Lydia and her household helped start the church at Thyatira. More likely, the church there was founded as an outreach of Paul's ministry at Ephesus (Acts 19:10).

The City
Thyatira (2:18a)

From Pergamum, northernmost of the seven cities, the Roman road curved east and then southeast to Thyatira, approximately forty miles away. Thyatira was located in a long north-south valley connecting the valleys of the Caicus and Hermus rivers. It was built in relatively flat country. While Pergamum's high hill provided a natural defense, Thyatira lacked natural fortifications against potential invaders.

Thyatira was founded by one of Alexander the Great's successors, Seleucus, as a military outpost guarding the north-south road. It later came under the rule of Lysimachus, who ruled Pergamum. Thyatira was the gateway to Pergamum, and the task of the defenders at Thyatira was to delay an attacker headed for Pergamum. Unfortunately, since Thyatira had no natural defenses, the garrison there could not hope to hold out for long. The city was repeatedly destroyed and rebuilt. Its brief references in ancient literature usually describe its conquest by an invading army.

About 190 B.C., Thyatira was conquered and annexed by the Romans, enjoying Roman peace. The city then became a flourishing commercial center. Its road became important in Roman times, as it connected Pergamum with Laodicea, Smyrna, and the interior regions. It also served as the Roman post road. At the time Revelation was written, Thyatira was just entering its period of greatest prosperity.

Thyatira was also known for its numerous guilds, similar to today's labor unions. Its main industry was wool and dyed-good production, but inscriptions also mention guilds for linen workers, makers of outer garments, dyers, leather workers, tanners, potters, bakers, slave dealers, and bronze smiths.[1]

Unlike Pergamum or Smyrna, Thyatira was not an important religious center. The primary god worshiped was the Greek sun god, Apollo. Nor does there appear to have been a sizable Jewish population. The pressure faced by the Christians in Thyatira came from the guilds. To hold a job or run a business, it was necessary to be a member of a guild. Each guild had a deity in whose honor feasts were held, including meat sacrificed to idols and sexual immorality. Christians faced the dilemma of participating or losing their job. How some in the Thyatira church were handling the situation caused Christ great concern.

The Commendation
I know your deeds, and your love and faith and service and perseverance, and that your deeds of late are greater than at first. (2:19)

Christ first commended the church at Thyatira before voicing His concerns about it. He assured them that He had not forgotten their righteous deeds (Hebrews 6:10), which He divided into four categories.

First, the believers at Thyatira were showing love for God and for one another. In some ways, Thyatira was strong where Ephesus was weak. Thyatira is the first of the seven churches commended for its love.

Second, Christ commended them for their faith. The Greek word for "faith" here is better translated "faithfulness." The true Christians in Thyatira were dependable, reliable, and consistent (2:25).

Out of faith and love grow "service and perseverance." Those who love will express it through helping others. Those who are faithful will steadfastly persevere in the faith (Matthew 16:24–26; 24:13).

Not only did the Thyatiran Christians possess these virtues, but their deeds of late were "greater than at first." Their loving service was becoming more consistent, and their faithful perseverance growing stronger. They were growing in grace and advancing the cause of Christ (2 Peter 1:8). For that behavior they were commended.

The Concern

But I have this against you, that you tolerate the woman Jezebel, who calls herself a prophetess, and she teaches and leads My bond-servants astray so that they commit acts of immorality and eat things sacrificed to idols. I gave her time to repent, and she does not want to repent of her immorality. Behold, I will throw her on a bed of sickness, and those who commit adultery with her into great tribulation, unless they repent of her deeds. And I will kill her children with pestilence, and all the churches will know that I am He who searches the minds and hearts; and I will give to each one of you according to your deeds. (2:20–23)

All was not well with the church at Thyatira. The problem was not external persecution, but internal compromise (Acts 20:29–30). Christ had noticed serious error, causing Him to warn "I have this against you." The use of the singular pronoun "you" points this phrase specifically to the leader of the church.

Their sin consisted of two parts. First, they violated the biblical teaching that women were not to be teachers or preachers in the church (1 Timothy 2:12). That led them to tolerate Jezebel, who called herself a prophetess. Second, they allowed her to teach error. As a result, Jesus declares, "she . . . leads My bond-servants astray so that they commit acts of immorality and eat things sacrificed to idols."

Jezebel was certainly not the woman's real name, but her actions resembled the infamous wife of King Ahab. Therefore Christ labeled her with the symbolic name Jezebel. The Old Testament Jezebel was an unspeakably vile woman. Through Jezebel's evil influence, Baal worship became widespread in Israel (1 Kings 16:30–31).

Likewise, the woman in Thyatira called Jezebel succeeded in leading

Christ's bond-servants astray so that they committed acts of immorality and ate things sacrificed to idols. Whatever the specific content of her false teaching, it led the majority of the Thyatiran believers astray from truth and righteousness.

The Bible teaches that true Christians can fall into sexual immorality (1 Corinthians 6:15–20) and idolatry (1 Corinthians 10:21). To lead other Christians into false doctrine or immoral living is a very serious sin, meriting the most severe punishment (Matthew 18:6–10).[2] In the case of the Old Testament Jezebel, her life ended in a gruesome death (2 Kings 9:30–37).

Graciously the Lord gave the false prophetess at Thyatira time to repent, but she did not want to repent of her immorality. Her blunt and final refusal to repent would lead to a terrible judgment, introduced by the arresting word "behold." Because Jezebel refused to repent, Christ declared, "I will throw her on a bed of sickness." The words "of sickness" are not part of the original Greek text but were supplied by the translators. In light of Jezebel's refusal to repent, it is more likely that the bed refers to death and hell, the ultimate resting place for those who refuse to repent.

Divine judgment was about to fall not only on Jezebel, but also on those who committed adultery with her. The Lord threatened to cast them "into great tribulation." This is not the tribulation described in Revelation 4–19, but distress or trouble. Since these were the sinning Christians who had believed her lies, the Lord does not threaten to send them to hell as He did the false prophetess. He promised to bring them severe chastening unless they repented of their deeds.

Then Christ declares, "I will kill her children with pestilence." Jezebel's children were her spiritual children. The church was about forty years old when John wrote, so her false teaching had been around long enough for a second generation to have arisen. As he did with Ananias and Sapphira, the Lord threatened to kill them with pestilence. It was too late for Jezebel since her heart was hardened in unrepentant sin. Still, Christ mercifully warned her followers to repent while there was still time.

It is not known how many in that church responded to Christ's warning, but, tragically, the Thyatira church as a whole apparently did not obey it. History records that it fell to the Montanist heresy, a movement led by a false prophet who claimed continuing revelation from God apart from Scripture. The church disappeared by the end of the second century.

Christ then addressed a word of comfort to those true believers in the Thyatira church: "I will give to each one of you according to your deeds." Christ's judgment would be based on each person's deeds. Those who were innocent would not be punished along with the guilty (Matthew 7:16; 16:27; Revelation 22:12). God is the righteous judge "who will render to each person according to his deeds" (Romans 2:6).

Works have always been the basis for divine judgment. That does not mean, however, that salvation is by works (Ephesians 2:8–9; 2 Timothy 1:9; Titus 3:5). Instead, people's deeds reveal their spiritual condition. That is what James meant when he said, "I will show you my faith by my works" (James 2:18). Upon salvation, Christians are new creatures (2 Corinthians 5:17), "created in Christ Jesus for good works, which God prepared beforehand so that we would walk in them" (Ephesians 2:10).

The Command

But I say to you, the rest who are in Thyatira, who do not hold this teaching, who have not known the deep things of Satan, as they call them—I place no other burden on you. Nevertheless what you have, hold fast until I come. (2:24–25)

Having warned those following false teaching to repent, Christ addressed words of comfort to the rest who were in Thyatira, who did not hold to Jezebel's teaching. He further defined the true believers as those "who have not known the deep things of Satan," as they called them. Jezebel and her followers claimed to discover the very depths of Satan's domain and remain spiritually unharmed. Since the spirit belongs to God, their twisted logic concluded, what does it matter if the body attends idolatrous feasts and engages in sexual immorality? They imagined themselves to be free to explore the satanic sphere and yet come to worship God.

To the true believers who had not experienced the alleged deeper knowledge claimed by these heretics, Christ said, "I place no other burden on you." Bearing the burden of false teaching and immoral living rampant in their church, along with personally resisting temptation themselves, was burden enough. Finally, Christ encourages them, "what you have, hold fast until I come." The use of the strong Greek word *krateō*, meaning "hold fast," indicates that it would not be easy. The coming of Christ as it related to the Thyatira church was His coming to them in judgment. Yet they were urged to "cling to what is good" (Romans 12:9) until Christ's return.

The Counsel

He who overcomes, and he who keeps My deeds until the end, to him I will give authority over the nations; and he shall rule them with a rod of iron, as the vessels of the potter are broken to pieces, as I also have received authority from My Father; and I will give him the morning star. He who has an ear, let him hear what the Spirit says to the churches. (2:26–29)

To the one "who overcomes" and "who keeps Christ's deeds until the end," Christ promises two things. First, Christ will give them "authority over the nations, and he shall rule them with a rod of iron, as the vessels of the potter are broken to pieces." That promise, taken from Psalm 2:7–9, is one of participation in the millennial kingdom. Those who remained faithful to Christ despite being beaten and despised in this life will rule with Him in His earthly kingdom. They will exercise authority over the nations, ruling them with a rod of iron (see Revelation 12:5; 19:15). Those nations in the millennial kingdom who rebel against Christ's rule and threaten His people will be destroyed. Those who rule with Him will help protect His people and promote holiness and righteousness. Christ will delegate authority to them as He also has received authority from His Father (John 5:22, 27).

Christ also promised to give to His faithful followers "the morning star." Some connect the morning star with such passages as Daniel 12:3 and Matthew 13:43. The promise would be that believers will reflect Christ's glory. While Christians will reflect Christ's glory, it is better to see the morning star as Christ Himself, a title He assumes in Revelation

22:16. Christ promised believers Himself in all His fullness (cf. 1 Corinthians 13:12).

The concluding words, "He who has an ear, let him hear what the Spirit says to the churches," are a charge to follow the message of the letter to the church at Thyatira. Three important truths stand out. First, this letter reveals the seriousness of practicing and tolerating sin, and that God will judge sin in the church. Second, a pattern of obedience marks true Christians. Finally, God's gracious promise is that, in spite of struggles with sin and error in churches, Christians will experience all the fullness of Christ as they reign with Him in His kingdom. Those churches, like Thyatira, who fail to obey the message will receive divine judgment. Those who do obey its message will receive divine blessing.

SARDIS: THE DEAD CHURCH

While the believers at Thyatira tolerated sin, those at Sardis were dead to sin. The church had a reputation for being alive with the light, but Christ pronounced it dead. The spiritual darkness of false teaching and sinful living had extinguished the light on the inside, though some of its reputation remained.

Like the rest of the seven churches, the church at Sardis was an actual, existing church in John's day. Yet it also symbolizes the dead churches that have existed throughout history, even in our own day.

The Correspondent
He who has the seven Spirits of God and the seven stars, says this: (3:1*b*)

The descriptions of the divine author in each of the seven letters are drawn from the vision of 1:12–17. The letter to Sardis draws an additional component from the salutation in 1:4, where the phrase "the seven Spirits" of God also appears. That phrase may refer to Isaiah 11:2, where the Holy Spirit is described as "the Spirit of the Lord . . . , the spirit of wisdom and understanding, the spirit of counsel and strength, the spirit of knowledge and the fear of the Lord." It may also refer to the symbolic depiction of the Holy Spirit as a lampstand with seven lamps presented in Zechariah 4:1–10. In either case, the reference is to the Spirit's fullness. Jesus Christ is represented in His church through the Holy Spirit.

The seven stars are the seven messengers or elders (1:20), one from each of the seven churches, who likely carried a copy of the book of Revelation back to their respective churches. The imagery shows Jesus Christ, the sovereign Lord of the church, ruling through godly leaders and pastors.

Christ's introduction of Himself does not hint at the severity of the situation in Sardis. Surprisingly, He did not introduce Himself as the divine Judge (as He did in 2:18), although the church at Sardis faced imminent judgment. Instead, He depicted Himself as the One who sovereignly works in His church through the Holy Spirit and godly leaders. That introduction served as a reminder to the Sardis church of what they lacked. Devoid of the Spirit, the church at Sardis was dead.

The Church
the church in Sardis (3:1a)

Though the details are not recorded in Scripture, the church at Sardis was probably founded as an outreach of Paul's ministry at Ephesus (Acts 19:10). The most prominent person from the church at Sardis known to history is Melito. He was an apologist, a defender of Christianity, who served as bishop of Sardis in the late second century. He also wrote the earliest known commentary on passages from Revelation. The letter does not speak of persecution, false doctrine, false teachers, or corrupt living. Yet some combination of those things was obviously present at Sardis, since the church had died.

The City
Sardis (3:1a)

To a striking degree, the history of the church at Sardis paralleled that of the city. Founded about 1200 B.C., Sardis had been one of the greatest cities in the ancient world, capital of the fabulously wealthy Lydian kingdom. Aesop, the famous writer of fables, may have been from Sardis. Much of Sardis's wealth came from gold taken from the nearby Pactolus River. Archaeologists have found hundreds of crucibles, used for refining gold, in the ruins of Sardis.[3] Gold and silver coins were apparently first minted at Sardis as well. The city also benefited from its location at the western end of the royal road that led east to the Persian capital city of Susa, and from its proximity to other important trade routes. It was also a center for wool production and the garment industry. Sardis even claimed to have discovered how to dye wool.

Sardis was located about thirty miles south of Thyatira in the fertile valley of the Hermus River. A series of spurs or hills jutted out from the ridge of Mount Tmolus, south of the Hermus River. On one of those hills, some fifteen hundred feet above the valley floor, stood Sardis. Its location made the city nearly invincible. The hill on which Sardis was built had smooth, nearly perpendicular rock walls on three sides. Only from the south could the city be approached, via a steep, difficult path. The one drawback to an otherwise ideal site was that there was limited room for the city to expand. Eventually, as Sardis grew, a new city sprang up at the foot of the hill. The old site remained a refuge to retreat into when danger threatened.

Its seemingly indestructible location caused the inhabitants of Sardis to become overconfident. That complacency eventually led to the city's downfall. Through carelessness, Sardis was conquered. The news of its downfall sent shock waves through the Greek world. One scholar relates the account of Sardis's fall:

> Despite an alleged warning against self-satisfaction by the Greek god whom he consulted, Croesus the king of Lydia initiated an attack against Cyrus king of Persia, but was soundly defeated. Returning to Sardis to recoup and rebuild his army for another attack, he was pursued quickly by Cyrus who laid siege against Sardis. Croesus felt utterly secure in his impregnable situation atop the acropolis and foresaw an easy victory over the Persians who were cornered among the perpendicular rocks in the

lower city, an easy prey for the assembling Lydian army to crush. After retiring one evening while the drama was unfolding, he awakened to discover that the Persians had gained control of the acropolis by scaling one-by-one the steep walls (549 B.C.). So secure did the Sardians feel that they left this means of access completely unguarded, permitting the climbers to ascend unobserved. It is said that even a child could have defended the city from this kind of attack, but not so much as one observer had been appointed to watch the side that was believed to be inaccessible.

History repeated itself more than three and a half centuries later when Antiochus the Great conquered Sardis by utilizing the services of a sure-footed mountain climber from Crete (195 B.C.). His army entered the city by another route while the defenders in careless confidence were content to guard the one known approach, the isthmus of land connected to Mount Tmolus on the south.[4]

Sardis never regained its independence, eventually coming under Roman control in 133 B.C. A catastrophic earthquake destroyed the city in A.D. 17, but it was rebuilt with the generous financial aid of Emperor Tiberius. In gratitude, the inhabitants of Sardis built a temple in his honor. The city's primary object of worship, however, was the goddess Cybele—the same goddess worshiped at Ephesus as Artemis (Diana). Hot springs not far from Sardis were celebrated as a spot in which the gods manifested their supposed power to give life to the dead—an ironic note for a city whose church was dead. In John's day Sardis was prosperous but decaying. Both the city and the church it contained had lost their vitality.

The Concern
I know your deeds, that you have a name that you are alive, but you are dead. . . . For I have not found your deeds completed in the sight of My God. (3:1c, 2b)

Because the Sardis church was spiritually dead, Christ skipped the usual commendation and turned directly to His concerns. Though its outward appearance may have fooled others, the Sardis church could not fool the all-knowing Christ. He said, "I know your deeds." With His infallible knowledge, He pronounced the Sardis church dead. It was defiled by the world, marked by inward decay, and populated by unbelieving people playing church.

Spiritual death in the New Testament is always connected with its sinful root. Ephesians 2:1 describes the unbelieving as "dead in trespasses and sins." The church at Sardis was like a museum where stuffed animals are exhibited in their natural habitats. Everything appears to be normal, but nothing is alive.

The church at Sardis was going through the motions. Christ declared that those deeds were not "completed in the sight of My God." Though sufficient to give the Sardis church a reputation among others, those deeds were unacceptable in God's sight. The spiritually dead members populating the Sardis church were living a lie. They had been weighed on the scales by the Righteous Judge and found wanting (cf. Daniel 5:27).

The Commendation
But you have a few people in Sardis who have not soiled their garments; and they will walk with Me in white, for they are worthy. (3:4)

Within this dead church of unbelievers, a few true Christians were scattered like flowers in a desert. There were not enough of them, however, to change Christ's overall evaluation of the church as dead. Yet He had not forgotten those who remained faithful to Him (Malachi 3:16–17; Hebrews 6:10).

God had His remnant even at Sardis. There were a few sincere followers of Christ. He described the faithful remnant as those who "have not soiled their garments." The Greek word translated "soiled" can also mean "to stain" or "to pollute." It was a word that would have been familiar to readers in Sardis because of the city's wool-dyeing industry. "Garments" symbolized character in Scripture (Isaiah 64:6; Jude 23). The faithful remnant could come into God's presence because they had not defiled or polluted themselves, but had shown godly character.

Specifically, Christ says of them that "they will walk with Me in white, for they are worthy." In ancient times, such garments were worn for celebrations and festivals. Because they refused to "defile their garments," Christ would replace those humanly preserved clean garments with divinely pure ones (7:14). The white robes of purity Christ promises here and in verse 5 are elsewhere worn by Christ Himself (Matthew 17:2; Mark 9:3) and the holy angels (Matthew 28:3; Mark 16:5; Acts 1:10). Those who have a measure of holiness and purity now will be given perfect holiness and purity in the future.

The Command

Wake up, and strengthen the things that remain, which were about to die. . . . So remember what you have received and heard; and keep it, and repent. Therefore if you do not wake up, I will come like a thief, and you will not know at what hour I will come to you. (3:2a, 3)

Christ addressed the command to the faithful remnant at Sardis. If their church was to survive, it desperately needed life. Christ laid out for them the path to spiritual restoration by giving them five steps to follow.

First, they needed to "wake up." There was no time for indifference. The believing remnant needed to look at what was happening in their church, evaluate the situation, confront sin, and make a difference.

Second, they needed to "strengthen the things that remain, which were about to die." "Things" here in the original language does not refer to people, but to spiritual realities. Christ exhorted the true Christians at Sardis to fan into flame the dying embers of the remaining spiritual graces in their church.

The third step was for the faithful remnant to remember what they had received and heard. They needed to go back to the truths of God's Word, remembering the gospel and the teaching of the apostles. By this time, Paul's letters were in circulation (2 Peter 3:15–16) and the rest of the New Testament had been written. The believers at Sardis needed to reaffirm their belief in the truth about Christ, sin, salvation, and holy living. Fourth, having gone back to the truths of Scripture, they needed to keep them. Correct beliefs apart from obedient lives would not bring about the necessary renewal.

Finally, they needed to repent. With great sorrow, the believers at Sardis were to confess and turn away from their sins. These five steps, if diligently practiced, would bring about revival.

The consequences if revival did not come would be severe. Christ warned them "if you do not wake up, I will come like a thief, and you will not know at what hour I will come to you." The picture of Jesus coming like a thief always carries the idea of imminent judgment (Matthew 24:43; Luke 12:39; 1 Thessalonians 5:2, 4). The threat here is not related to His second coming, but that the Lord would come and destroy the Sardis church if there was no revival.

The Counsel
He who overcomes will thus be clothed in white garments; and I will not erase his name from the book of life, and I will confess his name before My Father and before His angels. He who has an ear, let him hear what the Spirit says to the churches. (3:5–6)

Lastly, Christ described the rewards awaiting those who participated in the revival. True Christians will be "clothed in white garments." In the ancient world, white garments were also worn for festive occasions such as weddings. True Christians will wear theirs at the marriage supper of the Lamb (19:7–9). White robes were also worn by those celebrating victory in battle. All true Christians are victorious through Christ over sin, death, and Satan. However, white robes here primarily represent purity and holiness. Christ promises to clothe Christians in the brilliance of eternal purity and holiness.

Christ further promises every true Christian that He will not erase their name from the Book of Life, but "will confess [their] name before the Father and before His angels." Incredibly, although the text says just the opposite, some people assume that this verse teaches that a Christian's name can be erased from the Book of Life. They instead turn God's promise into a threat.

Some argue that Exodus 32:33 supports the idea that God may remove someone's name from the Book of Life. In that passage the Lord tells Moses that "whoever has sinned against Me, I will blot him out of My book." There is no contradiction, however, between that passage and Christ's promise in Revelation 3:5. The book referred to in Exodus 32:33 is not the Book of Life described here, in Philippians 4:3, and later in Revelation (13:8; 17:8; 20:12,15; 21:27). Instead, it refers to the book of the living, the record of those who are alive (Psalm 69:28). The threat, then, is not eternal punishment, but physical death.

In John's day, rulers kept a register of each city's citizens. If someone died or committed a serious crime, their name was erased from that register. Christ, the King of heaven, promises never to erase a true Christian's name from the list of those whose names were "written from the foundation of the world in the book of life of the Lamb who has been slain" (13:8). On the contrary, Christ will confess every believer's name before God the Father and before His angels. He will affirm that they belong to Him.

The letter to Sardis ends, like the other six, with an exhortation to follow the counsel, commands, and promises it contains: "He who has an ear, let him hear what the Spirit says to the churches." The spiritually dead people playing church needed to follow Christ's warning of impending judgment. The indifferent believers needed to wake up before it was too late to rescue their church. And the faithful few could take comfort in the knowledge that their salvation was eternally secure.

What happened to Sardis? Did they heed the warning? Did revival come? That such a prominent man as Melito served as bishop of Sardis several decades after John wrote argues that at least some revival took place in Sardis. Until Christ returns, it is never too late for other dying churches to find the path to spiritual renewal.

6

The Letters to the
BELIEVERS
at Philadelphia
and Laodicea

(3:7–22)

Occasionally I am asked by young men seeking a church to pastor if I know of a church without any problems. My response to them is "If I did, I wouldn't tell you; you'd go there and spoil it." The point is, *there are no perfect churches.* The church is not a place for people with no weaknesses. It is a fellowship of those who are aware of their weaknesses and long for the strength and grace of God to fill their lives. It is a spiritual hospital for those who know they are sick and needy.

PHILADELPHIA: THE FAITHFUL CHURCH

Like all churches, the one in Philadelphia had its imperfections. Yet the Lord commended its members for their faithfulness and loyalty. Along with Smyrna, they were the only two of the seven churches that did not receive condemnation from the Lord of the church. In spite of their struggles, the Christians at Philadelphia were faithful and obedient to the Lord. They provide an outstanding model of a loyal church.

The Correspondent
*He who is holy, who is true, who has the key of David, who opens and
no one will shut, and who shuts and no one opens, says this:* (3:7b)

The Lord Jesus Christ, the divine author of the seven letters, always introduces Himself with a description reflecting His character. In the previous
five letters, those descriptions had come from the vision recorded in
1:12–17. But this description of Him is unique and not drawn from that
earlier vision. It has distinctly Old Testament features.

"He who is holy" refers to God, who alone possesses absolute holiness.
The Old Testament repeatedly describes God as the Holy One (e.g., 2 Kings
19:22; Job 6:10; Psalms 71:22; 78:41). To say that God is holy is to say
that He is completely separate from sin. Therefore His character is absolutely flawless.

The title "Holy One" is used in the New Testament as a messianic title
for the Lord Jesus Christ. It is spoken by a demon (Mark 1:24), by an
angel speaking to Mary (Luke 1:35), and by Peter (John 6:69; Acts 3:14).
In John 6:69 Peter affirmed, "We have believed and have come to know
that You are the Holy One of God."

Jesus' identification of Himself as "He who is holy" reveals a direct
claim to deity. Christ possesses the holy and sinless nature of God. Because
Christ is holy, His church must be holy. As Peter wrote, "Like the Holy One
who called you, be holy yourselves also in all your behavior" (1 Peter 1:15).
That the omniscient Holy One gave no condemnation to the Philadelphia
church speaks very well of their view of Christ's holiness.

Christ also describes Himself as "He who is true." Truth is used in
combination with holiness to describe God in Revelation 6:10; 15:3; 16:7;
19:2, 11. The Greek word used here for "true" describes something that is
genuine, authentic, and real. In the midst of the falsehood and error that
fills the world, Jesus Christ is the truth (John 14:6).

Third, Christ describes Himself as the One who "has the key of David."
In Revelation 5:5 and 22:16, David symbolizes the role of the Messiah. A
"key" in Scripture represents authority. Whoever holds a key has control
(Revelation 1:18; 9:1; 20:1; Matthew 16:19). The term "the key of David"

also appears in Isaiah 22:22, where it refers to Eliakim, the prime minister to Israel's king. In his role, he controlled access to the top leader. As the holder of the key of David, Jesus alone has the authority to determine who enters His kingdom. Revelation 1:18 reveals that Jesus has the keys to death and hell. Here He is shown with the keys to salvation and blessing.

Finally, Jesus identifies Himself as He "who opens and no one will shut, and who shuts and no one opens." This description stresses Christ's ultimate power. "I act and who can reverse it?" declared the Lord in Isaiah 43:13. No one can shut the doors to the kingdom or to blessing if He holds them open. No one can force them open if He holds them shut. Based on the promise of verse 8, Christ could also be referring to opening and shutting doors for service. In either case, the emphasis is on His sovereign control over His church.

The Church
the church in Philadelphia (3:7a)

Little is known about the Philadelphia church apart from this passage. Like most of the other seven churches, it was probably founded during Paul's ministry at Ephesus (Acts 19:10). A few years after John wrote Revelation, the church father Ignatius passed through Philadelphia on his way to martyrdom at Rome. He later wrote the church a letter of encouragement and instruction. Some Christians from Philadelphia were martyred with Polycarp at Smyrna. The church lasted for centuries. The Christians in Philadelphia stood firm even after the region was overrun by the Muslims, until finally disappearing sometime during the fourteenth century.

The City
Philadelphia (3:7a)

From the Hermus River valley, where Sardis and Smyrna were located, a smaller valley near the Cogamis River branches off to the southeast. A road through this valley provided the best means of ascending the 2,500 feet from the Hermus valley to the vast central plateau. In this valley, about thirty miles from Sardis, was the city of Philadelphia.

Philadelphia was the youngest of the seven cities, founded sometime after 189 B.C. either by King Eumenes of Pergamum or his brother, Attalus II, who succeeded him as king. In either case, the city derived its name from Attalus II's nickname Philadelphus ("brother lover"), which his loyalty to his brother Eumenes had earned him.

Though situated on an easily defensible site on an eight-hundred-foot-high hill overlooking an important road, Philadelphia was not founded primarily as a military outpost. Its founders intended it to be a center of Greek culture and language. Philadelphia succeeded in its mission so well that by A.D. 19 the Lydian language had been completely replaced by Greek.

Philadelphia benefited from its location at the junction of several important trade routes, earning it the title "gateway to the East." The city was located on the edge of the Katakekaumene (the "burned land"), a volcanic region whose fertile soil was ideally suited for vineyards. Being near such a seismically active region had its drawbacks, however. In A.D. 17 a powerful earthquake rocked Philadelphia, along with Sardis and ten other nearby cities. Though the initial destruction was greater at Sardis, Philadelphia experienced frequent aftershocks during the coming years.

In gratitude for Caesar Tiberius's financial aid in rebuilding their city, the Philadelphians joined with several other cities in constructing a monument to him. Going beyond the other cities, Philadelphia actually changed its name to Neocaesarea for a number of years. Several decades later, the city again changed its name to Flavia, in honor of the ruling Roman imperial family. It would be known by both names, Philadelphia and Flavia, throughout the second and third centuries.

The Commendation

I know your deeds. Behold, I have put before you an open door which no one can shut, because you have a little power, and have kept My word, and have not denied My name. Behold, I will cause those of the synagogue of Satan, who say that they are Jews and are not, but lie—I will make them come and bow down at your feet, and make them know that I have loved you. Because you have kept the word of My persever-ance, I also will keep you from the hour of testing, that hour which is about to come upon the whole world, to test those who dwell on the earth. I am coming quickly; (3:8–11a)

Bypassing the concerns mentioned to five of the other churches, this let-ter moved on to commend the Christians at Philadelphia for four realities that characterized the church.

First, the Philadelphia church had "a little power." That was not a nega-tive comment about its weakness, but a commendation of its strength. The Philadelphia church was small in numbers, but had a powerful impact on its city. Most of its members may have been from the lower classes of society (1 Corinthians 1:26). Yet despite its small size, spiritual power flowed in the Philadelphia church.

The believers at Philadelphia were also marked by obedience; "you have kept My word." Like Martin Luther, on trial before the Imperial Diet, they could say, "My conscience is captive to the Word of God." They did not deviate from the pattern of obedience, proving the genuineness of their love for Christ (John 14:23–24; 15:13–14).

Third, they had "not denied [His] name," despite the pressures they faced to do so. They remained loyal regardless of the cost. Revelation 14:12 describes the tribulation saints who refused to take the mark of the beast: "Here is the perseverance of the saints who keep the command-ments of God and their faith in Jesus." Like them, the Philadelphia church would not turn from its faith.

Finally, the church had kept "the word of [His] perseverance." The New International Version's translation clarifies Christ's meaning: "You have kept my command to endure patiently." The Christians at Philadelphia persevered faithfully through all of their difficulties.

Because of its faithfulness, Christ made the Philadelphia church some astounding promises. First, He put before them an "open door which no one can shut." Their salvation was secure. Their entrance into the blessings of salvation by grace and Christ's future kingdom was guaranteed. The picture of Christ's opening the door also symbolizes His giving the faithful Philadelphia church opportunities for service. In Scripture an open door depicts freedom to proclaim the gospel (1 Corintians 16:8–9; 2 Corintians 2:12; Colossians 4:2–3). Their city's strategic location provided the Christians at Philadelphia with an excellent opportunity to spread the gospel.

Verse 9 records a second promise made by Christ to the Philadelphia church: "Behold, I will cause those of the synagogue of Satan, who say that they are Jews and are not, but lie—I will make them come and bow down at your feet, and make them know that I have loved you." As was the case in Smyrna (2:9), Christians in Philadelphia faced hostility from unbelieving Jews. Ignatius later debated some hostile Jews during his visit to Philadelphia. Because of their rejection of Jesus as the Messiah, they were not a synagogue of God, but a synagogue of Satan. Though they claimed they were Jews, their claim was a lie. They were Jews physically, but not spiritually (Romans 2:28–29).

Amazingly, Christ promised that some of the very Jews who were persecuting the Christians at Philadelphia would come and bow down at their feet. Bowing at someone's feet depicts total submission. The Philadelphia church's enemies would be completely humbled and defeated. This imagery comes from the Old Testament, which describes the future day when unbelieving Gentiles will bow down to the believing remnant of Israel (Isaiah 45:14; 49:23; 60:14). The Philadelphia church's faithfulness would be rewarded by the salvation of some of the very Jews who were persecuting it.

Verse 10 contains a final promise to the faithful Philadelphia church: "Because you have kept the word of My perseverance, I also will keep you from the hour of testing, that hour which is about to come upon the whole world, to test those who dwell on the earth." Because the believers in Philadelphia had successfully passed so many tests, Jesus promised to spare them from the ultimate test. The sweeping nature of that promise extends far beyond the Philadelphia congregation to encompass all faithful churches throughout history. This verse promises that the church will be delivered from the tribulation, thus supporting a pretribulation rapture.

The rapture is the subject of three passages in the New Testament (John 14:1–4; 1 Corinthians 15:51–54; 1 Thessalonians 4:13–17), none of which speak of judgment but rather of the church being taken up to heaven. There are three views of the timing of the rapture in relation to the tribulation: that it comes at the end of the tribulation (posttribulationism), in the middle of the tribulation (midtribulationism), and the view that seems to be supported by this text, that the rapture takes place before the tribulation (pretribulationism).

Several aspects of this wonderful promise may be noted. First, the test is still for the future. Second, the test is for a limited time. Jesus described it as "the hour of testing." Third, it is a test or trial that will expose people for what they really are. Fourth, the test is worldwide in scope, since it will "come upon the whole world." Finally, and most significantly, its purpose is to test "those who dwell on the earth"—a phrase used as a technical term in the book of Revelation for unbelievers (6:10; 8:13; 11:10; 13:8, 12, 14; 17:2, 8). The hour of testing is Daniel's Seventieth Week (Daniel 9:25–27), the time of Jacob's trouble (Jeremiah 30:7), the seven-year tribulation period. The Lord promises to keep His church out of the future time of testing that will come on unbelievers.

Unbelievers will either pass the test by repenting, or fail it by refusing to repent. Revelation 6:9–11; 7:9–10, 14; 14:4; and 17:14 describe those who repent during the tribulation and are saved, passing the test. Revelation 6:15–17; 9:20; 16:11; and 19:17–18 describe those who refuse to repent, failing the test.

There has been much debate over the meaning of the phrase translated "keep from." Those who argue that the church will go through the tribulation hold that this phrase means preservation through the time of judgment. They believe the church will go through the tribulation judgments and that God will preserve it in the midst of them. That view is unlikely, however, both on linguistic and biblical grounds. The basic meaning of the Greek preposition translated "from" (*ek*) is "from," "out from," or "away from." If the Lord intended to convey that the church would be preserved in the midst of the tribulation, a different Greek preposition meaning "in" (*en*) or through" (*dia*) would have been more appropriate.

Another clear objection to interpreting this as a promise of preservation in the tribulation is that believers in the tribulation will not be preserved. In fact, many will be martyred (6:9–11; 7:9–14). Some hold that the promise of deliverance is only from God's wrath during the tribulation. But a promise that God will not kill believers but will allow Satan and Antichrist to do so would provide small comfort to the suffering church at Philadelphia.

The coming that Christ refers to differs from those promised to others of the seven churches (2:5, 16; 3:3). Those earlier promises were warnings of impending judgment on sinning churches (Acts 5:1–11; 1 Corinthians 11:28–30). The coming spoken of here is to bring the hour of testing that culminates in Christ's second coming. It is Christ's coming to deliver the church (2 Thessalonians 2:1), not to bring judgment to it. "Quickly" depicts the imminency of Christ's coming for His church. It could happen at any time.

The Command
hold fast what you have, so that no one will take your crown. (3:11b)

Because of the Lord's imminent return for His church, believers must hold fast what they have. The members of the Philadelphia church had been faithful to Christ. He commanded them to remain faithful. Those who persevere to the end thereby prove the genuineness of their salvation (Matthew 10:22; 24:13).

It is true that believers are eternally secure because of the power of God. Yet He secures them by providing believers with a persevering faith. Christians are saved by God's power, but not apart from their constant, undying faith (Colossians 1:22–23). According to 1 John 2:19, those who abandon the faith reveal that they were never truly saved to begin with: "They went out from us, but they were not really of us; for if they had been of us, they would have remained with us; but they went out, so that it would be shown that they all are not of us."

Christ's promise to the one who faithfully perseveres is "no one will take your crown." Revelation 2:10 defines this crown as the "crown of life," or as the Greek text literally reads, "the crown which is life." The crown for those who faithfully endure to the end is eternal life with all its rewards. Second Timothy 4:8 describes it as a crown of righteousness, and 1 Peter 5:4 as one of glory. In our glorified state, we will be able to perfectly reflect God's glory. Those whose faithful perseverance marks them as true children of God never need to fear losing their salvation.

The Counsel

He who overcomes, I will make him a pillar in the temple of My God, and he will not go out from it anymore; and I will write on him the name of My God, and the name of the city of My God, the new Jerusalem, which comes down out of heaven from My God, and My new name. He who has an ear, let him hear what the Spirit says to the churches. (3:12–13)

As He concluded the letter to the faithful church at Philadelphia, Christ promised four eternal blessings to the one "who overcomes."

The first promise is that Christ will make him "a pillar in the temple of My God, and he will not go out from it anymore." A pillar represents stability and permanence. Pillars can also represent honor. In pagan temples they were often carved to honor a particular deity. The marvelous promise Christ makes to believers is that they will have an eternal place of honor in the temple of God. To people used to fleeing their city because of earthquakes and enemies, the promise that they will not go out from heaven was understood as security in eternal glory.

Christ's second promise is that He "will write on him the name of My God." That depicts ownership, signifying that all true Christians belong to God. It also speaks of the intimate personal relationship we have with Him forever.

Third, Christ promises to write on believers "the name of the city of My God, the New Jerusalem, which comes down out of heaven from My God." Christians have eternal citizenship in heaven's capital city, the New Jerusalem, described in detail in Revelation 21. That is yet another promise of security, safety, and glory.

Finally, Christ promises believers His "new name." Christ's name represents the fullness of His person. In heaven, believers will "see Him just as He is" (1 John 3:2), and whatever we may have known of Him will not compare with the reality in which we will then see Him. The new name by which we will be privileged to call Him will reflect that glorious revelation of His Person.

The exhortation "He who has an ear, let him hear what the Spirit says to the churches" closes all seven letters. Believers must obey the truths found in each letter, since the seven churches represent the types of churches that have existed throughout history. The letter to the faithful Philadelphia church reveals that the holy, omnipotent God pours out His blessings on churches that remain loyal to Him.

LAODICEA: THE LUKEWARM CHURCH

The church at Laodicea was the last—and worst—of the seven churches written to by Christ. This church was a totally unchanged, deceitful assembly. It has the grim distinction of being the only church of the seven for which Christ offers nothing positive. Due to the drastic nature of the situation at Laodicea, this is also the most threatening of the seven letters.

The Correspondent
The Amen, the faithful and true Witness, the Beginning of the creation of God, says this: (3:14b)

As in the letter to the church at Philadelphia, Christ did not identify Himself using any of the phrases from the vision recorded in 1:12–17. Instead, He identified Himself using three divine titles.

First, the Lord Jesus Christ described Himself as "The Amen." That unique title, used only here in Scripture to describe Christ, is similar to Isaiah 65:16, where God is twice called the "God of truth." *Amen* is from the Hebrew word meaning "truth," "affirmation," or "certainty." It refers to something firm, fixed, and unchangeable. Amen is often used in Scripture to affirm the truthfulness of a statement. Christ is certainly the Amen in the sense that He is the God of truth incarnate. He is the Amen because He is the One who confirmed all of God's promises (2 Corinthians 1:20).

Christ also identified Himself as "the faithful and true Witness." That title further expresses the thought communicated in the first title. Not only is Jesus the Amen because of His work, but also because everything He speaks is the truth. He is completely trustworthy and reliable. Jesus Christ is "the way, and the truth, and the life" (John 14:6). This was an appropriate way to begin the letter to the Laodiceans because it affirmed to them that Christ had accurately assessed their spiritual condition. It also affirmed that His offer of fellowship and salvation in verse 20 was true, because God's promises were confirmed through His work.

Finally, Christ referred to Himself as "the Beginning of the creation of God." The English translation is somewhat ambiguous and misleading. As a result, some have attempted to use this verse to prove that Jesus is a created being. There is no ambiguity in the Greek text, however. It does not mean that Christ was the first person God created, but rather that Christ Himself is the source of creation (Revelation 22:13). Through His power everything was created (John 1:3; Hebrews 1:2). Yet the same heresy plaguing the Colossians likely had made its way to Laodicea (cf. Colossians 4:16). A form of incipient gnosticism taught that Christ was a created being, one of a series of emanations from God. Its proponents also claimed that they possessed a secret, higher spiritual knowledge above and beyond the simple words of Scripture.

The Church
the church in Laodicea (3:14a)

The New Testament does not record anything about the founding of the church at Laodicea. Like most of the other six churches, it was likely established during Paul's ministry at Ephesus (Acts 19:10). Paul did not found it, since when he wrote Colossians some years later he still had not visited Laodicea (Colossians 2:1). Since Paul's coworker Epaphras founded the church in nearby Colossae (Colossians 1:6–7), he may well have founded the Laodicean church as well. Some have suggested that Archippus, Philemon's son (Philemon 2), was its pastor (Colossians 4:17), since the fourth-century *Apostolic Constitutions* names Archippus as the bishop of Laodicea.

The City
Laodicea (3:14a)

One of a triad of cities in the Lycus valley, about one hundred miles east of Ephesus, Laodicea was the southeasternmost of the seven cities, about forty miles from Philadelphia. Its sister cities were Colossae, about ten miles to the east, and Hierapolis, about six miles to the north. Located on a plateau several hundred feet high, Laodicea was geographically nearly impenetrable. Its only vulnerability to attack was due to the fact that it had to pipe in its water from several miles away through aqueducts that could easily be blocked or diverted by besieging forces.

Laodicea was founded by the Seleucid ruler Antiochus II and named after his first wife. Since he divorced her in 253 B.C., the city was most likely founded before that date. Though its original settlers were largely from Syria, a significant number of Jews also settled there. A local governor once prohibited the Jews from sending the temple tax to Jerusalem. When they attempted to do so in spite of the prohibition, he confiscated the gold they intended for that tax. From the amount of the seized shipment, it has been calculated that 7,500 Jewish men lived in Laodicea. There would have been several thousand more women and children.

Under the Roman Empire's leadership, Laodicea prospered. It was strategically located at the junction of two important roads: the east-west road leading from Ephesus into the interior, and the north-south road from Pergamum to the Mediterranean Sea. That location made it an important commercial city. That the first-century B.C. Roman statesman and philosopher Cicero cashed his letters of credit there reveals Laodicea to have been a strategic banking center. The city was so wealthy that it paid for its own reconstruction after a devastating earthquake in A.D. 60, rejecting offers of financial aid from Rome.

The city was also famous for the soft, black wool it produced. The wool was made into clothes and woven into carpets, both highly valued. Laodicea was also an important center of ancient medicine. The nearby temple of the Phrygian god Men Karou had an important medical school associated with it. That school was most famous for an eye salve that it had developed, which was exported all over the Greco-Roman world. All three industries, finance, wool, and the production of eye salve, come into play in this letter to the Laodicean church.

The Concern

I know your deeds, that you are neither cold nor hot; I wish that you were cold or hot. So because you are lukewarm, and neither hot nor cold, I will spit you out of My mouth. Because you say, "I am rich, and have become wealthy, and have need of nothing," and you do not know that you are wretched and miserable and poor and blind and naked, (3:15–17)

Since there was nothing positive to mention for the church at Laodicea, Christ launched directly into His concerns. "Deeds" always reveal a person's true spiritual state, as indicated by the Lord's words "You will know them by their fruits" (Matthew 7:16; Romans 2:6–8). Though salvation is by God's grace alone through faith alone, deeds confirm or deny the presence of genuine salvation (James 2:14ff). Christ knew that the Laodiceans' deeds indicated an unbelieving church.

Christ rebuked them for being "neither cold nor hot" but "lukewarm." His language is drawn from Laodicea's water supply. Because it traveled several miles through an underground aqueduct before reaching the city, the water arrived dirty and warm. It was not hot enough to relax and restore, like the hot springs at Hierapolis. Nor was it cold and refreshing, like the stream water at Colossae. Laodicea's lukewarm water was repulsive to its people.

Comparing its spiritual state to the city's water, Christ gave the Laodicean church a powerful, shocking rebuke: "because you are lukewarm, and neither hot nor cold, I will spit you out of My mouth." Some churches make the Lord weep. Others make Him angry. The Laodicean church made Him sick.

Hot people are those who are spiritually alive and possess the fervency of a transformed life. The spiritually cold are those who reject Jesus Christ. They have no interest in Christ, His Word, or His church. And they make no pretense about it; they are not hypocrites.

The lukewarm do not fit into either category. They are not genuinely saved, yet they do not openly reject Christ. They attend church and claim to know the Lord. Like the Pharisees, they are content to practice a self-righteous religion. They are hypocrites playing games (cf. Matthew 7:22–23).

The Laodiceans' lukewarmness was compounded by their self-deception. Christ rebuked them for their disastrously inaccurate self-assessment: "You say, 'I am rich, and have become wealthy, and have need of nothing,' and you do not know that you are wretched and miserable and poor and blind and naked."

Laodicea was a very wealthy city. That wealth gave the members of its church a false sense of security as they imagined that their spiritual wealth mirrored their city's material wealth. They were rich in spiritual pride but bankrupt in saving grace. Believing they were to be envied, they were in fact to be pitied. Their inaccurate beliefs (taking the form of incipient gnosticism) led them to think they had attained a higher level of knowledge. They no doubt looked down on the unsophisticated people who fully accepted and were satisfied with the biblical teaching of Jesus Christ. However, the reality was that they were spiritually "wretched and miserable and poor and blind and naked."

The Command
I advise you to buy from Me gold refined by fire so that you may become rich, and white garments so that you may clothe yourself, and that the shame of your nakedness will not be revealed; and eye salve to anoint your eyes so that you may see. Those whom I love, I reprove and discipline; therefore be zealous and repent. Behold, I stand at the door and knock; if anyone hears My voice and opens the door, I will come in to him and will dine with him, and he with Me. (3:18–20)

Christ could have instantly judged and destroyed this church filled with unbelieving hypocrites. Instead, He graciously offered them genuine salvation. Christ's three-part appeal played on the three features the city of

Laodicea was most noted for: its wealth, wool industry, and production of eye salve. Christ offered them spiritual gold, spiritual clothes, and spiritual sight.

The Lord, of course, did not teach that salvation could be earned by good works. Lost people have no way to buy salvation (Isaiah 64:5–6). The buying here is the same as the invitation in Isaiah 55:1: "Ho! Every one who thirsts, come to the waters; and you who have no money come, buy and eat. Come, buy wine and milk without money and without cost." All sinners have to offer is their hopelessly lost condition. In exchange, Christ offers His righteousness to those who truly repent.

Christ advised the Laodiceans to buy from Him three things, all of which symbolize true redemption. First, they needed to purchase "gold refined by fire" so they could become rich. They needed gold that was free of impurities, representing the priceless riches of true salvation. Christ offered the Laodiceans a pure, true salvation that would bring them into a real relationship with Him.

Second, Christ advised them to "buy white garments" so they could clothe themselves. This would cover the shame of their nakedness. Laodicea's famed black wool symbolized the dirty, sinful garments that cover the unsaved (see Isaiah 64:6; Zechariah 3:3–4). In contrast, God clothes the redeemed with white garments, symbolizing the righteous deeds that always accompany genuine saving faith (19:8).

Finally, Christ offered them eye salve to anoint their eyes so they could see. Though they prided themselves about their supposed higher spiritual knowledge, the Laodiceans were in fact spiritually blind. Blindness represents a lack of understanding and knowledge of spiritual truth (Matthew 15:14; 23:16–17). Like all unregenerate people, the Laodiceans desperately needed Christ to "open their eyes so that they [might] turn from darkness to light and from the dominion of Satan to God, that they [might] receive forgiveness of sins and an inheritance among those who have been sanctified by faith in [Him]" (Acts 26:18).

Some argue that the language of Christ's direct appeal to the Laodiceans in verse 19, "Those whom I love, I reprove and discipline," in-dicates that they were believers. Verses 18 and 20, however, seem better suited to indicate that they were unbelievers desperately in need of the gold of true spiritual riches, the garments of true righteousness, and the eye salve that brings true spiritual understanding (verse 18).

"To reprove" means to expose and convict. It is a general term for God's dealings with sinners (John 3:18–20; 16:8; 1 Corinthians 14:24). "Discipline" refers to punishment and is used of God's convicting of unbelievers (see 2 Timothy 2:25). The wording of verse 19 does not mean that Christ is speaking to believers. The Lord compassionately, tenderly called those in this church to come to saving faith. Otherwise, He would convict and judge them (see Ezekiel 18:30–32; 33:11).

In order for the Laodiceans to be saved, they would have to "be zealous and repent." This would include an attitude of mourning over sin and hungering and thirsting for the righteousness of which Jesus spoke (Matthew 5:4, 6). The New Testament call to salvation always includes a call to repentance (e.g., Matthew 3:2, 8; 4:17; Mark 6:12). In repentance, the sinner turns from his sin to serve God (1 Thessalonians 1:9). The Lord Jesus Christ followed the call to repentance in verse 19 with a tender, gracious invitation in verse 20. The Laodicean church could only have expected Christ to come in judgment. But the startling reality, introduced by the arresting word "behold," was that Christ stood at the door of the Laodicean church and knocked. If anyone in the church would hear His "voice and open the door, [He would] come in to him and dine with him, and he with [Christ]."

Though this verse has been used in many evangelistic booklets and messages to depict Christ's knocking on the door of the sinner's heart, the meaning is much broader. The door on which Christ is knocking is not the door to a single human heart, but to the Laodicean church. Christ was outside this apostate church and wanted to come in—something that could happen only if the people repented.

The invitation is a personal one, since salvation is individual. But He is knocking on the door of the church, calling many to saving faith, so that He can enter the church. If one person—"anyone"—opened the door by repentance and faith, Christ would enter that church through that individual. The picture of Christ outside the Laodicean church seeking

entrance strongly implies that there were few believers there or no believers at all.

Christ's offer to dine with the repentant church speaks of fellowship,
communion, and intimacy. Sharing a meal in ancient times symbolized
the union of people in loving fellowship. Believers will dine with Christ
at the marriage supper of the Lamb (19:9), and in the millennial kingdom
(Luke 22:16, 29–30). "Dine" is from the Greek word indicating the
evening meal, the last meal of the day (Luke 17:8; 22:20; 1 Corinthians
11:25). Christ urged them to repent and have fellowship with Him before
the night of judgment fell and it was too late forever.

The Counsel

*He who overcomes, I will grant to him to sit down with Me on My throne,
as I also overcame and sat down with My Father on His throne. He who
has an ear, let him hear what the Spirit says to the churches.* (3:21–22)

"He who overcomes" (all believers) receives a wonderful promise: Christ
will grant to that person to sit down with Him on His throne, as He "also
overcame and sat down with the Father on His throne." To enjoy fellowship with Christ in the kingdom and throughout eternity is sufficient
blessing beyond all comprehension. But Christ offers more, promising to
seat believers on the throne He shares with the Father (see Matthew
19:28; Luke 22:29–30). That symbolizes the truth that we will reign with
Him (1 Corinthians 6:3; 2 Timothy 2:12; Revelation 5:10; 20:6).

As did the other six letters, the letter to the Laodiceans closed with
Christ's exhortation, "He who has an ear, let him hear what the Spirit says
to the churches." The message to this hypocritical church is obvious:
Repent, and open up to Christ before the night of judgment falls. The implication for true believers is that, like Christ, we must compassionately call
those in the unbelieving church to repent and receive salvation in Jesus
Christ.

PART

3

"The Things Which Will Take Place After This"

(4:1–22:21)

JUDGMENTS AND BLESSINGS IN REVELATION

	JUDGMENTS			BLESSINGS
	SEVEN SEALS	**SEVEN TRUMPETS**	**SEVEN BOWLS**	**SEVEN BEATITUDES** *On Those Who...*
1.	Antichrist (Rev. 6:1–2)	Vegetation Burned (Rev. 8:7)	Terrible Sores (Rev. 16:2)	Read and Heed This Book (Rev. 1:3)
2.	War (Rev. 6:3,4)	Sea Life Destroyed (Rev. 8:8,9)	Seas Turned to Blood (Rev. 16:3)	Die in the Lord (Rev. 14:13)
3.	Famine (Rev. 6:5,6)	Waters Made Bitter (Rev. 8:10,11)	Fresh Water to Blood (Rev. 16:4–7)	Wait for His Coming (Rev. 16:15)
4.	Pestilence and Death (Rev. 6:7,8)	Heavens Struck (Rev. 8:12,13)	Sun Scorches Men (Rev. 16:8, 9)	Are Invited to the Supper (Rev. 19:9)
5.	Martyrs (Rev. 6:9–11)	Demonic "Locusts" (Rev. 9:1–12)	Darkness and Pain (Rev. 16:10,11)	Are Resurrected to Life (Rev. 20:6)
6.	Cosmic Disasters (Rev. 6:12–17)	Deadly Plagues (Rev. 9:13–21)	Euphrates Dries Up (Rev. 16:12–16)	Keep These Words (Rev. 22:7)
7.	The Seven Trumpets (Rev. 8:1–6)	The Seven Bowls (Rev. 11:15–19)	Final Destruction (Rev. 16:17–21)	Do His Commandments (Rev. 22:14)

The Throne of
GOD
(4:1–11)

In contrast to the bizarre accounts of those who falsely claim to have visited heaven, the Bible records accounts of two people who actually were taken there in visions. In 2 Corinthians 12, the apostle Paul wrote of being transported to the "third heaven," though he was forbidden to speak of what he saw there (verse 4). The apostle John also had the special privilege of visiting heaven. Unlike Paul, John was permitted to provide a detailed description of his vision in Revelation 4 and 5.

The Bible refers to heaven more than five hundred times, and others, such as Paul (2 Corinthians 12) and Ezekiel (Ezekiel 1), have written descriptions of it. Yet John's words in Revelation 4 and 5 are the most informative in all of Scripture. Readers are carried far beyond this world's understanding into a picture of heaven's realities. Through John's vision, believers have the privilege of previewing the place where they will live forever.

The first occurrence of the phrase "after these things" (verse 1) relates to John's personal chronology. It notes that this second vision followed immediately after John's vision of the risen, glorified Christ (1:9–20) and the letters to the seven churches (2:1–3:22). The phrase "after these things" is used throughout Revelation to mark the beginning of a new vision.

THE THRONE AS PROLOGUE TO FUTURE EVENTS

The second occurrence of "after these things" at the end of verse 1 relates to God's chronology. Its use marks an important transition in the book of Revelation from the church age described in chapters 2–3, to the third great division of the book found in chapters 4–22. The scene shifts from matters concerning the church on earth (which is nowhere mentioned in chapters 4–19) to a dramatic scene in heaven. This new scene focuses on the throne of God and forms the prologue to the future, historical events that unfold in chapters 6–22. In keeping with the Lord's promise to spare His church from the hour of testing given in 3:10, the church will be raptured before that time of tribulation begins.

As John looked, to his astonishment he saw "a door standing open in heaven" (Revelation 4:1; cf. Ezekiel 1:1; Acts 7:56). That door admitted John into the third heaven to the very throne room of God. It was heaven where Christ ascended after His resurrection and where He has since been seated at the right hand of God. Heaven became John's vantage point for most of the remainder of Revelation.

After noticing the open door, the first voice John heard was the familiar voice "like the sound of a trumpet" that had spoken to him in his first vision (in 1:10). This was the voice of the risen, exalted Christ. His voice is likened to the sound of a trumpet because of its commanding, authoritative quality. The Lord specifically ordered John to "come up here," meaning to heaven. John was not swept away into some mystical fantasyland, but transported spiritually into the reality of heaven.

The central theme of John's vision is the "throne of God," mentioned eleven times in this chapter. All the features of the chapter can be outlined based on how they relate to that throne of divine glory.

THE THRONE

Immediately I was in the Spirit; and behold, a throne was standing in heaven (4:2*a*)

Today most people who claim to have visions of heaven tend to emphasize its most bizarre aspects. Yet John's vision focused on the glorious throne of God and the majesty of the One who sits on it. John was amazed and astounded by what he saw, causing him to exclaim, "behold."

The cause of John's amazement was the throne of God that he saw "standing in heaven." This was not a piece of furniture, but a symbol of God's sovereign rule and authority located in the temple in heaven (7:15; 16:17). According to Revelation 21:22 the heavenly temple is not an actual building: "The Lord God the Almighty and the Lamb" are the temple. The use of the term "temple" symbolizes God's presence. The throne was said to be standing because God's sovereign rule is fixed, permanent, and unshakable. A vision of God's immovable throne reveals He is in permanent, unchanging, and complete control of the universe. That is a comforting realization in light of the horror and trauma of the end-time events about to be revealed (chapters 6–19).

ON THE THRONE

and One sitting on the throne. And He who was sitting was like a jasper stone and a sardius in appearance; (4:2*b*–3*a*)

Random chance does not control the universe. Instead, the all-powerful Creator of the universe is sitting on His throne as its ruler. Unlike its use in Hebrews (1:3; 10:12; 12:2), where it depicts Christ's posture of rest, the term "sitting" indicates the posture of reigning. Jesus is not resting because the work of redemption has been accomplished, but reigning because judgment is about to take place.

Though John does not name the One sitting on the throne, it is obvious who He is. He is the One Isaiah saw in his vision: "I saw the Lord sitting on a throne, lofty and exalted, with the train of His robe filling the temple" (Isaiah 6:1). The prophets Micaiah, Daniel, and Ezekiel also saw Him on His glorious throne (1 Kings 22:19; Daniel 7:9–10; Ezekiel 1:26–28). In sharp contrast to the casual accounts of those today who claim visions of God, these prophets were terrified and humbled by their visions.

John described "He who was sitting" on the throne as being "like a jasper stone and a sardius in appearance." That description is reminiscent of the flashing light, blazing fire, and vivid colors in Ezekiel's vision. Revelation 21:11 describes jasper as "crystal-clear." Therefore, it is best to identify this stone as a diamond. All the shining, flashing facets of the glory of God are compared to a diamond, brilliantly refracting all the colors of the spectrum. A sardius, the origin of the name for the city of Sardis, is a fiery, bloodred ruby. It also expresses the shining beauty of God's glory, and may also symbolize God's blazing wrath, about to be poured out on the rebellious world (Revelation 6–19).

There is a possible further symbolism in the choice of these two stones. The sardius and the jasper were the first and last stones on the high priest's breastplate (Exodus 28:17–20), representing the firstborn and lastborn of the twelve sons of Jacob. It may be that those stones depict God's covenant relationship with Israel. His wrath and judgment will not destroy that relationship.

John's vision of God's throne is not one of peace and comfort. Its flashing, splendorous magnificence reveals the terrors of God's judgment.

AROUND THE THRONE

and there was a rainbow around the throne, like an emerald in appearance. Around the throne were twenty-four thrones; and upon the thrones I saw twenty-four elders sitting, clothed in white garments, and golden crowns on their heads. (4:3b–4)

Moving away from his description of the throne to describe what was around it, John first noted that there was a rainbow around it. That John described it as being "like an emerald in appearance" reveals that green was the dominant color. This again is introduced to show the many-splendored glory of God (Ezekiel 1:28). The rainbow provides a comforting balance to the fiery flashings of judgment earlier seen from God's throne. According to Genesis 9:13–17, a rainbow symbolizes God's covenant faithfulness, mercy, and grace. God's attributes always operate in perfect harmony. His wrath never operates at the expense of His faithfulness.

John also saw around the throne twenty-four elders sitting upon twenty-four other thrones, "clothed in white garments, and golden crowns on their heads." The identity of the twenty-four elders has been much debated. While some see them as an order of angelic beings, it seems best to view them as human representatives of the church. Why? First, the reference to the twenty-four thrones they sit upon indicates that they reign with Christ. Nowhere in Scripture do angels sit on thrones, nor are they pictured as reigning. The church, on the other hand, is repeatedly promised to rule with Christ (2:26–27; 3:21; 5:10; 20:4; Matthew 19:28; Luke 22:30; 1 Corinthians 6:2–3; 2 Timothy 2:12).

The Greek word translated "elders" is never used in Scripture to refer to angels, but always to men. It is used to speak of older men in general, and the rulers of both Israel and the church. There is also no clear use of this word outside of Revelation to refer to angels. Further, "elder" would be an inappropriate term to describe angels, who do not age.

While angels do appear in white (John 20:12; Acts 1:10), white garments more commonly are the dress of believers. That is particularly true in the immediate context of Revelation. Christ promised the believers at Sardis that they would "be clothed in white garments" (3:5). He advised the Laodiceans to "buy from Me . . . white garments so that you may clothe yourself" (3:18). At the marriage supper of the Lamb, His bride will "clothe herself in fine linen, bright and clean" (19:8). White garments symbolize Christ's righteousness imputed to believers at salvation.

That the elders wore golden crowns on their heads provides further evidence that they were humans. Crowns are never promised to angels in the Bible, nor are angels ever seen wearing them. This crown in Greek refers to the victor's crown, worn by those who successfully competed and won the victory. Christ promised this crown to the loyal believers at

Smyrna (2:10; cf.1 Corinthians 9:25; 2 Timothy 4:8; James 1:12).

If the twenty-four elders are humans, who do they represent? In the Bible, the number twenty-four is used in Scripture to speak of completion and representation. There were twenty-four officers of the sanctuary representing the twenty-four courses of the Levitical priests (1 Chronicles 24:4–5, 7–18), as well as twenty-four divisions of singers in the temple (1 Chronicles 25). Whoever the twenty-four elders are, then, they likely represent a larger group.

Some believe the elders represent Israel. But while individual Jews have been and will continue to be redeemed throughout history, at the time of this vision the nation as a whole had not yet been redeemed. The elders also cannot be tribulation saints, since they too had not yet been converted. Others split the twenty-four elders into two groups of twelve, one representing the church and the other Israel. Yet in all their appearances in Revelation, they appear as a unified group of twenty-four, never as two groups of twelve.

The most likely option is that they represent the raptured church, which sings the song of redemption (5:8–10). They have their crowns and live in the place prepared for them, where they have gone to be with Jesus (John 14:1–4).

FROM THE THRONE

Out from the throne come flashes of lightning and sounds and peals of thunder. (4:5a)

"Flashes of lightning and sounds and peals of thunder" are associated with God's presence in Exodus 19:16 and Ezekiel 1:13. They are also associated with God's judgment during the tribulation. In Revelation 8:5, "The angel took the censer and filled it with the fire of the altar, and threw it to the earth; and there followed peals of thunder and sounds and flashes of lightning" (11:19; 16:18).

Thus John saw a preview of the divine wrath that will be poured out on the earth, described in chapters 6–19.

BEFORE THE THRONE

And there were seven lamps of fire burning before the throne, which are the seven Spirits of God; and before the throne there was, something like, a sea of glass like crystal; (4:5b–6a)

John saw two things before the throne. First were "seven lamps of fire." Unlike the lampstands mentioned in 1:12–13, these were outdoor torches, giving off the fierce, blazing light of a fiery torch. John identifies them as "the seven Spirits of God." This phrase describes the Holy Spirit in all His fullness (Isaiah 11:2; Zechariah 4:1–10). Torches are associated with war in Judges 7:16, 20 and Nahum 2:3–4. John's vision depicts God as ready to make war on sinful, rebellious humanity and the Holy Spirit as His war torch. The Comforter of those who love Christ will be the Consumer of those who reject Him.

Second, he saw "something like, a sea of glass like crystal." That sea is metaphorical, since there is no sea in heaven (21:1). What John saw at the base of the throne was a vast pavement of glass, shining brilliantly like crystal. Exodus 24:10 records a similar scene when Moses, Aaron, and the elders of Israel saw the God of Israel. Heaven is a world of brilliant light, refracting and shining as through jewels and crystal in a manner beyond our ability to describe or imagine (cf. Revelation 21:10–11, 18).

IN AND AROUND THE THRONE

and in the center and around the throne, four living creatures full of eyes in front and behind. The first creature was like a lion, and the second creature like a calf, and the third creature had a face like that of a man, and the fourth creature was like a flying eagle. And the four living creatures, each one of them having six wings, are full of eyes around and within; (4:6b–8a)

This passage introduces the four living creatures who will play a significant role in the events of Revelation. That they are said to be both "in the center and around the throne" means that their station is in the inner circle nearest the throne. Ezekiel 1:12, 17 suggests they are in constant motion about it. The translation "living creatures" is somewhat misleading, since these are not animals. The phrase derives from a single word in the Greek text that can mean "living ones."

Ezekiel gives a detailed description of these incredible beings and of the glorious magnificence of heaven and God's throne in Ezekiel 1:4–25. Both Ezekiel's description and that in Revelation 4 describe what could be called the divine war machine ready to unleash judgment.

Ezekiel 10:15 specifically identifies them: "Then the cherubim rose up. They are the living beings that I saw by the river Chebar." The four living creatures are cherubim, an exalted order of angels frequently associated in Scripture with God's holy power.

John said the living creatures were "full of eyes in front and behind," symbolizing their awareness, alertness, and comprehensive knowledge. Nothing pertaining to their duties escapes their scrutiny.

Ezekiel's description of these angels notes that each one possessed all four facial features (Ezekiel 1:6). From John's point of view, the first was like a lion, the second like a calf, the third had a face like that of a man, and the fourth was like a flying eagle. Those descriptions view the four cherubim in relation to the created world. The lion represents wild creatures, the calf domestic animals, the eagle flying creatures, and man the pinnacle of creation. It is also significant that the twelve tribes of Israel camped under these four banners; some with Reuben (symbolized by a man), others with Dan (symbolized by an eagle), others with Ephraim (symbolized by the calf, or ox), and the rest with Judah (symbolized by a lion).

Their six wings denote that their supreme responsibility and privilege is to constantly worship God. From Isaiah's vision, we learn that the seraphim used their six wings in the following manner: "with two [they] covered [their faces], and with two [they] covered [their] feet, and with two [they] flew" (Isaiah 6:2). Four of their six wings related to worship. Worship is their privilege and permanent occupation.

TOWARD THE THRONE

and day and night they do not cease to say, "Holy, holy, holy is the Lord God, the Almighty, who was and who is and who is to come." And when the living creatures give glory and honor and thanks to Him who sits on the throne, to Him who lives forever and ever, the twenty-four elders will fall down before Him who sits on the throne, and will worship Him who lives forever and ever, and will cast their crowns before the throne, saying, "Worthy are You, our Lord and our God, to receive glory and honor and power; for You created all things, and because of Your will they existed, and were created." (4:8b–11)

This scene in heaven ends in worship directed toward God on His throne. Here and in chapter 5 are five great hymns of praise, each gradually increasing in the number of singers—from a quartet (the four living creatures) with the twenty-four elders joining in (verse 10), then myriads of angels adding their voices (verse 11), and finally, all created beings in the universe filling in the mighty chorus of praise to God (verse 13). This mighty oratorio of praise and worship can be divided into two movements: the hymn of creation (chapter 4), and the hymn of redemption (chapter 5).

This hymn of creation, the first movement, may be divided into several elements. The four living creatures begin by focusing on God's *holiness*: "day and night they do not cease to say, 'Holy, holy, holy is the Lord God.'" The threefold repetition of *holy* is also found in Isaiah 6:3. Holiness is the only one of God's attributes repeated in this way, since it is the summation of all that He is.

Next, the four living creatures refer to God's *power*. He is the Almighty, a title by which God identified Himself to Abraham (Genesis 17:1). That term identifies God as the most powerful being, devoid of any weakness, whose conquering power and overpowering strength none can oppose. Because God is Almighty, He can effortlessly do whatever His holy will purposes to do (cf. Isaiah 40:28).

God's power is seen in creation. Psalm 33:9 says, "He spoke, and it was done; He commanded, and it stood fast." Having created the universe, God also controls it. But as was the case with His holiness, the aspect of God's power most clearly in view here is His power exhibited in judgment. For example, He judged Satan and the sinning angels, expelling them from heaven; destroyed Sodom, Gomorrah, and the cities of the plain; drowned Pharaoh's army; and shattered the most powerful king in the world, Nebuchadnezzar, reducing him to eating grass like an animal for seven years. And it will be God's power that unleashes the terrible, irresistible judgments on sinful mankind during the tribulation before the Lord's return.

The four living creatures also praise God for His eternity, extolling Him as "He who was and who is and who is to come." Scripture repeatedly affirms God's eternity, that He has neither beginning nor ending (e.g., Psalms 90:2; 93:2; Isaiah 57:15; 1 Timothy 1:17).

The praise of the four living creatures, as they give glory and honor and thanks to Him who sits on the throne, triggers a response from the twenty-four elders. They will "fall down before Him who sits on the throne, and will worship Him who lives forever and ever." This is the first of six times the elders bow before God (5:8, 14; 7:11; 11:16; 19:4). This is a posture of reverential worship, a natural response to the majestic glory of God.

Amazingly, after prostrating themselves the twenty-four elders "cast their crowns before the throne." They are not concerned about their own holiness, honor, or reward. All those things pale into insignificance and become meaningless in light of the glory of God.

The elders add their own note to the chorus of praise, crying out, "Worthy are You, our Lord and our God, to receive glory and honor and power; for You created all things, and because of Your will they existed, and were created." The Greek word for "worthy" was used of the Roman emperor when he marched in a triumphal procession. The focus of the elders' song is on God's glory in creation. He is presented as Creator throughout Scripture (10:6; cf. Genesis 1:1; Exodus 20:11). The elders are acknowledging that God has the right both to redeem and to judge His creation. Their song anticipates paradise lost becoming paradise regained.

8

The
WORTHY
One
(5:1–14)

The events of chapter 5 follow immediately after those of chapter 4. The scene is once again the throne of God in heaven. The cherubim, the twenty-four elders, and the Holy Spirit in His sevenfold glory are all present. The events described in these two chapters anticipate the divine judgment about to strike the earth (Revelation 6–19). Awestruck by the majesty of God's throne, the cherubim and elders begin a series of hymns to God. Those hymns celebrate God as creator and redeemer, and rejoice that He is about to take back what is rightfully His.

As that moment approaches, God begins to stir. The opening phrase "I saw" introduces the various scenes described in this chapter and stresses John's status as an eyewitness. In his vision, John saw in the right hand of Him who sat on the throne a book written inside and on the back, sealed up with seven seals. God stretched out His hand, as it were, and in it He held a book. The Greek word here refers to a scroll. A scroll was a long piece of papyrus or animal skin, rolled from both ends into the middle. Scrolls were commonly used before the invention of the modern book.

While Roman wills were sealed up with seven seals, this scroll is not a will but a deed or contract. Jeremiah 32 provides a good illustration of the use of such a document. In the waning days of the southern kingdom, shortly before the fall of Jerusalem, Jeremiah's cousin Hanamel approached him. Hanamel was desperate to sell a field he owned in Jeremiah's hometown of Anathoth, near Jerusalem. Hanamel knew the land would be seized once the Babylonian army conquered. Jeremiah, in obedience to God's command (Jeremiah 32:6–7), purchased the field in spite of its potential loss as a sign that the Babylonian captivity would not be permanent

The scroll John saw in God's hand is the title deed to the earth. Unlike other such deeds, however, it does not record the descriptive detail of what Christ will inherit, but rather how He will regain His rightful inheritance. It will occur by the divine judgments about to be poured out on the earth. While the scroll is a scroll of doom and judgment, it is also a scroll of redemption. It tells how Christ will redeem the world from Satan and those with him. Ezekiel describes this same scroll in his vision of heaven (Ezekiel 2:9–10).

THE SEARCH FOR THE WORTHY ONE

And I saw a strong angel proclaiming with a loud voice, "Who is worthy to open the book and to break its seals?" And no one in heaven or on the earth or under the earth was able to open the book or to look into it. Then I began to weep greatly because no one was found worthy to open the book or to look into it; (5:2–4)

The strong angel (also in 10:1; 18:21) is not named. Some identify him as Gabriel, others as Michael, but he is anonymous. He spoke with "a loud voice" so that his proclamation would penetrate every corner of the universe. The angel sought someone both "worthy to open the book and to break its seals."

As the echoes of his cry end, there is silence. No one "in heaven or on the earth or under the earth was able to open the book or to look into it."

A search of the entire universe turns up no one worthy to open the scroll.

Overwhelmed with grief at this turn of events, John began to weep. "Weep" is the same Greek word used to describe Jesus' weeping over Jerusalem (Luke 19:41), and Peter's bitter weeping after betraying the Lord (Luke 22:62). It is a word that expresses strong, unrestrained emotion. Interestingly, this is the only time in Scripture that tears are seen in heaven.

John's weeping, though sincere, was premature. God was about to take action. John wept because he wanted to see the world without evil, sin, and death. He wanted to see God's kingdom established on earth. Yet John did not need to weep, because the search for the one worthy to open the scroll was about to end.

THE SELECTION OF THE WORTHY ONE

and one of the elders said to me, "Stop weeping; behold, the Lion that is from the tribe of Judah, the Root of David, has overcome so as to open the book and its seven seals." And I saw between the throne (with the four living creatures) and the elders a Lamb standing, as if slain, having seven horns and seven eyes, which are the seven Spirits of God, sent out into all the earth. And He came and took the book out of the right hand of Him who sat on the throne. (5:5–7)

Because his tears were unnecessary, one of the elders told John to stop weeping. Then he drew John's attention to a new Person emerging on the scene: "the Lion that is from the tribe of Judah, the Root of David." No human or angel can redeem the universe, but there is One who can— Jesus Christ. The title "the Lion that is from the tribe of Judah" derives from Jacob's blessing on the tribe of Judah given in Genesis 49:8–10. Out of the lionlike tribe of Judah would come a strong, fierce, and deadly ruler.

The Jews of Jesus' day expected the Messiah to be powerful and to liberate them from the heavy hand of their Roman oppressors. It was partly because Jesus failed to live up to those expectations that they rejected Him. Tragically, the Jews completely misjudged their Messiah. He is a lion, and will tear up and destroy their enemies. But He will do so according to His timetable, not theirs. His lionlike judgment of His enemies awaits the yet-future day that He has chosen.

Jesus is also seen here as "the Root of David." This title derives from Isaiah 11:1, 10. As Matthew 1 and Luke 3 reveal, Jesus was a descendant of David both on His father's and mother's side. In Romans 1:3 the apostle Paul said that Jesus was "born of a descendant of David according to the flesh."

Jesus is the One worthy to take the scroll because of who He is—the rightful King from David's descendants—and what He is—the Lion from Judah's tribe with the power to destroy His enemies.

As he looked at the incredible scene before him, John found his attention irresistibly drawn to what he saw between the throne with the four living creatures and the elders. Instead of the anticipated mighty Lion of the Tribe of Judah, John saw a Lamb. The Lord Jesus could not be the Lion of judgment, or the King of glory, unless He was first "the Lamb of God who takes away the sin of the world" (John 1:29).

The Greek word used here for "lamb" refers to a little lamb or pet lamb. The imagery derives from the Passover, when Jewish families were required to keep the sacrificial lamb as a household pet for four days before sacrificing it (Exodus 12:3–6). While every lamb sacrificed under the Old Covenant pointed toward Christ, He is only referred to as a lamb once in the Old Testament (Isaiah 53:7). In the New Testament outside of Revelation, He is only called a lamb four times (John 1:29, 36; Acts 8:32; 1 Peter 1:19). In Revelation He appears as the Lamb thirty-one times.

Several features indicate that this was no ordinary lamb. First, He was standing, alive, on His feet, yet looking as if He had been slain. The scars from the deadly wound this Lamb received were clearly visible, yet He was alive. Though demons and wicked men conspired against Him and killed Him, He rose from the dead, defeating and triumphing over His enemies.

Another feature about this Lamb that John noted was that it had seven horns. In imagery drawn from the animal world, horns in Scripture symbolize strength and power. Seven, the number of perfection, symbolizes the Lamb's complete, absolute power. The Lamb in John's vision also had seven eyes, again denoting perfect and complete understanding and knowledge. The eyes represented the seven Spirits of God, sent out into all the earth. The phrase "seven Spirits of God" describes the Holy Spirit in all His fullness.

Verse 7 records the final, monumental act in the heavenly scene. Everything John has been describing since this vision began in 4:1 had been building toward this moment. This views the great, culminating act of history, the act that will signal the end of man's day. The ultimate goal of redemption is about to be seen; paradise will be regained, Eden restored. Before John's wondering eyes the Lamb came and took the book out of the right hand of Him who sat on the throne.

The worthy One has arrived to take back what is rightfully His.

THE SONG OF THE WORTHY ONE

When He had taken the book, the four living creatures and the twenty-four elders fell down before the Lamb, each one holding a harp and golden bowls full of incense, which are the prayers of the saints. And they sang a new song, saying, "Worthy are You to take the book and to break its seals; for You were slain, and purchased for God with Your blood men from every tribe and tongue and people and nation. You have made them to be a kingdom and priests to our God; and they will reign upon the earth." Then I looked, and I heard the voice of many angels around the throne and the living creatures and the elders; and the number of them was myriads of myriads, and thousands of thousands, saying with a loud voice, "Worthy is the Lamb that was slain to receive power and riches and wisdom and might and honor and glory and blessing." And every created thing which is in heaven and on the earth and under the earth and on the sea, and all things in them, I heard saying, "To Him who sits on the throne, and to the Lamb, be blessing and honor and glory and dominion forever and ever." And the four living creatures kept saying, "Amen." And the elders fell down and worshiped. (5:8–14)

The appearance of the Lamb as He moves to take the scroll causes praise to break out from everywhere in the universe. To the two majestic praises of chapter 4 are added three more in chapter 5. The spontaneous outburst of worship results from the realization that the long-anticipated defeat of sin, death, and Satan is about to be accomplished. Christ will return to earth in triumph and establish His glorious millennial kingdom. The curse will be reversed, the believing remnant of Israel will be saved, and the church will be granted the privilege of reigning with Christ.

As they began their song of praise and worship, the four living creatures and the twenty-four elders fell down before the Lamb. That they offer the same worship to Christ that they did to the Father in 4:10 offers convincing proof of Christ's deity, since only God is to be worshiped (19:10; Matthew 4:10).

As they prostrated themselves before the Lamb in worship, John noticed that each one of the twenty-four elders was "holding a harp and golden bowls full of incense, which are the prayers of the saints." Harps were frequently associated in the Old Testament with worship (e.g., 2 Samuel 6:4–5; Psalms 33:2; 71:22), but they were also closely linked to prophecy (2 Kings 3:15; 1 Chronicles 25:1). The harps held by the elders probably symbolize all of prophecy, which culminates in the momentous events about to take place.

In addition to the harps, the elders were also holding "golden bowls full of incense." These wide-mouthed bowls were used in the tabernacle and the temple (1 Kings 7:40, 45, 50; 2 Kings 12:13–14), where they were connected with the altar. They symbolized the priestly work of intercession for the people. Scripture associates the burning of incense with the prayers of the saints in Psalm 141:2, Luke 1:9–10, and Revelation 8:3–4. The incense in these bowls represents the prayers of believers through the ages. Taken together, the harps and the bowls indicate that all that the prophets ever prophesied and all that God's children ever prayed for is finally to be fulfilled.

As the elders brought before God the desires and prayers of the saints, they "sang a new song." Since (with the possible exception of Job 38:7) the Bible nowhere records angels singing, it is best to see only the elders as singing here. That is consistent with the rest of Scripture, which pictures the redeemed singing praise to God (e.g., Acts 16:25; Ephesians 5:19) and angels speaking it (Luke 2:13–14). Throughout Scripture the new song is a song of redemption (Psalms 33:3; 40:3; 96:1; 98:1).

The song opens with a reaffirmation that Christ is "worthy . . . to take the book and to break its seals." He is worthy because He is the Lamb, the Lion of the tribe of Judah, and the King of Kings and Lord of Lords. To break the book's seals means to enact the judgments written in it.

Then, further reinforcing Christ's worthiness, the song continues, "for You were slain, and purchased for God with Your blood men from every tribe and tongue and people and nation." That phrase elaborates on the statement of verse 6 that the Lamb had been slain, explaining the significance of His death. "Purchased" is from a Greek word for redemption that pictures slaves purchased in the marketplace and then set free. At the cross, Jesus Christ paid the purchase price—His own blood (1 Peter 1:18–19)—to redeem from the slave market of sinful humanity those "from every tribe [descent] and tongue [language] and people [race] and nation [culture]." Those four terms appear together also in Revelation 7:9; 11:9; 13:7; and 14:6 and encompass all of humanity.

The song moves on to express the results of redemption: "You have made them to be a kingdom and priests to our God; and they will reign upon the earth." The use of "them" instead of "us" indicates the vastness and comprehensiveness of redemption. The twenty-four elders move beyond themselves to sweep up all the saints of all the ages into praise and adoration. The redeemed are a part of God's kingdom (1:6), a community of believers under God's sovereign rule. They are also priests to our God (20:6), signifying their complete access to God's presence for worship and service. The present priesthood of believers (1 Peter 2:5, 9) foreshadows that future day when we will have total access to and perfect communion with God. During the millennial kingdom, believers will reign upon the earth with Christ (20:6; 2 Timothy 2:12).

In verse 11 John says for the fourth time in the chapter that he "saw something." To the voices of the four living creatures and the twenty-four elders are now added those of innumerable angels. *Myriad* means "ten thousand," apparently the highest number the Greeks had in their language. The phrase "myriads and myriads" describes an uncountable host. Hebrews 12:1 also says that the number of holy angels cannot be counted. They number at least twice as many as the fallen angels according to Revelation 12:3–4.

The vast host began saying with a loud voice, "Worthy is the Lamb that was slain to receive power and riches and wisdom and might and honor and glory and blessing." Once again, the emphasis is on Christ's death providing a perfect redemption. He is worthy to receive recognition because of His power and the spiritual and material riches He possesses (Psalm 50:10–12). He is also worthy to receive recognition because of His wisdom and omniscience. For all those things and all His other absolute perfections, Jesus Christ is worthy of all honor and glory and blessing.

As the great hymn of praise reaches a crescendo, "every created thing which is in heaven and on the earth and under the earth and on the sea, and all things in them" join together. This all-inclusive statement is reminiscent of Psalm 69:34: "Let heaven and earth praise Him, the seas and everything that moves in them," and the concluding verse of the Psalms, "Let everything that has breath praise the Lord. Praise the Lord!" (Psalm 150:6). This mighty chorus cries out, "To Him who sits on the throne, and to the Lamb, be blessing and honor and glory and dominion forever and ever." Endless worship belongs to God the Father and the Lord Jesus Christ. The creation is unable to contain its joy over its upcoming redemption.

Lost in praise, the four living creatures could only keep saying, "Amen." That solemn affirmation means "let it be," "make it happen" (cf. 1:6–7).

Soon, this mighty host would march out of heaven to execute judgment, gather God's people, and return with Christ when He sets up His earthly kingdom. The stage for God's ultimate plan has been set in the throne room of God.

9

The Tribulation's
SEAL
Judgments
(6:1–17)

In Revelation 5:1–7, Christ received a scroll sealed with seven seals. The scroll contained the title deed to the earth. Unlike normal title deeds, it did not contain a description of Christ's inheritance, but details of how He will reclaim what is rightfully His. Beginning in chapter 6, the scroll is unrolled and its seals broken. The unrolling of the scroll marks the beginning of God's judgment.

Each of the scroll's seven seals represents a specific divine judgment that will be poured out sequentially on earth. The seals encompass the entire tribulation (3:10), ending with the return of Christ. It seems best to understand the first four seals as taking place during the first half of the tribulation, the fifth stretching from the first into the second half, the "great tribulation" in 7:14, and the sixth and seventh taking place during that "great tribulation." Apparently the seventh seal contains the seven trumpet judgments (8:1–11:19) and the seventh trumpet (11:15) contains the seven bowl judgments (16:1–21). The seven seals contain all the judgments until the end, when Jesus Christ returns.

The unfolding of the seven seals parallels our Lord's chronology of tribulation events found in His own message in Matthew 24. (See the chart "The Coming Seven Seal Judgments.")

Just as a mother's birth pains increase in frequency and intensity as the time to give birth approaches, so the judgments will intensify throughout the tribulation until the arrival of Christ in judgment glory. The first four seals cover the period Jesus described as "the beginning of birth pangs" (Matthew 24:8). As terrible as those four judgments are, they are but the preliminary outpouring of God's final wrath in the last three seals.

THE COMING SEVEN SEAL JUDGMENTS

JESUS' WORDS	THE SEAL	ITS CONTENTS
Matthew 24:4–5	1st Seal	False peace
Matthew 24:6–7	2nd Seal	Worldwide war
Matthew 24:7	3rd Seal	Famine
Matthew 24:7	4th Seal	Earthquakes—death
Matthew 24:9	5th Seal	Divine judgment
Matthew 24:29	6th Seal	Cosmic darkness—physical destruction
Matthew 24:37ff	7th Seal	Cataclysmic events (the seven trumpets)

THE FIRST SEAL: FALSE PEACE

Then I saw when the Lamb broke one of the seven seals, and I heard one of the four living creatures saying as with a voice of thunder, "Come." I looked, and behold, a white horse, and he who sat on it had a bow; and a crown was given to him, and he went out conquering and to conquer. (6:1–2)

Chapters 4–5 described the praise offered in heaven to the Father and Jesus. As the seals begin to be opened in chapter 6, the praise ceases in anticipation of the coming judgment. The scene now shifts from heaven to earth, the focus of events through the return of Christ in chapter 19 and His earthly kingdom in chapter 20.

Having received from His Father the title deed to the earth (5:7), the

Lamb broke the first of the seven seals. As each seal is broken in the vision, what is written on the scroll is not read, but acted out. Immediately, John heard one of the four living creatures saying with a powerful voice of thunder, "Come." In response to the angelic summons, a white horse came forth bearing its rider.

The first four seals involve horses and riders, the four horsemen of the Apocalypse. Horses in Scripture are associated with triumph, majesty, power, and conquest (19:11, 14; Job 39:19–25; Proverbs 21:31).

Some, seeing a parallel with 19:11, identify the one who sat on the white horse as Christ. But since Christ opens the sealed scroll, He cannot be the rider. Further, this rider wears a crown won as a prize. In 19:12 Christ wears many royal crowns. Unlike this rider, who carries a bow, Christ carries a sword (19:15). Finally, Christ returns at the end of the tribulation, not at its beginning.

Others identify the rider as Antichrist. But since the other three riders represent impersonal forces (war, famine, and death), it is best to view the first one as a force as well. That force is best defined as a worldwide peace, shattered during the second seal by the second rider (6:4).

So before the terrors of the tribulation break loose and lead to the battle of Armageddon, there will come a period of world peace. But it will be a deceptive peace, as the world is lulled into a false sense of security followed by war, famine, and death. The world's desperate desire for international peace will serve as the bait for the satanic trap. That longing for security and safety will play into the hands of Antichrist, Satan's ruler, who will convince the world that he can provide them.

That the rider had a bow but no arrows, and that he was honored with a crown that was freely given to him, reveals that his conquering will involve bloodless victories. His crown is a winner's crown. He is not a real king, but has won a crown from the world for his triumphant achievements leading to world peace. He will not conquer by military force, but by deceit (2 Thessalonians 2:9–11). His conquest will be a peace won by agreement, not conflict (Daniel 9:24–27). Even as the final doom of the world approaches, Antichrist will promise a golden age of peace and prosperity. In gratitude, the world will honor him and elevate him to the position of supreme leadership. Yet his promises and the peace will be short-lived.

THE SECOND SEAL: WAR

When He broke the second seal, I heard the second living creature saying, "Come." And another, a red horse, went out; and to him who sat on it, it was granted to take peace from the earth, and that men would slay one another; and a great sword was given to him. (6:3–4)

The world's attitude of peace and harmony will be shattered as the second horse and rider appear on the scene. As the Lamb broke the second seal, John heard the second living creature summoning the second horseman, saying, "Come." Immediately "a red horse went out." Red, the color of fire and blood, depicts war. God's judgment descends and the false peace led by Antichrist dissolves into war.

Concerning the rider, John first notes that "to him . . . it was granted to take peace from the earth." All that happens will be under God's control. He allows the false peace, and He ends it by bringing war on the earth. Contrary to the teaching of some, the judgments of the tribulation do not reflect the wrath of humanity or the wrath of Satan. They express God's wrath poured out on the world. Describing this time, Jesus said, "You will be hearing of wars and rumors of wars. . . . Nation will rise against nation, and kingdom against kingdom" (Matthew 24:6–7). Men will kill one another on an unprecedented scale. While Scripture does not give the details, the advances in modern weapons suggest a terrible destruction.

John also noted that "a great sword was given" to the rider. The Greek word for "sword" here refers to the short, stabbing sword a Roman soldier carried into battle. It was also a weapon used by assassins. The vision depicts a great sword to describe the extent of the war. Antichrist's false peace will dissolve in battle and revolt.

Antichrist will play a major role in the wars that follow. When wars break out all over the world he will have no choice but to resort to war in order to preserve his power. He will be as skillful at war as he was at promoting false peace (cf. Daniel 8:24). Among his victims will be many of God's people (cf. 6:9; Matthew 24:9).

Antichrist's setting up of the abomination of desolation (Daniel 11:31; 12:11; Matthew 24:15) will touch off a massive conflict (see Daniel 11:36–45).

As the head of a Western confederacy, Antichrist will initially portray himself as a champion of peace. He will even appear to bring peace to the troubled Middle East. He will make a treaty with Israel, posing as their protector and defender. Soon afterwards, however, his desire for dominance will provoke rebellion. Antichrist's attempts to crush his enemies will last throughout the remainder of the tribulation. Finally, when Jesus Christ, returns, Antichrist will be cast into the lake of fire forever (20:10).

THE THIRD SEAL: FAMINE

When He broke the third seal, I heard the third living creature saying, "Come." I looked, and behold, a black horse; and he who sat on it had a pair of scales in his hand. And I heard something like a voice in the center of the four living creatures saying, "A quart of wheat for a denarius, and three quarts of barley for a denarius; and do not damage the oil and the wine." (6:5–6)

As the Lamb broke the third seal, the mighty voice of the third living creature announced the coming of the third horse and rider. John's use of the word "behold" reveals how startled he was by the rider's appearance. The color black is associated with famine (Lamentations 5:10 KJV). Famine is a logical consequence of worldwide war as food supplies are destroyed. Jesus also predicted this future famine (Matthew 24:7). God has used famine as a means of judgment in the past, but this will be the most devastating famine in all of human history.

The pair of scales the rider carried in his hand pictures the rationing that will result from the famine. Following the appearance of the black horse and its rider, John heard "something like a voice" in the center of the four living creatures. Since the four living creatures were stationed around the throne (4:6), this is likely the voice of God, the One sitting on the throne (4:2–3). God also speaks in connection with the fifth seal (6:11). He speaks here as a reminder that the famine is a direct judgment from Him.

The famine's severity can be seen in the example given. A quart of wheat is barely enough to sustain one person for one day, while a denarius represents one day's wages for an average worker. The average worker's salary will barely provide enough food for himself for each day and not enough to feed his family. Those with families will be able to purchase three quarts of barley for a denarius. That will provide food for their families, but barley was low in nutritional value and often fed to livestock. God cautions people not to waste the oil and the wine. Basic food staples will become priceless luxuries. Olive oil and wine, used in the preparation and cooking of food, as well as the purification of water, will need to be carefully protected.

THE FOURTH SEAL: DEATH

When the Lamb broke the fourth seal, I heard the voice of the fourth living creature saying, "Come." I looked, and behold, an ashen horse; and he who sat on it had the name Death; and Hades was following with him. Authority was given to them over a fourth of the earth, to kill with sword and with famine and with pestilence and by the wild beasts of the earth. (6:7–8)

The Lamb broke the seal and the fourth living creature summoned the fourth horse and its rider. John described the final horse as an ashen horse. "Ashen" refers to a sickly, pale, yellow-green color. The horse's color vividly portrays the pale-green pallor of death characteristic of the decomposition of a corpse. The rider who sat on it had the name Death. Death on a massive scale is the inevitable consequence of widespread war and famine. In this terrifying scene, John saw Hades following with Death.

The extent of the death and destruction brought by war and famine is given. Authority was given to Death and Hades to destroy a fourth of the world's population. At the world's current population, that would amount to the staggering total of nearly 1.5 billion deaths. Death will use four tools in his grim task. The first three elements, the sword, famine, and pestilence, are often linked together in Scripture (1 Chronicles 21:12; 2 Chronicles 20:9; Jeremiah 14:12), and all four elements appear in Ezekiel 14:12–21.

The sword (war) and famine have already been discussed in connection with the second and third seals. The fourth seal expands these conditions. "Pestilence" here may primarily refer to disease as the cause of death (2:23; 18:8) but is broad enough to encompass natural disasters such as the earthquakes predicted by Jesus (Matthew 24:7), floods, and volcanic eruptions. It could even refer to the effects of biological and chemical weapons.

At first glance, the inclusion of "wild beasts" with war, famine, and disease seems puzzling, since most creatures dangerous to man are either extinct or isolated in unpopulated regions. But one explanation may be that the most deadly creature of all, the rat, thrives in all populated areas. Rats have been responsible for uncounted millions of deaths throughout history by spreading disease. The most devastating occurrence of rat-borne disease was a fourteenth-century outbreak of bubonic plague that wiped out one-fourth to one-third of Europe's population. In a world ravaged by war, famine, and disease, the rat population may run wild.

THE FIFTH SEAL: DIVINE JUDGMENT

When the Lamb broke the fifth seal, I saw underneath the altar the souls of those who had been slain because of the word of God, and because of the testimony which they had maintained; and they cried out with a loud voice, saying, "How long, O Lord, holy and true, will You refrain from judging and avenging our blood on those who dwell on the earth?" And there was given to each of them a white robe; and they were told that they should rest for a little while longer, until the number of their fellow servants and their brethren who were to be killed even as they had been, would be completed also. (6:9–11)

The fifth seal marks the midpoint of the tribulation, bridging the gap between the beginning of God's wrath in the first half of the tribulation and its full fury revealed in the second half. Like the horsemen of the first four seals, it also portrays a force. That force is the prayers of God's saints. Three features become evident.

The Persons (6:9)

First, John saw underneath the altar the souls of those who had been slain. These are martyrs, killed during the time of the judgments. In addition to divine judgment, there will be widespread persecution of believers led by Satan, his demons, and the final Antichrist.

The persecution of believers, which will begin early in the first half of the tribulation, will intensify dramatically after Antichrist sets himself up as God. At that time he will "make war with the saints and . . . overcome them" (13:7). With the whole world worshiping Antichrist as God, believers will be considered blasphemers for opposing him. That will bring upon them persecution from Antichrist's false religious system. Revelation 9:21 speaks of the proliferation of murders at this time; many of the victims will no doubt be believers, the victims of mob violence.

John described the martyrs he saw underneath the altar as souls because their bodily resurrection had not yet taken place (20:4). They are the firstfruits of those who will be saved during the tribulation. Some will be Jewish, foreshadowing the salvation of Israel as a whole at the end of the tribulation (Zechariah 12:10; 14:1; Romans 11:26–29).

The text does not define which altar is in view, nor does the scene in heaven parallel the earthly temple or tabernacle. The altar John saw is most likely comparable to the altar of incense in the Old Testament (Exodus 40:5), because of the association of incense with prayer (5:8; 8:3–4; Psalm 141:2; Luke 1:10).

John gives two reasons why the martyrs will be slain: "because of the word of God, and because of the testimony which they had maintained." They will correctly interpret what they see going on around them, calling on people to repent and believe the gospel. Antichrist and his followers will not tolerate their bold preaching and will kill them. "Because of the testimony" which they had maintained refers to their loyalty to Jesus Christ (1:2, 9; 12:17; 19:10; 20:4), demonstrated by their proclamation of God's Word despite life-threatening hostility.

The Petitions (6:10)

The fifth seal is not martyrdom, as some suggest, because martyrdom could not be judgment from God. The seals depict God's wrath and judgment on the evil, not His children. The force, then, that is involved in the fifth seal is the prayers of the tribulation martyrs for God to enact vengeance on their murderers.

Prayer will play a vital role in God's judgments on the earth. This prayer of the martyrs is similar to the imprecatory psalms. A prayer for pardon is appropriate in a time of grace. But when judgment comes, prayers for divine judgment are fitting. Such prayers are not from a desire for revenge, but a protest against all that is sinful and dishonoring to God.

God's hand of judgment will move in response to the martyrs because their prayers will be urgent and consistent with His purpose. The word translated "cried out" emphasizes the urgent need and denotes strong emotions. The twenty-four elders and the angels loudly praised God (5:12), and the tribulation martyrs will petition Him with a loud voice. In keeping with their call for vengeance and justice, they address Him as the "Lord, holy and true." The word translated "Lord" speaks of God the Father's power and authority.

The martyrs' question "How long . . . will You refrain from judging and avenging our blood on those who dwell on the earth?" does not reflect a personal vendetta. They are asking Him the question because they have a holy desire to see Satan and Antichrist destroyed. "How long" is a well-known cry of suffering Israel, reflecting the perplexing question of the righteous asking when their pain will end (Psalms 13:1; 35:17). The phrase "those who dwell on the earth" is a technical one used throughout Revelation for the ungodly. As was the case with murdered Abel, the very ground cries out for their blood.

The Promise (6:11)

Two elements make up God's response to His martyred saints: a symbolic gift, and a spoken word. The gift given to each of them was a white robe. These long, brilliant white robes were a reward of grace (7:9, 14), symbolizing God's gift of eternal righteousness. They symbolize all the glory that redeemed saints will enjoy in heaven. These were not actual robes, since this vision is before the resurrection of the bodies of the redeemed, which occurs for tribulation saints at Christ's return (20:4–5).

Along with this gift came God's spoken word, that they should "rest for a little while longer." That is not a rebuke for impatience, but an invitation to stop the cry for vengeance and enjoy heavenly rest until God's wrath arrives. The phrase "for a little while longer" (John 7:33; 12:35) indicates that the time will not be delayed. This seal is best seen as describing a period in the middle of the seven years of tribulation. There is a verbal similarity to the phrase in Revelation 10:6, "there will be delay no longer." Some time will clearly elapse between 6:11 and 10:6. God's day of judgment and vengeance is about three and a half years ahead, and will not come until the number of the martyrs' fellow servants would be completed.

"Fellow servants and brethren" are two classes of people. The first group was alive and willing to die like the martyrs, though they would not. The second group were those who will be killed.

THE SIXTH SEAL—PHYSICAL DESTRUCTION

I looked when He broke the sixth seal, and there was a great earthquake; and the sun became black as sackcloth made of hair, and the whole moon became like blood; and the stars of the sky fell to the earth, as a fig tree casts its unripe figs when shaken by a great wind. The sky was split apart like a scroll when it is rolled up, and every mountain and island were moved out of their places. Then the kings of the earth and the great men and the commanders and the rich and the strong and every slave and free man hid themselves in the caves and among the rocks of the mountains; and they said to the mountains and to the rocks, "Fall on us and hide us from the presence of Him who sits on the throne, and from the wrath of the Lamb; for the great day of their wrath has come, and who is able to stand?" (6:12–17)

Three features describe the overwhelming fear associated with the sixth seal: the reason for fear, the range of fear, and the reaction of fear.

The Reason for Fear (6:12–14)

Unlike the first five seals, each of which involved humans in one way or another, God acts alone with the sixth seal. By the time this seal is opened, the tribulation's midpoint has passed and the world is in the "great tribulation" (Matthew 24:21). By then the final Antichrist has desecrated the temple in Jerusalem (the "abomination of desolation"), the world worships him, and a massive persecution of Jews and Christians has broken out. Incredibly, in the midst of all the turmoil and chaos from the divine judgments on the world, it will be business as usual for most people (Matthew 24:37–39). But the sixth seal will be so devastating and terrifying that it will be attributable only to God.

First, will be a great earthquake. There have been many earthquakes in recorded history and more during the first half of the tribulation (Matthew 24:7). Yet the event John saw in this seal is to be far more powerful and devastating than any previous earthquake. In fact, this one will shake more than just the earth (6:13–14). The Greek word translated here as "earthquake" literally means "a shaking." In Matthew 8:24 it describes a great storm on the Sea of Galilee. God has often made His presence felt in human history by shaking the earth (Exodus 19:18; Psalm 68:8; 1 Kings 19:11–12; Matthew 27:51, 54). This event, however, causes far more than the earth to be shaken. It will shake the heavens as well as the earth.

On the heels of the earthquake comes a second disaster, as the "sun became black as sackcloth made of hair." Sackcloth was rough cloth worn by mourners, usually made from the hair of black goats. Following the violent earthquake that devastates the earth, the sun will turn as black as a mourner's robe.

The prophet Joel spoke of these same phenomena in connection with the day of the Lord: "The sun will be turned into darkness and the moon into blood before the great and awesome day of the Lord comes" (Joel 2:31). Darkness is associated with judgment elsewhere in Scripture (Exodus 10:21–22; Matthew 27:45).

The third disaster is closely connected with the darkening of the sun, as the whole "moon became like blood." There will be vast clouds of ash and smoke spewed out by the volcanic activity associated with the great worldwide earthquake. That ash and smoke will eclipse the moon, coloring it bloodred as it attempts to pierce the smoke-darkened sky.

Isaiah also described this strange and terrifying phenomenon, writing in Isaiah 13:10, "The sun will be dark when it rises and the moon will not shed its light." Joel adds, "The sun and the moon grow dark" (Joel 2:10, 31). These phenomena will affect every aspect of life as the normal cycle of daylight and darkness is disrupted. The total eclipse of the sun and moon will add more reason for the world to be in panic.

Then, out of the darkened sky comes the fourth disaster; John records that the stars of the sky fell to the earth. The word translated "stars" can refer to actual stars, but it can also describe any heavenly body other than the sun and the moon. In this context it does not refer to actual stars, since they are far too large to fall to the earth and would incinerate it long before striking it. Also, the stars are still in place later when the fourth trumpet sounds (8:12). This is most likely a reference to asteroid or meteor showers bombarding the earth.

The fifth disaster in this seal affects the earth's atmosphere, because the sky appears to split apart like a scroll when it is rolled up. This is the human perception of the magnitude of this judgment, but is not the final dissolving of heaven, which comes later (21:1; 2 Peter 3:10). John likens the sky to an unrolled scroll that splits in the middle and rolls up on either side (cf. Isaiah 34:4).

John describes a sixth devastating natural phenomenon, noting that every mountain and island were moved out of their places. The whole unstable crust of the earth begins to move and shift.

The devastating natural disasters accompanying the sixth seal will be the most terrifying events ever to affect the earth. Their cumulative impact will be far more destructive than any of the current doomsday scenarios about asteroids hitting the earth.

The Reaction of Fear (6:15–17)

The debilitating fear caused by the disasters associated with the sixth seal will affect all unbelievers. These seven categories embrace all classes of society. "The kings of the earth" refers to the heads of state throughout the world. "The great men" are the high-ranking officials in government. "The commanders" are the military leaders, while "the rich" are those who control commerce and business, and "the strong" may well be the influential. Together, they comprise the elite elements of human society. Ironically, these are the very people who ignored the warnings of God's impending judgment and persecuted believers. "Every slave" and "every free man" encompass all other individuals.

The reaction of the unbelieving world to the terrors unleashed by the sixth seal will not be repentance, but panic. They will finally acknowledge that the disasters they have experienced are God's judgment. Yet they will continue to follow Antichrist. As a result, God will abandon them (see 2 Thessalonians 2:11–12). Those who repeatedly harden their hearts will have their hearts hardened by God.

The panic-stricken sinners will react irrationally, foolishly attempting to hide themselves "in the caves and among the rocks of the mountains" (cf. Isaiah 2:17–21)—the very places that are being shaken. They are no doubt seeking refuge from the swarms of meteors and asteroids bombarding the earth. But in light of the massive earthquake and its continuing aftershocks, the widespread volcanic eruptions, and the other disturbances to the earth's crust, such hiding places will offer no safety. The terrifying events prompt a worldwide prayer meeting, but the prayers are to Mother Nature, not to God. They will say to the mountains and to the rocks, "Fall on us and hide us from the presence of Him who sits on the throne, and from the wrath of the Lamb; for the great day of their wrath has come, and who is able to stand?"[1] People will be so terrified that they would rather die than face the wrath of a holy God.

"Him who sits on the throne" refers to God (4:2, 3, 9, 10). They will have, by then, come to a clear understanding that God has been behind all the judgments. More specifically, they "fear the wrath of the Lamb." The Lamb, Jesus Christ (5:6–8), is the agent of direct judgment. The wrath of the incarnate Jesus has displayed only twice before (John 2:13–17; Matthew 21:12–13). In the future, He will judge like a lion (5:5).

"The great day of their wrath" is another term for the day of the Lord. These "day of the Lord" horrors precede the coming of the Lord and even anticipate the worst that is yet to come in the seventh seal, which includes the trumpet (8:1–9:21) and bowl (16:1–21) judgments.

The scene closes with the asking of the rhetorical question "Who is able to stand?" The answer is "No one."

This picture, horrifying and frightening as it is, is not altogether hopeless. The church will be delivered from that time (3:10). Great multitudes of people will be saved in the midst of the terrors of divine judgment, both Gentiles (7:9) and Jews (Romans 11:26). But for the rest the words of Hebrews will apply: "It is a terrifying thing to fall into the hands of the living God" (Hebrews 10:31).

10

The
TRIBULATION
Saints

(7:1–17)

Revelation 7 forms a parenthetical section between the sixth (6:12–17) and seventh (8:1) seals to answer the question, "The great day of their wrath has come, and who is able to stand?" (6:17). It introduces two groups who will survive the fury of divine judgment. The first (described in verses 1–8) are the Jewish evangelists who will be preserved on earth. They will survive the divine wrath unleashed by the seal, trumpet, and bowl judgments. God will also protect them from the murderous efforts of Antichrist to wipe out believers. Having survived the wars, famines, and unprecedented natural disasters, they will enter the millennial kingdom alive. The second group to escape divine fury (7:9–17) constitutes those who will be martyred.

THE 144,000 JEWS

Wrath Restrained
After this I saw four angels standing at the four corners of the earth, holding back the four winds of the earth, so that no wind would blow on the earth or on the sea or on any tree. (7:1)

The use of "after this" here signifies that the vision of the sixth seal has ended and John is about to see a new vision. It may also indicate that this new vision depicts events that come after the sixth seal chronologically. The scene now shifts from judgment on the ungodly to special protection for the godly.

As the vision unfolded, John first saw four angels. These four are given power over the elements of nature (14:18; 16:5). They are seen "standing at the four corners of the earth holding back the four winds of the earth." Unsophisticated skeptics imagine that John's poetic reference to the four corners of the earth reflects a primitive notion that the earth is flat and square. But the phrase actually refers to the whole earth by designating the four primary points on the compass (north, south, east, and west).

From their key positions on the earth, these powerful angels ensured that no wind would blow on the earth, sea, or any tree. The four winds are often associated in Scripture with God's judgment (Jeremiah 49:36; Daniel 7:2; Hosea 13:15).

"Holding back" is from a strong word that suggests the winds are struggling to break free from their restraint. The angelic restraining of the wind also symbolizes the withholding of the plagues associated with the upcoming trumpet judgments (8:5ff.). So the next phase of God's wrath is restrained for the moment.

Saints Sealed

And I saw another angel ascending from the rising of the sun, having the seal of the living God; and he cried out with a loud voice to the four angels to whom it was granted to harm the earth and the sea, saying, "Do not harm the earth or the sea or the trees until we have sealed the bond-servants of our God on their foreheads." (7:2–3)

The reason for the temporary restraining of God's judgment becomes clear as John sees another angel in addition to the four holding back the winds. Some have identified this angel as Jesus Christ, but that is unlikely because "another" here means another of the same kind as the first four angels.

John saw the angel ascending "from the rising of the sun." That is a poetic way of saying from the east, the point of the compass in which the sun rises. From John's perspective on the island of Patmos, the east would be toward the land of Israel, the land where God's promised salvation came through Jesus.

The angel had with him "the seal of the living God." This seal (from the Greek *sphragis*) often referred to a signet ring. Kings or other officials would use such rings to stamp into wax on documents or other items, affirming their authenticity and guaranteeing their security (Genesis 41:42; Esther 3:10; 8:2, 8; Daniel 6:17; Matthew 27:66).

In contrast to the seals of earthly rulers, the seal borne by the angel belonged to "the living God." The Bible frequently identifies God as the living God to distinguish Him from the dead idols worshiped by unbelievers. The most prominent false deity of the tribulation period, Antichrist, will seal his followers (13:16–17; 14:9–11; 16:2; 19:20; 20:4), and the true and living God will seal His. Revelation 14:1 identifies the mark left by God's seal as the names of Christ and the Father.

Urgently, the fifth angel cried out with a loud voice to the other four angels, "Do not harm the earth or the sea or the trees until we have sealed the bond-servants of our God on their foreheads." The harm that will come to the earth, the sea, and the trees will occur when the four angels suddenly release the judgment they have been restraining. But that judgment had to wait until the angels had sealed the bond-servants of God on their foreheads. That they are referred to as bond-servants indicates they are already redeemed. At this point they are to be protected so they can continue to witness about Christ. After the sealing is complete the judgments can begin. Revelation 14:1–5 describes their morally pure, undefiled character and devotion to Christ. They are also described as having been "purchased from among men as first fruits to God and to the Lamb" (14:4). They will be the most effective missionaries the world has ever seen, and will be instrumental in the conversion of both their own countrymen and the nations.

Israelites Identified

And I heard the number of those who were sealed, one hundred and forty-four thousand sealed from every tribe of the sons of Israel: from the tribe of Judah, twelve thousand were sealed, from the tribe of Reuben twelve thousand, from the tribe of Gad twelve thousand, from the tribe of Asher twelve thousand, from the tribe of Naphtali twelve thousand, from the tribe of Manasseh twelve thousand, from the tribe of Simeon twelve thousand, from the tribe of Levi twelve thousand, from the tribe of Issachar twelve thousand, from the tribe of Zebulun twelve thousand, from the tribe of Joseph twelve thousand, from the tribe of Benjamin, twelve thousand were sealed. (7:4–8)

The 144,000 are not all Jewish believers at that time, but a unique group selected to proclaim the gospel in that day (12:17; 14:1–5). Despite the plain and unambiguous declaration of the text that the one hundred and forty-four thousand who are to be sealed will come from every tribe of the sons of Israel, many persist in identifying them as the church. But the identification of Israel with the church in those passages is tenuous and disputed. The fact is that "no clear-cut example of the church being called 'Israel' exists in the [New Testament] or in ancient church writings until A.D. 160. . . . This fact is crippling to any attempt to identify Israel as the church in Revelation 7:4."[1] The term Israel must be interpreted in accordance with its normal biblical usage as a reference to the physical descendants of Abraham, Isaac, and Jacob.

That there were 12,000 sealed from every tribe of the sons of Israel speaks of God's elective purpose. Mere random human choice would not come up with such an even division. While the tribal records were lost when the Romans sacked Jerusalem in A.D. 70, God knows who belongs to each tribe.[2]

The specific tribal names in this list raise three interesting questions. Why is Judah listed first, even though Reuben was the firstborn? Why is the tribe of Dan omitted, and why is Ephraim omitted in favor of his father, Joseph? Reuben forfeited his birthright as punishment for his sexual misconduct with his father's concubine (1 Chronicles 5:1). The omission of the tribe of Dan in favor of the priestly tribe of Levi probably is due to the tribe's reputation for idolatry (Deuteronomy 29:18–21). While Dan will share in the millennial blessings (Ezekiel 48:1–2, 32), the tribe will not be selected for this duty nor protected during the tribulation. Similarly, the name of Ephraim is omitted in favor of his father Joseph because Ephraim defected from the ruling house of Judah (Isaiah 7:17). Like Dan, Ephraim was consumed with idolatry (Hosea 4:17). His brother Manasseh is included because he was the faithful son of Joseph.

This critical passage reinforces the biblical truth that God is not through with the nation of Israel (see Romans 9–11). Though Israel failed in its mission to be a witness nation, that will not be the case in the future. From the Jewish people will come the greatest missionary force the world has ever known.

THE BELIEVERS OF THE TRIBULATION

Description
After these things I looked, and behold, a great multitude which no one could count, from every nation and all tribes and peoples and tongues . . . clothed in white robes, and palm branches were in their hands; (7:9a, c)

Revelation 7:9–17 describes that vast multitude of people from all the nations of the world who will be saved during the coming tribulation. This could include those of Israel who are saved during the preaching of the 144,000. There is nothing in the terminology of the passage that excludes Jews. Rather, the phrase "every nation" could include them.

As it does throughout Revelation, the phrase "after these things" introduces a new vision, distinct from the one in 7:1–8. The exclamation "behold" reveals this vision to be a shocking, startling one to John. The aged apostle, the last survivor of the Twelve, must have felt isolated and alone in his exile on the isle of Patmos. He had seen Gentiles come to Christ through his own ministry in Asia Minor and the ministries of Paul, Timothy, Titus, and others. Gentile churches had been founded, yet they were for the most part small, beleaguered, and persecuted. This vision must surely have renewed his joy and hope, as he realized that the church would survive and, in the end, people from the nations would be saved in great numbers.

That the group introduced in this passage is distinct from the 144,000 (7:1–8) is evident from several considerations. First, the phrase "after these things" introduces a new vision. Second, this group is described as "a great multitude which no one could count." No specific number is mentioned. Third, the 144,000 came from the twelve tribes of Israel (7:4–8), while this group came from every nation, tribe, people, and language. Finally, the 144,000 are beyond the reach of persecutors because they are sealed for protection from persecution on earth (7:3). Yet this second group is beyond the reach of any persecutors because it is already in heaven. Verse 14 describes and identifies them: "These are the ones who come out of the great tribulation, and they have washed their robes and made them white in the blood of the Lamb."

The redeemed were "clothed in white robes." "Robes" is from a Greek word that depicts a long, full-length robe and are the same ones worn by the martyrs in 6:9–11. That fact suggests that the group in view here is part of that earlier group of martyred believers. As the tribulation wears on, the number of martyrs will increase, as will the number of believers who die naturally or violently, eventually accumulating into the vast, uncountable multitude in this passage. The white robes are symbolic rather than literal, since the saints do not yet have their resurrected bodies (6:9; 20:4). Such white robes, also symbolic of holiness, are reserved for Christ (Matthew 17:2; Mark 9:3), His angels (Matthew 28:3; Mark 16:5), and the glorified church (19:8, 14).

The saints also held "palm branches . . . in their hands." Palm branches are associated in Scripture with celebration, deliverance, and joy. They were especially prominent during the Feast of Tabernacles (Leviticus 23:40), being employed in the construction of the booths the people lived in during that feast (Nehemiah 8:15–17). During Jesus' triumphal entry the joyous crowd waved palm branches as they welcomed Him into Jerusalem, shouting, "Hosanna! Blessed is He who comes in the name of the Lord, even the King of Israel" (John 12:13). The palm branches in the hands of these redeemed saints are a fitting celebrative symbol of Christ's salvation.

Location
standing before the throne and before the Lamb (7:9b)

John saw this vast crowd of victorious, joyous saints standing before the throne of God in heaven. They were also in the presence of the Lamb, whom John saw in his earlier vision standing near the throne (5:6). Many had suffered death at the hands of Antichrist (cf. 20:4) for refusing to take his mark or worship him. They are no longer seen under the altar praying for divine vengeance (6:9–11), which has already begun, but standing triumphantly before the throne of God.

Action
and they cry out with a loud voice, saying, "Salvation to our God who sits on the throne, and to the Lamb." (7:10)

The redeemed martyrs constantly cry out with a loud voice in joyous, exuberant worship. The Lord desires loud praise (Psalms 66:1; 100:1). Their prayers of intercession have ceased and they are glorifying and praising God. Salvation is the theme of their worship, as it is throughout Revelation. In 12:10 John "heard a loud voice in heaven, saying, 'Now the salvation, and the power, and the kingdom of our God and the authority of His Christ have come, for the accuser of our brethren has been thrown down, he who accuses them before our God day and night.'" The occupation of those in heaven is continual, eternal praise of the Almighty God and the Lamb. They identify God as "our God," claiming God as their own.

Association
And all the angels were standing around the throne and around the elders and the four living creatures; and they fell on their faces before the throne and worshiped God, saying, "Amen, blessing and glory and wisdom and thanksgiving and honor and power and might, be to our God forever and ever. Amen." (7:11–12)

The innumerable believers before God's throne were not alone in their loud worship. An uncountable number of angels (first reported in the earlier vision of 5:11) joined them. The angels ringing God's glorious, magnificent throne (4:1–6, 5:1, 6) also surrounded the other two groups involved in worshiping God, the elders and the four living creatures. In 5:8–10, the twenty-four elders sang the song of redemption, while here they are seen praising the God of redemption. The four living creatures are cherubim, an exalted order of angels and often appear together with these elders (5:6, 8, 11, 14; 14:3; 19:4).

Overwhelmed by God's glory, all present fell on their faces before the throne and worshiped God. Then, recognizing God's sovereignty and holiness, the worshipers utter a benediction bracketed front and back with the affirmation "Amen," meaning, "so let it be." Their prayer is that "blessing and glory and wisdom and thanksgiving and honor and power and might be attributed to our God forever and ever" (4:11; 5:12).

The phrase "forever and ever" indicates, as did the doxology of 5:13ff., that this praise is not temporary or momentary, but will continue eternally. What is described here is worship that will never cease through all of endless eternity.

Origination
Then one of the elders answered, saying to me, "These who are clothed in the white robes, who are they, and where have they come from?" I said to him, "My lord, you know." And he said to me, "These are the ones who come out of the great tribulation, and they have washed their robes and made them white in the blood of the Lamb." (7:13–14)

John then became an active participant in the vision when one of the twenty-four elders questioned him. The elder was not asking for information because he did not know the answer, but to emphasize his point. The elder's question specifies and emphasizes the truth that people will be saved during the tribulation.

Some argue that the redeemed tribulation martyrs and others seen in heaven will be people who never lived during the church age. That cannot be true, however, since the tribulation lasts seven years (Daniel 9:27) and the great tribulation half of that (Revelation 11:2–3; 12:6; 13:5). They would all have to be younger than seven years of age. Others hold that these are people who never heard the gospel during their lifetimes and received the opportunity to repent after death. That interpretation is also impossible, "inasmuch as it is appointed for men to die once and after this comes judgment" (Hebrews 9:27). People have the opportunity only during their lifetimes. These are people whose lifetimes will extend past the rapture into the tribulation.

John's reply to the elder is emphatic: "My lord, you know." It includes both a confession of ignorance and a request for further revelation. John's calling the elder "lord" did not ascribe deity to him. He was using the Greek equivalent of "sir" as a title of great respect (19:10; 22:8–9). The heavenly elder's reply confirmed the identity of these believers as "the ones who come out of the great tribulation." They lived into it, were redeemed during it, and have now come out of it through death. The Greek phrase translated "the ones who come out" depicts a prolonged process. This group will keep growing as people keep dying during the tribulation. Therefore the rapture of the church is not in view here, since it is an instantaneous event (1 Corinthians 15:51–52). The description of these believers clearly distinguishes them from any other group of redeemed people in history.

The elder further described how the tribulation believers gained the privilege of being in the presence of God and His angels. It is because they are clothed in the white robes, which they have washed and made white in the blood of the Lamb. Here their white robes indicate holiness, and purity. "Soiled garments" in Scripture symbolize the defilement of sin (Isaiah 64:6; Zechariah 3:3), and salvation is often pictured as a washing (Psalm 51:7; Isaiah 1:18; Titus 3:5; Revelation 22:14). That anything could be cleansed by washing it in blood seems strange to consider, but not to those familiar with the Old Testament. Such a washing was required for spiritual cleansing (Hebrews 10:4). Christ's substitutionary death atoned for the tribulation believers' sins, and by repentant faith they were justified and reconciled to God (Romans 5:10; 2 Corinthians 5:18–21).

Function
For this reason, they are before the throne of God; and they serve Him day and night in His temple; (7:15a)

The reason these tribulation believers were allowed to stand before the throne of God is that they were purified and cleansed from their sins by the sacrifice of the Lamb of God on their behalf. They were thus fitted for the presence of God that they might serve Him day and night. "Serve" is from a word often used to describe priestly service (Luke 2:37; Hebrews 8:5; 13:10). "Day and night" is an idiomatic way to indicate their continuous occupation. There is no actual night and day in God's eternal heaven (22:3–5). The location of that service is in His temple. There is currently a temple in heaven, and there will be one on earth during the millennial kingdom of Christ on earth (Ezekiel 40–48). In the eternal state, however, there will no longer be a need for a temple, "for the Lord God the Almighty and the Lamb are its temple" (Revelation 21:22). The heavenly temple currently is the holy domain where God's presence dwells outside the fallen universe, but that will be unnecessary in the new heavens and new earth where sin has been forever done away with. There will no longer be a temple building, because God will occupy all places, and all believers everywhere throughout the eternal state will continue to worship and serve Him forever.

Protection
and He who sits on the throne will spread His tabernacle over them. (7:15b)

In a wonderful, comforting picture, God, described as He who sits on the throne (cf. 4:1–3; 5:1, 13; 7:10), promises to spread the tabernacle, or tent (cf. 21:3), of His *shekinah* presence over these persecuted believers. "Tabernacle" is a word John likes to use (cf. 13:6; 15:5; 21:3; the related verb translated "dwelt" appears in John 1:14), which reflects the sheltering presence of the Lord. It corresponds to the Old Testament promises of God's protective presence (cf. Leviticus 26:11–12; Ezekiel 37:27;

Zechariah 2:10–11; 8:3, 8). These believers will have witnessed unspeakable suffering and indescribable horrors as God's judgments were poured out on the world. They will have suffered terrible persecution at the hands of Antichrist and his followers. But when they enter God's presence, they will come to a heavenly sanctuary, the most secure place. There they will receive shelter from the terrors of the fallen world that are to come as God continues to unleash His devastating and destructive judgments.

Provision
They will hunger no more, nor thirst anymore; nor will the sun beat down on them, nor any heat; for the Lamb in the center of the throne will be their shepherd, and will guide them to springs of the water of life; and God will wipe every tear from their eyes. (7:16–17)

This comforting promise of further provision is drawn from and almost identical to the words of Isaiah 49:10. As they experienced the horrors of the tribulation, these sufferers had endured hunger, thirst, and scorching heat as the sun beat down on them, a phenomenon which will occur in the tribulation (Revelation 16:9). Yet now they will enjoy eternal satisfaction, for the Lamb in the center of the throne (5:6) will be their shepherd, and will guide them to springs of the water of life. The picture of God as the Shepherd of His people is one of the most beloved and common in the Old Testament, and Jesus is depicted as the Shepherd of His people.[3] Interestingly, the other three uses of *shepherd* in Revelation (2:27; 12:5; 19:15) reveal Christ crushing sinners with a rod of iron (Psalm 2:9). The Great Shepherd will guide His flock to springs of the water of life and wipe every tear from their eyes. In heaven there will be no pain or sorrow.

In this age when Christianity is under siege on all sides, it is comforting to be reassured of the ultimate triumph of God's saving grace. God will redeem His people. That thought should bring all believers great comfort, and motivate us to praise God for the greatness of His plan.

The Six
TRUMPET
Judgments
(8:1–9:21)

When the Lamb opens the seventh and last seal on the little scroll that is the title deed to the earth (5:1), the judgments of the day of the Lord will intensify and expand dramatically.

This final seal contains within it all of the remaining judgments of the time of the great tribulation, including the trumpet and bowl judgments. Though some believe the events of the trumpet and bowl judgments happen simultaneously with those of the sixth seal, it seems better to understand them as telescoping out of each other sequentially. That the seventh seal contains the seven trumpet judgments seems clear, since there is no description of judgment in the seventh seal, but an anticipation of severe judgment followed immediately in the text by the seven trumpet judgments. In a similar manner, the seventh trumpet does not describe a judgment (10:7; 11:15–17), but rather contains the anticipation of heavenly rejoicing over the judgment to come.

The progressive judgments within the seventh seal will take place over an indefinite period of time. The effects of the fifth trumpet, for example, will last for five months (9:10). While the exact timetable for

the trumpet and bowl judgments is not revealed, their escalating devastation indicates that they all occur during the last half of the tribulation.
Therefore, the seventh seal encompasses all of God's final wrath up to the
return of Christ.

THE OPENING OF THE SEVENTH SEAL (8:1–6)

Silence
**When the Lamb broke the seventh seal, there was silence in heaven for
about half an hour** (8:1)

When Jesus broke the seventh seal a unique response occurred—silence.
A review of the visions up to this point makes it clear that John had heard
much noise in heaven. Beginning in Revelation 4, "sounds and peals of
thunder" emanated from God's throne, (verse 5) and "the four living creatures . . . [did] not cease to say, 'Holy, holy, holy is the Lord God, the
Almighty, who was and who is and who is to come'" (verse 8). Later John
heard a "strong angel proclaiming with a loud voice, 'Who is worthy to
open the book and to break its seals?'", the cries of the martyrs for
vengeance (6:9–10), the loud roar of a powerful earthquake (6:12), and
an angel who "cried out . . . saying, 'Do not harm the earth or the sea or
the trees until we have sealed the bond-servants of our God on their foreheads'" (7:2–3).

But after all that loudness, when the judgment becomes visible on the
scroll, both the redeemed and the angels are reduced to silence. They face
the reality of the future destruction they see written and answer with the
silence of foreboding and awe at what God is about to do.

While eternal heaven has no time, the apostle John, who is seeing the
vision, does. Each minute of that half hour of silence must have increased
the sense of suspense for John. Heaven, which had resounded with loud
praises from the vast crowd of people and angels, became strangely still.
The greatest event since the fall is about to take place. All heaven is seen
waiting in great expectancy.

Sounding

***And I saw the seven angels who stand before God, and seven trumpets
were given to them.*** (8:2)

Following the half hour of heaven's silence, John experienced the seven
angels who stand before God. The use of "the" appears to set them apart
as a unique group, which some have called the presence angels. The Greek
verb translated "stand" indicates that they were in the presence of God
and had been there for a time. Scripture describes various ranks and
orders of angels, such as cherubim (Genesis 3:24), seraphim (Isaiah 6:2),
archangels (1 Thessalonians 4:16; Jude 9), thrones, dominions, rulers,
authorities (Colossians 1:16), and powers (Ephesians 6:12). These seven
appear to be one such order of high-ranking angels. Gabriel may have
been one of them (Luke 1:19).

As John watched, seven trumpets were given to these angels, in
preparation for the trumpet judgments that would shortly follow. As they
did in the seal judgments (6:1, 3, 5, 6, 7) and will in the bowl judgments
(16:2, 3, 4, 8, 10, 12, 17), angels participate in the trumpet judgments.
That involvement is consistent with the teaching of Jesus that angels will
play an important role in God's future judgments (Matthew 13:39–41,
49–50; 16:27; 25:31).

Each of the seven trumpets unleashes a specific judgment of greater
intensity than the first six seals, yet not as destructive as the seven bowls
(16:1–21). The first four trumpets destroy the earth's ecology (8:6–12),
the next two produce demonic destruction of humanity (8:13; 9:1–11,
13–19), and the seventh trumpet introduces the final outpouring of
God's wrath contained in the seven bowl judgments.

Having been introduced and given their trumpets, the seven angels
did not immediately blow them. They had to wait for other important
events to transpire.

Supplication

***Another angel came and stood at the altar, holding a golden censer; and
much incense was given to him, so that he might add it to the prayers of***

all the saints on the golden altar which was before the throne. And the
smoke of the incense, with the prayers of the saints, went up before God
out of the angel's hand. (8:3–4)

John's attention was drawn from the seven angels with their trumpets to
another angel who came and stood at the altar of incense (cf. 6:9). Some
identify him as Christ. However, this is unlikely because: (1) Christ is
already identified in the heavenly scene as the Lamb (5:6; 6:1; 7:17);
(2) Jesus is nowhere identified as an angel in the New Testament; (3) the
angel in verse 3 is described as another of the same kind, like those in
verse 2; and (4) everywhere He appears in Revelation, Jesus is clearly
identified. If He were the One at the altar, it is reasonable to assume that
He would be specifically identified.

John notes that "the angel came and stood at the altar." That altar is
the heavenly counterpart to the altar of incense in the temple, which also
was made with gold (Exodus 30:3). It was the same golden incense altar
seen by Isaiah in his vision (Isaiah 6:6) and by Ezekiel (Ezekiel 10:2). The
further description of this altar as "before the throne" assures John's readers that the altar of incense was the earthly counterpart to this heavenly
incense altar. That is evident because the altar of incense in the tabernacle and the temple was the nearest thing to the Holy of Holies where
God's glory dwelt (Exodus 30:6). Consistent with that identification is
that the angel held a golden censer, or firepan. In the Old Testament, the
priests would twice daily take hot, fiery coals from the brazen altar and
transport them into the Holy Place to the incense altar (Exodus 30:7, 8).
The angel took the incense symbolizing the multiplied prayers of God's
people (5:8; 6:9–11) that was given to him. Though it does not say who
gave the angel the incense, the verb "was given" frequently refers in
Revelation to something given by God. This was so that he might add it
to the prayers of all the saints already rising from the altar. Those prayers
were for Satan to be destroyed, sin to be defeated, their deaths to be
avenged (6:9–11), and Christ to come. As the angel added his incense to
that already burning on the altar, the smoke of the incense, with the
prayers of the saints, went up before God out of the angel's hand. These

are undoubtedly the cries of believers in the great tribulation against their persecutors and all who blaspheme God and Christ in that time.

Storm

Then the angel took the censer and filled it with the fire of the altar, and threw it to the earth; and there followed peals of thunder and sounds and flashes of lightning and an earthquake. (8:5)

"The censer . . . filled with the fire of the altar," usually linked with the prayers of God's people, becomes here a symbol of divine wrath. The angel's act of throwing it to earth reveals that God's judgment will come in direct response to those prayers. The cumulative effect of the prayers of innumerable righteous men will be very powerful (see James 5:16).The immediate effects of the firestorm of wrath that bursts upon the earth are "peals of thunder and sounds and flashes of lightning and an earthquake," in direct contrast to the silence (8:1). "Peals of thunder and sounds and flashes of lightning" are associated with the awesome majesty of God's glorious throne in (4:5; 11:19; 16:18; Exodus 19:16–19). No details are given about the earthquake, but it will probably be at least as powerful as the one associated with the sixth seal (6:12).

THE FIRST TRUMPET

The first sounded, and there came hail and fire, mixed with blood, and they were thrown to the earth; and a third of the earth was burned up, and a third of the trees were burned up, and all the green grass was burned up. (8:7)

Hail is frequently associated in Scripture with divine judgment (e.g., Exodus 9:13–25; Job 38:22–23), as is fire (Genesis 19:24; Psalm 11:6; Ezekiel 38:22). The combination of fire mixed with blood is reminiscent of Joel 2:30, which also describes the day of the Lord. The specific cause of the hail and fire is not revealed, but from a scientific standpoint an earthquake of the magnitude and extent of the one in verse 5 would likely trigger worldwide volcanic eruptions. Besides spewing vast quantities of flaming lava (which could be bloodred in appearance) into the atmosphere, the atmospheric disturbances caused by those eruptions could trigger violent thunderstorms that would produce large hail. Such thunderstorms would be in keeping with the imagery of verse 5. The blood may be actual blood, or John may be using descriptive language. Regardless, this deluge of death was thrown to the earth by God with devastating effects. The shocking result was that a third of the earth was burned up, making the soil unusable. Then a third of the trees were burned up, destroying fruit all over the earth. Finally all the green grass was burned up. The effects of such catastrophic fires would be widespread and devastating, including destruction of crops, death of animals on a massive scale, loss of wood for construction, and the destruction of watersheds.

THE SECOND TRUMPET

The second angel sounded, and something like a great mountain burning with fire was thrown into the sea; and a third of the sea became blood, and a third of the creatures which were in the sea and had life, died; and a third of the ships were destroyed. (8:8–9)

The judgment of the first trumpet fell on the land, that of the second trumpet on the sea. God created the sea to be a blessing to humanity, but people have repaid God's gracious provision with ingratitude and idolatry, revering the sea as the supposed source of their remotest evolutionary ancestors. As He had devastated the land environment, the true God judges the sea.

The massive object plunging through the sky looked to the terrified observers on earth "like a great mountain burning with fire." This is evidently a giant meteorite or asteroid, surrounded by flaming gases set ablaze by the friction of the earth's atmosphere. The current doomsday scenarios about an asteroid hitting the earth will come true with a vengeance. Everyone will see it, either live or on television. As the world's telescopes see it coming, many predictions will no doubt be made about whether it will hit the earth or not. It will strike somewhere in the world's oceans with an explosive power far greater than that of an atomic bomb. Because all the world's oceans are connected, the devastation will spread across one-third of the ocean waters, causing a third of the sea to become blood.

Three catastrophic, supernaturally designed effects result from the collision: (1) one-third of the sea became blood; (2) as a result of that effect one-third of the creatures which were in the sea died; and (3) giant waves will destroy a third of the ships on the world's oceans, capsizing huge vessels and completely swamping ports. The resulting disruption of commerce and transportation will cause economic chaos.

So the first two trumpets will bring devastating judgment on both the land and the sea, which are the beginning of the final catastrophes God will unleash on a rebellious world.

THE THIRD TRUMPET

The third angel sounded, and a great star fell from heaven, burning like a torch, and it fell on a third of the rivers and on the springs of waters. The name of the star is called Wormwood; and a third of the waters became wormwood, and many men died from the waters, because they were made bitter. (8:10–11)

As the third angel sounded his trumpet, another flaming object hurtled toward the earth. John described it as a great star that fell from heaven. The Greek word here for "star" can refer to any celestial body other than the sun and moon. The massive object that smashed into the ocean remained intact, but this object disintegrated as it reached Earth's atmosphere. The fact that it is described as burning like a torch supports that it is likely a meteor or comet, since torches were used in ancient times to describe meteors and comets. Its fiery debris fell on a third of the rivers and on the springs of waters, polluting the fresh water around the globe.

Because of its deadly effects, the star will be called Wormwood. Wormwood is mentioned only here in the New Testament. It is a shrub whose leaves are used in the manufacture of absinthe, a liqueur so toxic that its manufacture is banned in many countries. Wormwood is mentioned eight times in the Old Testament, where it is associated with bitterness, poison, and death (Deuteronomy 29:18; Proverbs 5:4; Jeremiah 9:15; 23:15; Lamentations 3:15, 19; Amos 5:7; 6:12). In three of those uses, wormwood is connected with poisoned water. Whatever the poison represented by the name *Wormwood* is, it destroys a third of the fresh waters. The repeated pattern of one-third destruction demonstrates that these are not natural events, but divine judgments.

With the third trumpet judgment, John records that many men died from the waters, because they were made bitter. The rivers will run with deadly poison. The wells will become springs of death. The lakes and reservoirs will be filled with toxic waters. Yet, the worst is yet to come.

THE FOURTH TRUMPET

The fourth angel sounded, and a third of the sun and a third of the moon and a third of the stars were struck, so that a third of them would be darkened and the day would not shine for a third of it, and the night in the same way. Then I looked, and I heard an eagle flying in midheaven, saying with a loud voice, "Woe, woe, woe to those who dwell on the earth, because of the remaining blasts of the trumpet of the three angels who are about to sound!" (8:12–13)

As the fourth angel sounded, the focus of divine judgment shifted from the earth to the heavens. The heavenly bodies are hit with a plague from God so that a third of them would be darkened and the day would not shine for a third of it, and the night in the same way. This partial eclipse is temporary, as God will later increase the amount of heat coming from the sun (16:8–9). At this point, the loss of heat from the sun will cause temperatures to plunge drastically all over the world. That will severely disrupt the earth's weather patterns and the seas' tides, leading to violent, unpredictable storms and tides, the destruction of crops, and further loss of animal and human lives.

The Old Testament prophets associated such signs in the heavens with the day of the Lord. Speaking through the prophet Ezekiel, God declared, "I will cover the heavens and darken their stars; I will cover the sun with a cloud and the moon will not give its light. All the shining lights in the heavens I will darken over you and will set darkness on your land" (Ezekiel 32:7–8). Isaiah, Joel, and Amos also wrote of the sun going dark (Isaiah 13:9–10; Joel 2:10, 31; 3:15; Amos 8:9). The Lord Jesus Christ added His own prediction, warning that "there will be signs in sun and moon and stars" (Luke 21:25; cf. Mark 13:24).

The dimming of the celestial lights sets the stage for a startling and ominous announcement. As John looked, he heard "an eagle flying in midheaven, saying with a loud voice, 'Woe, woe, woe to those who dwell on the earth, because of the remaining blasts of the trumpet of the three angels who are about to sound!'" The imagery is that of a strong bird of prey rushing to consume its victim. In this case, it refers to the rapid approach of God's final vengeance. Depicted in the vision as flying in midheaven, the bird would be at the height of the midday sun, visible to all. His loud voice assures that everyone will be able to hear his pronouncements. The eagle's dire warning is that the last three trumpet judgments will be even more devastating than the first four.

While double woes are used for emphasis (cf. 18:10, 16, 19; Ezekiel 16:23), the eagle's triple pronouncement of "woe, woe, woe" introduces one threat for each of the remaining three trumpets about to sound (9:1–21; 11:15ff.). *Woe* is used throughout Scripture as an expression of judgment, destruction, and condemnation. God's wrath and judgment will come upon "those who dwell on the earth," a descriptive phrase used in Revelation for those who reject the gospel (6:10; 11:10; 13:8, 12, 14; 17:2, 8). Although they will acknowledge that the disasters have come from God (6:15–17), they will not repent. They will be destroyed because they fail to listen to the warning God addresses to all sinners (cf. Hebrews 3:7–8).

THE FIFTH TRUMPET (9:1–12)

Each of the first four trumpet judgments affect the physical universe in some way, but with the sounding of the fifth trumpet the focus will shift from the physical to the spiritual realm.

The Pit Unlocked

Then the fifth angel sounded, and I saw a star from heaven which had fallen to the earth; and the key of the bottomless pit was given to him. He opened the bottomless pit, and smoke went up out of the pit, like the smoke of a great furnace; and the sun and the air were darkened by the smoke of the pit. *(9:1–2)*

When the fifth angel sounded his trumpet, John saw a star from heaven that had fallen to the earth. In his visions, the apostle had already seen several heavenly bodies plunge to earth (6:13; 8:8, 10). Unlike them, however, this star was not an inanimate piece of celestial matter, but an angelic being (cf. Job 38:7). That he was said to have fallen to the earth suggests that this is a reference to Satan—the leader of all the fallen angels (cf. Isaiah 14:12–15; Ezekiel 28:12–16; Luke 10:18).

The fall of Satan described in 9:1 is not his original rebellion. Though he and the angels who fell with him (12:4) were banished from heaven, Satan retains access to God's presence, where he constantly accuses believers (12:10; Job 1:6). During the tribulation he and his demon hosts will unsuccessfully battle Michael and the holy angels. As a result of their defeat, they will be permanently cast down to the earth (12:7–9). Satan will then seek to marshal all of his demonic hosts—those already on earth, those cast to earth with him, and those incarcerated in the bottomless pit (literally "the pit of the abyss"). *Abussos* ("bottomless") appears seven times in Revelation, always in reference to the abode of incarcerated demons (9:2, 11; 11:7; 17:8). Satan himself will be held prisoner there during the millennium, chained and locked up with the other demonic prisoners (20:1, 3).

After Satan received the key to the abyss from its keeper, Jesus Christ

(1:18), he opened the bottomless pit and released its inmates. When the abyss opened, smoke arose like the smoke of a great furnace. "Smoke" in Revelation may refer to holy things (8:4; 15:8), but is usually associated with judgment (9:17–18; 14:11; 18:9, 18; 19:3). Such a vast volume of smoke issued from the abyss that the sun and the air were darkened by it. The smoke polluting the sky symbolizes the corruption of hell belched forth from the abyss to pollute the world.

The Power Unleashed

Then out of the smoke came locusts upon the earth, and power was given them, as the scorpions of the earth have power. They were told not to hurt the grass of the earth, nor any green thing, nor any tree, but only the men who do not have the seal of God on their foreheads. And they were not permitted to kill anyone, but to torment for five months; and their torment was like the torment of a scorpion when it stings a man. And in those days men will seek death and will not find it; they will long to die, and death flees from them. (9:3–6)

Out of the vast, billowing, ominous cloud of smoke that darkened the sky and caused panic among earth's inhabitants, John saw a new terror emerge. Vile demons, taking on a visible form resembling locusts, swarmed out of the abyss to plague the earth. The imagery of smoke is a fitting depiction of a locust plague, since millions of the grasshopper-like insects swarm so thickly that they can darken the sky and blot out the sun, turning day into night. One swarm over the Red Sea in 1889 was reported to have covered 2,000 square miles. The destruction they can cause to crops and other vegetation is staggering (2 Chronicles 7:13).

Yet these were not ordinary locusts, but demons, who, like locusts, bring swarming destruction. Describing them in the form of locusts symbolizes their uncountable numbers and massive destructive capabilities. The fact that three times in the passage (verses 3, 5, 10) their power to inflict pain is compared to that of scorpions indicates they are not actual locusts, since locusts have no stinging tail as scorpions do. But the devastating pain inflicted by these demons will be far worse than that of actual scorpions. In this judgment God brings demons into direct contact with the unrepentant people. The fact that these locust- and scorpion-like creatures come from the pit and that their leader is the "angel of the abyss" (9:11) indicates that demons must be in view in this scene. Sadly, even the horrifying experience of this demon infestation will not cause many to repent (9:20–21), if any.

Strict limitations were placed on the activities of this demonic host. This judgment, unlike the first four trumpet judgments, is not on the physical world. God forced the locust horde not to hurt the grass of the earth, nor any green thing, nor any tree (8:7). That again shows that they were not actual insects, since real locusts devour plant life. The reference to the grass of the earth suggests that some time has passed since the first trumpet judgment scorched all the grass that was then in season (8:7). The damaged grass has grown again and is to remain untouched in this plague, indicating that enough time has elapsed for a partial recovery of the earth's environment.

Certainly Satan would want to kill all the unregenerate to keep them from repenting. But God, in His mercy, will give people torment for five months (the normal life span of locusts, usually from May to September), during which they cannot die but will be given the opportunity to repent and embrace the gospel. That five-month period will be one of intense spiritual and physical suffering inflicted on unbelievers by the judgment of God. That fearful judgment is likened to the torment inflicted by a scorpion when it stings a man. Unbelievers will also hear the message of salvation in Jesus Christ preached by the 144,000 Jewish evangelists, the two witnesses, and other believers. The five months will be for many people the last opportunity to repent and believe (9:20–21; 16:9, 11).

So intense will be the torment inflicted on unbelievers in those days that "people will seek death and will not find it." The earth people have loved will have been devastated, the land ravaged by earthquakes, fires, and volcanoes, the atmosphere polluted with gases and showers of heavenly debris. The dream of a worldwide utopia under the leadership of Antichrist (the Beast of 13:1ff.) will have died. There will be no escape from the agony inflicted by the demons or from divine judgment.

The Appearance Unveiled

The appearance of the locusts was like horses prepared for battle; and on their heads appeared to be crowns like gold, and their faces were like the faces of men. They had hair like the hair of women, and their teeth were like the teeth of lions. They had breastplates like breastplates of iron; and the sound of their wings was like the sound of chariots, of many horses rushing to battle. They have tails like scorpions, and stings; and in their tails is their power to hurt men for five months. (9:7–10)

These demons are described as locusts because they bring massive, devastating, rapid judgment from God. John can give only an approximation of what this spiritual army looked like, as the repeated use of the terms "like" (used eight times in this passage) and "appeared to be" indicates. To describe the supernatural and unfamiliar demon horde, John chooses natural and familiar analogies.

The general appearance of the locusts was "like horses prepared for battle." They were warlike, powerful, and defiant, like horses straining at the bit and pawing the ground in their eagerness to charge forward on their mission of death. On their heads John saw what appeared to be crowns like gold. The crowns they wore are victors' crowns, indicating that the demon host will be invincible. People will have no weapon that can harm them and no cure for the terrible torment they inflict. That their faces were like the faces of men indicates they are rational beings, not actual insects. The description of their hair as being like the hair of women likely emphasizes their seductiveness. The glory or beauty of a woman is her hair, which she may decorate to become more alluring. Having teeth like the teeth of lions, they will be fierce and powerful, tearing apart their victims. Breastplates of iron, designed to protect the vital organs of the soldier, here symbolize the demon horde's invulnerability. In a further metaphor drawn from the battlefield, John compares the sound of their wings to a moving army, noting that it "was like the sound of chariots, of many horses rushing to battle." There will be no escaping their massive, worldwide onslaught. The threefold comparison of the demons to scorpions stresses that their sole mission is to hurt people.

The Prince Unmasked
They have as king over them, the angel of the abyss; his name in Hebrew is Abaddon, and in the Greek he has the name Apollyon. The first woe is past; behold, two woes are still coming after these things. (9:11–12)

Unlike real locusts, the demons had a king over them. John calls him the angel of the abyss. Some identify this angel as Satan, but his domain is the heavenlies (Ephesians 6:12). He is not associated with the abyss until he is cast into it (20:1–3). This angel is better viewed as a high-ranking demon in Satan's hierarchy. John notes that "his name in Hebrew is Abaddon, and in the Greek he has the name Apollyon." John uses both names to emphasize his impact on both ungodly Jews and Gentiles. Both words mean "destroyer," an apt name for the head of the devastating army of demons that rises from the abyss.

Having described the first woe (8:13; the fifth trumpet judgment), John cautions that God's wrath has not run its course. Two woes (the sixth and seventh trumpet judgments, including all the bowl judgments) are still coming after these things, so there will be nothing more than a brief sigh of relief before still more fearful judgments follow.

THE SIXTH TRUMPET

Like the fifth trumpet, the sounding of the sixth trumpet heralds another, more severe demonic attack on sinful mankind. This attack, unlike the previous one, brings death.

The Release of Demons
Then the sixth angel sounded, and I heard a voice from the four horns of the golden altar which is before God, one saying to the sixth angel who had the trumpet, "Release the four angels who are bound at the great river Euphrates." (9:13–14)

The sixth angel sounded his mighty trumpet. Immediately, John "heard a voice." The Greek text literally reads "one voice." The voice is not identi-

fied, but it is possibly that of the Lamb, Jesus Christ. He was pictured earlier standing near the throne (5:6), when He took the seven-sealed scroll
from the Father's hand (5:7) and broke its seals (6:1). This could also be
the voice of the angel whom John had seen standing near the golden altar
of incense (8:3).

While identifying the source of the voice is not possible, its location
came from the four horns of the golden altar before God. John had seen
this altar twice before in his visions. In the tabernacle and temple, this
altar was a place where incense was burnt, symbolizing the peoples'
prayers for mercy rising to God. But in John's vision the golden altar
became an altar of intercession, as the martyred saints pleaded with God
for vengeance on their murderers (6:9–11).

The voice coming from the surface of the altar between the four pro-
truding corners commanded the sixth angel who had the trumpet,
"Release the four angels who are bound at the great river Euphrates." That
the four angels are bound indicates that they are demons (20:1ff.; 2 Peter
2:4; Jude 6), since holy angels are nowhere in Scripture said to be bound.

Because holy angels always perfectly carry out God's will, there is no
need for Him to restrain them from opposing His will. God's control over
demonic forces is complete—they are bound or loosed at His command.
The perfect tense of the participle translated "bound" implies that these
four angels were bound in the past with continuing results; they were in
a state or condition of bondage until God's determined time came for
them to be released to execute their function as instruments of divine
judgment.

The use of the definite article "the" suggests that these four angels
form a specific group. Their precise identity is not revealed, but they may
be the demons that controlled the four major world empires of Babylon,
Medo-Persia, Greece, and Rome. Daniel 10 provides insight into the warfare between holy angels and the demons that influence individual
nations. Whoever they are, these four powerful fallen angels control a
huge demonic army set to wage war against fallen mankind when God
releases them to do so.

The Return of Death

And the four angels, who had been prepared for the hour and day and month and year, were released, so that they would kill a third of mankind. The number of the armies of the horsemen was two hundred million; I heard the number of them. And this is how I saw in the vision the horses and those who sat on them: the riders had breastplates the color of fire and of hyacinth and of brimstone; and the heads of the horses are like the heads of lions; and out of their mouths proceed fire and smoke and brimstone. A third of mankind was killed by these three plagues, by the fire and the smoke and the brimstone which proceeded out of their mouths. For the power of the horses is in their mouths and in their tails; for their tails are like serpents and have heads, and with them they do harm. (9:15–19)

Death, which had taken a holiday under the fifth trumpet (9:5–6), now returns with a vengeance. The shocking purpose for the release of these four demon leaders and their hordes was so that they would kill a third of mankind. The judgment of the fourth seal killed one quarter of the earth's population (6:8). This additional third brings the death toll from these two judgments alone to more than half the earth's pretribulation population. That staggering total does not include those who died in the other seal and trumpet judgments.

The terrible slaughter will completely disrupt human society. The problem of disposing of the dead bodies alone will be inconceivable. The sickly stench of decaying corpses will permeate the world, and it will take an enormous effort on the part of the survivors to bury them in mass graves or burn them.

To slaughter well over a billion people will require an unimaginably powerful force. John reported that the number of the armies of the horsemen was an astonishing two hundred million. This is likely an exact number, or more general specifications, such as those used in 5:11 and 7:9, would have been used. Then, as if anticipating that some skeptical readers would doubt that huge number, John emphatically insisted, "I heard the number of them." The use of the plural "armies" may imply that the attacking force will be divided into four armies, each commanded by one of the formerly bound demons.

Some have suggested that this is the human army referred to in 16:12 and led by "the kings from the east," noting that the Red Chinese army reportedly numbered two hundred million during the 1970s. But no reference is made to the size of the army led by the kings of the East. Further, that army arrives on the scene during the sixth bowl judgment, which takes place during the seventh trumpet, not the sixth. Though there may be at that time an existing standing army of two hundred million, the impossibility of marshaling, supplying, and transporting such a vast human force all over the globe also argues against this army being a human army. The figurative language used to describe this army's horses suggests that this is a supernatural rather than human force.

John briefly described those who sat on the horses. "The riders had breastplates the color of fire and of hyacinth and of brimstone." The color of fire is red; that of hyacinth, dark blue or black like smoke; that of brimstone, a sulfurous yellow, describing the rock which, when ignited, produces a burning flame and suffocating gas. Those are the very colors and features of hell (14:10; 19:20; 20:10; 21:8).

Horses are frequently associated with warfare in Scripture, but it is clear that these are not actual horses. Using the descriptive language of his vision, John noted that the heads of the horses were like the heads of lions. John noted three ways that the demon horses killed their victims, all of which picture the violent, devastating fury of hell. They incinerated them with fire, and asphyxiated them with smoke and the gas given off by the heated brimstone.

John saw that the devastating result of this deadly demonic assault was that "a third of all people were killed by these three plagues."

It may be noted that the word "plagues" will appear frequently in the remainder of Revelation (11:6; 15:1, 6, 8; 16:9, 21; 18:4, 8; 21:9; 22:18) as a term for the destructive final judgments. As if the description he has already given were not frightening enough, John sees more about the deadly power of the demons. He is made aware that not only is the power of the horses in their mouths, but also in their tails. Having likened the horses' heads to savage lions, John notes that "their tails are like [deadly, venomous] serpents and have heads, and with them they do harm." These images describe the supernatural deadliness of this demon force in terms that are commonly understood in the natural realm. Unlike the scorpion stings inflicted during the previous demonic assault (9:5), the snakebites inflicted by this host will be fatal.

The Reaction of Defiance

And the rest of mankind, who were not killed by these plagues, did not repent of the works of their hands, so as not to worship demons, and the idols of gold and of silver and of brass and of stone and of wood, which can neither see nor hear nor walk; and they did not repent of their murders nor of their sorceries nor of their immorality nor of their thefts. (9:20–21)

The death of one-third of the earth's remaining population will be the most catastrophic disaster to strike the earth since the flood. Yet in an amazing display of hardness of heart, the rest of mankind not killed by these plagues still refuses to repent. Tragically, those remaining will choose to worship the dragon and the beast (Antichrist) instead of the Lamb (13:4–8).

As he concludes his account of this amazing vision, John lists five sins representative of the defiance of those who refused to repent. First, they "did not repent of the works of their hands," worshiping other gods and demons. Second, violent crimes like "murders" will be rampant. Without any sense of morality, unrepentant people will imitate the demon horde's murderous blood lust.

Third, John mentions "sorceries," a Greek word from which the English words "pharmacy" and "pharmaceuticals" derive. Drugs were and still are believed to induce a higher religious state of communion with deities.[1] Fourth, "immorality" will prevail. The Greek word is a general term that can include any sexual sin. Indescribable sexual perversions will be rampant in that day.

Finally, people will refuse to repent of thefts. Like morality, honesty will be nonexistent, as people compete for the increasingly scarce supplies of food, clothing, water, shelter, and medicines.

Under the influence of the massive demon forces, the world will descend into a morass of false religion, murder, sexual perversion, and crime unparalleled in human history. It is sobering to realize that the Lord will one day come "to execute judgment upon all" (Jude 15). In light of that coming judgment, it is the responsibility of all believers to faithfully proclaim the gospel to unbelievers, thereby "snatching them out of the fire" (Jude 23).

The Little Book and
TWO GREAT
Witnesses
(10:1–11:14)

Before the seventh trumpet sounds there will be an interlude, which stretches from Revelation 10:1 to 11:14, allowing John to pause and assimilate the startling truths that have just been revealed to him. The interlude between the sixth and seventh trumpets parallels similar interludes in the seal and bowl judgments. These interludes encourage God's people in the midst of the fury and horror of divine judgment. During the interludes God comforts His people with the knowledge that He has not forgotten them, and that they will ultimately be victorious.

That is especially true in the longest of the three interludes, this one between the sixth and seventh trumpets. Believers alive during that time will endure the unimaginable horrors of a sin-infected world. God will comfort and reassure them that He has not forgotten them and that He still controls events and protects His own.

THE INTERLUDE'S FIRST HALF:
FIVE UNUSUAL EVENTS

Chapter 10 describes the opening events of this interlude preparing for the final trumpet blast by highlighting five unusual occurrences: an unusual angel, an unusual act, an unusual answer, an unusual announcement, and an unusual assignment.

An Unusual Angel

I saw another strong angel coming down out of heaven, clothed with a cloud; and the rainbow was upon his head, and his face was like the sun, and his feet like pillars of fire; and he had in his hand a little book which was open. (10:1–2a)

As it does throughout Revelation, John's words "I saw" mark the beginning of a new vision. Following his vision of the first six trumpets, John saw a vision of someone new. This strong angel is distinct from the seven angels who sound the seven trumpets. Noting the similarities between his description and that of Christ in 1:12–17, and that he, like Christ, descends in a cloud (1:7), some identify this angel as Jesus Christ. However, this is very unlikely. First, the Greek word for "another" indicates another of the same kind, like the previously mentioned trumpet angels. Second, whenever Jesus Christ appears in Revelation, John gives Him an unmistakable title. Third, other strong angels appear in Revelation (5:2; 18:21). Fourth, Christ could not take the action of verses 5 and 6, raising "his right hand to heaven, and [swearing] by Him who lives forever and ever, who created heaven and the things in it, and the earth and the things in it, and the sea and the things in it." Since He is God, the risen, Jesus Christ would swear by Himself (cf. Hebrews 6:13). Finally, this angel came down out of heaven to the earth. To identify him as Christ is to add another coming of Christ to the earth.

Having introduced this powerful angel, John describes his spectacular attire. He was clothed with a cloud, wearing the drapery of the sky over his mighty shoulders. That symbolizes his power and the fact that he comes bringing judgment. Clouds are elsewhere associated with the second coming of Christ in judgment (1:7; 14:14–16; Matthew 24:30; Mark 13:26; 14:62; Luke 21:27).

John also saw a "rainbow upon his head." Iris (rainbow) was the Greek goddess who personified the rainbow and served as a messenger of the gods. In classical Greek *iris* was used to describe any bright halo surrounding another object, such as the circle surrounding the eyes on a peacock's tail, or the iris of an eye. Here it describes the brilliant, many-colored rainbow around the angel's head, which reflects his glorious splendor.

While the cloud symbolizes judgment, the rainbow represents God's covenant mercy in the midst of judgment (4:3). After the flood, God gave the rainbow as the sign of His promise never again to destroy the world by water (Genesis 9:12–16). The rainbow with which the angel is crowned will reassure God's people of His mercy in the midst of coming judgments.

Moving on to describe the angel's appearance, John notes first that "his face was like the sun." His brilliant, radiant glory lit up the earth like the blazing sun. John next described the angel's feet and legs as being like firm, stable, immovable pillars of fire. That symbolizes his unbending holiness in stamping out his judgment on the earth, pictured here as fire that consumes the ungodly.

The angel held "in his hand a little book which was open." This is probably the same book described in Revelation 5:1, "sealed up with seven seals" and then opened in Revelation 6. Some argue that the use of the diminuitive "little" in 10:2 distinguishes this book from the book of 5:1. Rather than distinguishing this book from the one in chapter 5, the diminutive form merely adds a further description of it in this vision. The book needed to be made smaller for the sake of the symbolism of this vision, since John was to eat it (10:9–10). Further, the use of the perfect participle form—"which was open"—emphasizes the idea of the scroll being open; having been opened, it is to remain open. That further identifies it with the fully unrolled scroll of 6:1ff as seal after seal is broken. The little book lying open in this unusual angel's hand unveils all the terrors of divine judgment yet to come.

An Unusual Act

He placed his right foot on the sea and his left on the land; and he cried out with a loud voice, as when a lion roars; and when he had cried out, the seven peals of thunder uttered their voices. (10:2b–3)

That the angel put one foot on the sea and the other on the land shows his massive size from the perspective of John's vision. This action of the angel demonstrates God's sovereign authority to judge the entire earth (cf. 7:2; Exodus 20:11; 1 Corinthians 10:26), which He will soon take back from Satan. The angel's act also symbolically anticipates the coming judgments of the seventh trumpet and the seven bowls on the whole earth.

In keeping with his huge size, the angel "cried out with a loud voice, as when a lion roars." His loud cry reflects the power and authority of God. The Old Testament prophets also connect a loud, lionlike roaring voice with judgment (Jeremiah 25:30; Hosea 11:10; Joel 3:16; Amos 1:2; 3:8).

After the angel cried out, an amazing thing happened—"the seven peals of thunder uttered their voices." "Seven" speaks of completeness and perfection. "Thunder" is often a mark of judgment in Scripture (8:5; 11:19; 16:18; 1 Samuel 2:10; 2 Samuel 22:14). These seven loud, powerful voices cry out for vengeance and judgment upon the sinful earth. The thunder was separate from the angel's voice and may have represented the voice of God (1 Samuel 7:10; Psalm 18:13). The text does not reveal what the thunder said, but hearing it certainly would have added to the terror of the scene of judgment (see also 8:5; 11:19; 16:18).

An Unusual Answer

When the seven peals of thunder had spoken, I was about to write; and I heard a voice from heaven saying, "Seal up the things which the seven peals of thunder have spoken and do not write them." (10:4)

The seven peals of thunder did not merely make a loud noise, but communicated information that John was about to write. In obedience to

God's commands, John had already written much of what he saw in his visions. Later in Revelation, John would once again be commanded to write what he saw in his visions (14:13; 19:9; 21:5).

But before John could record the message of the seven peals of thunder, he heard a voice from heaven saying, "Seal up the things which the seven peals of thunder have spoken and do not write them." Whether the voice was that of the Father, Jesus Christ, or an angel is not revealed. The command, however, clearly originated with God. The reason John was forbidden to record the message is not revealed. It may be that the judgment is simply too terrifying to be recorded. Any speculation as to the specific content of their message is pointless. If God had wanted it to be known, He would not have forbidden John to write it. They are the only words in the book of Revelation that are sealed.

An Unusual Announcement

Then the angel whom I saw standing on the sea and on the land lifted up his right hand to heaven, and swore by Him who lives forever and ever, who created heaven and the things in it, and the earth and the things in it, and the sea and the things in it, that there will be delay no longer, but in the days of the voice of the seventh angel, when he is about to sound, then the mystery of God is finished, as He preached to His servants the prophets. (10:5–7)

In a solemn act, the angel whom John "saw standing on the sea and on the land" (verse 2) "lifted up his right hand to heaven"—the standard gesture for taking a solemn vow (Deuteronomy 32:40; Daniel 12:7). To take such a vow is to affirm before God that one is going to speak the truth. That vow indicated that what the angel was about to say was of the utmost importance and truthfulness.

The angel took his vow in the name of "Him who lives forever and ever, who created heaven and the things in it, and the earth and the things in it, and the sea and the things in it." That designation of God stresses His eternity and sovereign power in and over all creation. This identification of God as Creator echoes the praise song of the twenty-four elders recorded in 4:11: "Worthy are You, our Lord and our God, to receive glory and honor and power; for You created all things, and because of Your will they existed, and were created."

The specific content of the angel's oath was that there will be delay no longer, answering the question of the martyrs, "How long?" (6:10), and the prayers of the saints in 8:3–5. The phrase "but in the days of the voice of the seventh angel, when he is about to sound" indicates that the judgment of the seventh trumpet is about to come and that it is not a single event, but covers days, indicating a period of time. This period includes the seven bowl judgments (16:1–21), which would appear to require some weeks or months to unfold. The sounding of the seventh trumpet brings the final judgment depicted in the bowls of fury poured out on the earth. The time of God's patience is seen as having ended. The time for the final acts of judgment is seen as being at hand. The time anticipated in the disciples' questions recorded in Matthew 24:3 and Acts 1:6 has come.

At that time "the mystery of God is finished." Mystery in Scripture refers to truths God has hidden and will reveal in His time. Mysteries hidden in the past that the New Testament reveals include the "mysteries of the kingdom" (Matthew 13:11), the mystery of Israel's blindness (Romans 11:25), the mystery of the rapture (1 Corinthians 15:51), the "mystery of lawlessness" (2 Thessalonians 2:7), the "mystery of Christ" and of "Christ and the church" (Ephesians 3:4; 5:32), the mystery of Christ in the believer (Colossians 1:26–27), and the mystery of the incarnation (1 Timothy 3:16). Paul saw himself as a "steward" or guardian of these great mysteries (1 Corinthians 4:1), to "bring to light" these mysteries "which for ages [have] been hidden in God" (Ephesians 3:9).

The mystery of God of which the angel spoke is that of "the summing up of all things in Christ, things in the heavens and things on the earth" (Ephesians 1:10). It is the consummation of God's plan in bringing His glorious kingdom in Christ to fulfillment. It involves the salvation of the elect and their place in His glorious kingdom and all that goes with that. It includes the judgment of men and demons. The mystery previously hidden refers to all the unknown details that are revealed from this point to the end of Revelation, when the new heavens and new earth are created. To believers living at that time in a world overrun by demons and unparalleled natural disasters, the realization that God's glorious plan is on schedule will bring great comfort and hope in the midst of judgment.

An Unusual Assignment

Then the voice which I heard from heaven, I heard again speaking with me, and saying, "Go, take the book which is open in the hand of the angel who stands on the sea and on the land." So I went to the angel, telling him to give me the little book. And he said to me, "Take it and eat it; it will make your stomach bitter, but in your mouth it will be sweet as honey." I took the little book out of the angel's hand and ate it, and in my mouth it was sweet as honey; and when I had eaten it, my stomach was made bitter. And they said to me, "You must prophesy again concerning many peoples and nations and tongues and kings." (10:8–11)

The voice John had earlier heard from heaven (verse 4) forbidding him to record the words of the seven peals of thunder spoke to him again. As he had earlier (1:17; 4:1; 5:4–5; 7:13–14), John again became an active participant in this vision. He left the place of an observer to become an actor in the drama. The voice said to him, "Go, take the book which is open in the hand of the angel who stands on the sea and on the land." This third reference to the location of the angel emphasizes strongly the unusual authority he has over the earth. Then, in a graphic illustration of what a proper response on the part of believers to God's impending judgment should be, John was told, "Take it and eat it; it will make your stomach bitter, but in your mouth it will be sweet as honey." The angel knew what John's reaction to this truth would be. Obediently, like Ezekiel before him (Ezekiel 2:9–3:3), John in the vision symbolically took the little book out of the angel's hand and ate it.

The act of eating the scroll symbolized the absorbing and assimilating of God's Word (cf. Psalm 19:10; Jeremiah 15:16; Ezekiel 3:1–3). When John took in the divine words concerning the remaining judgments as the Lord took possession of the universe, he found them both "sweet as honey" and "bitter." Sweet because John, like all believers, wanted the Lord to act in judgment to take back the earth that is rightfully His and be exalted and glorified as He deserved. Yet the realization of the terrible doom awaiting unbelievers turned that initial sweet taste into bitterness.

All who love Jesus Christ can relate to John's ambivalence. Believers long for Christ to return in glory, for Satan to be destroyed, and the glorious kingdom of our Lord to be set up on earth, in which He will rule in glory while establishing in the world righteousness, truth, and peace. But they, like Paul (Romans 9:1–3), mourn bitterly over the judgment of the ungodly.

In keeping with his bittersweet experience, John was told, "You must prophesy again concerning many peoples and nations and tongues and kings." The use of "again" indicates John was being commissioned a second time (1:19) to write the rest of the prophecies God was going to give him. What he was about to learn would be more devastating than anything yet revealed—and more glorious. He was to be faithful to his duty to record all the truth he had seen and would soon see. The prophecies John would receive would relate to everyone everywhere. John is to warn of all the bitter judgments coming in the seventh trumpet and the seven bowls.

As an exile on Patmos (1:9), he had no opportunity to preach to all nations, but he was to write the prophecies and distribute them, so as to warn all people of the bitterness of judgment to come, and of death and hell. Sinners everywhere may know because John recorded these prophecies that, while judgment is presently restrained, a future day is coming when the seventh angel will sound his trumpet and sin's dominion will be broken, the freedom of Satan and his demons will come to an end, godless men will be judged, and believers will be glorified.

THE INTERLUDE'S SECOND HALF:
TWO UNUSUAL WITNESSES

Throughout history God has faithfully sent His spokesmen to call sinners to repentance. During the long, dark years of Israel's rebellion, "the Lord warned Israel and Judah through all His prophets" (2 Kings 17:13; cf. 2 Chronicles

36:15). Prophets such as Elijah, Elisha, Isaiah, Jeremiah, Jonah, and the others confronted both wayward Israel and sinful Gentile nations. In the future, God will raise up two exceptional and powerful preachers.

The Fearless Witnesses

These two witnesses will fearlessly proclaim the gospel during the last half of the seven-year tribulation. During that time of horrific divine judgments on the earth, their gospel preaching will be part of a final expression of God's grace offered to repentant and believing sinners.

In addition to preaching the gospel, these two preachers will proclaim God's judgment on the wicked world. Their ministry will likely stretch from the midpoint of the tribulation until just before the sounding of the seventh trumpet. They will declare that the disasters falling on the world are the judgments of God. They will participate in fulfilling the words that the "gospel of the kingdom shall be preached in the whole world for a witness to all the nations, and then the end will come" (Matthew 24:14). They will also be used by God to bring salvation to Israel.

The Measured Temple

Then there was given me a measuring rod like a staff; and someone said, "Get up and measure the temple of God and the altar, and those who worship in it. Leave out the court which is outside the temple and do not measure it, for it has been given to the nations; and they will tread under foot the holy city for forty-two months." (11:1–2)

After his renewed commission to write the prophecies yet to come in Revelation (10:11), John again became involved in one of the visions he was recording. He was given a "measuring rod like a staff," by either the same angel in 10:8 or the strong angel in 10:9–11. The Greek word translated "measuring rod" refers to a reedlike plant that grew in the Jordan Valley to a height of fifteen to twenty feet. It had a stalk that was hollow and lightweight, yet rigid enough to be used as a walking staff or to be shaved down into a pen. The stalks, because they were long and lightweight, were ideal for use as measuring rods. In Ezekiel's vision, an angel used such a rod to measure the millennial temple (Ezekiel 40:3–43:17).

John was told to measure the temple of God, including "the altar, and those who worship in it." Obviously, this was not an effort to determine its physical dimensions, since none are given, but was conveying some important truth beyond architecture. It could have indicated, as in the Old Testament, that God sometimes marks things out for destruction (2 Samuel 8:2; 2 Kings 21:13; Isaiah 28:17; Amos 7:7–9). However, John's measuring is better understood as signifying ownership, defining the parameters of God's possessions (21:15; Zechariah 2:1–5). This measuring signified something good, since what was not measured was evil (verse 2). It is best to see it as God's measuring off Israel for salvation and His special protection, preservation, and favor. The prophecies yet to be given to John will distinguish between God's favor toward Israel and His wrath on the world.

The Greek word for "temple" does not refer to the entire temple complex, but to the inner temple, made up of the Holy Place and the Holy of Holies. The altar is probably the brazen altar, located outside the inner sanctuary in the courtyard, since that is where those who worship in the temple would have gathered. The people were never permitted into the inner temple. Only the priests could enter the Holy Place. The worshipers in John's vision depict a remnant of believing Jews worshiping God during the tribulation.

The tribulation temple will be built early in the first half of the tribulation under the influence of Antichrist. Many orthodox Jews today dream of rebuilding their temple, but its site is now occupied by the Islamic Dome of the Rock. Because Muslims believe it to be the place from which Muhammad ascended to heaven, it is among the most sacred shrines in the Islamic world. For the Jews to take that site from the Muslims and build their temple there would be unthinkable in today's political climate. But during the tribulation, under the protection of Antichrist (Daniel 9:24–27), they will be able to rebuild the temple.

John's instructions on measuring the temple included a significant omission. He was commanded, "Leave out the court which is outside the temple and do not measure it." The reference is to the court of the

Gentiles, located outside the courtyard containing the brazen altar. It marked the boundary where Gentiles were forbidden to go. In New Testament times, the Romans had given the Jews the right to execute any Gentile who went beyond the court of the Gentiles. For a Gentile to do so was to defile the temple (Acts 21:28–29).

John was told not to measure the outer court because "it has been given to the nations; and they will tread under foot the holy city for forty-two months." The forty-two months (three and one-half years) correspond to the overtly evil career of Antichrist, which dominates the last half of the tribulation (13:5). That period will be the culmination of the "times of the Gentiles" (Luke 21:24)—the thousands of years during which Gentile nations have in various ways occupied and oppressed Jerusalem.

SALVATION THROUGH TWO WITNESSES

During this same forty-two-month period, God will shelter many Israelites in a place He has prepared for them in the wilderness (some speculate the rock city of Petra). Revelation 12:6 reads, "Then the woman [Israel] fled into the wilderness where she had a place prepared by God, so that there she would be nourished for one thousand two hundred and sixty days." Many Jews will follow Jesus' warning to flee to safety.

The rest who remain will face terrible persecution from the forces of Antichrist. At that time, God will bring salvation to Israel, using the two powerful preachers who will appear in Jerusalem (verse 3), and will also suffer hostility and hatred (verses 7–8).

The connection between this vision of the two preachers and the previous passage (verses 1–2) should be clear. They are among God's unique witnesses who will proclaim His message of judgment during the final stages of the tribulation. They will preach the gospel so the Jewish remnant can believe and enjoy God's protection.

Their Duty
And I will grant authority to my two witnesses, and they will prophesy for twelve hundred and sixty days. (11:3a)

The speaker who will grant authority to the two witnesses is not identified, but could be only God the Father or Jesus. "Witnesses" is the plural
form from which the English word "martyr" derives, since so many witnesses of Jesus Christ in the early church paid with their lives. Since it is
always used in the New Testament to refer to persons, the two witnesses
must be actual people. There are two witnesses because the Bible requires
the testimony of two people to confirm a fact or verify truth
(Deuteronomy 17:6; 19:15; Matthew 18:16).

It will be their responsibility to prophesy. Prophecy in the New
Testament does not necessarily refer to predicting the future. Its primary
meaning is "to speak forth," "to proclaim," or "to preach." The two witnesses will proclaim that the disasters occurring during the last half of the
tribulation are from God. They will warn that God's final outpouring of
judgment and eternal hell will follow. At the same time, they will preach
the gospel, calling people to repentance and faith in Jesus Christ. The
period of their ministry is twelve hundred and sixty days, the last three
and one-half years of the tribulation.

Their Attitude
clothed in sackcloth. (11:3*b*)

Sackcloth was rough, heavy, coarse cloth worn in ancient times as a symbol of mourning, distress, grief, and humility (Genesis 37:34; 2 Samuel
3:31; 1 Chronicles 21:16; 2 Kings 6:30). The two witnesses will put on
sackcloth as an object lesson to express their great sorrow for the unbelieving world. They will also mourn because of the desecration of the temple, the oppression of Jerusalem, and the rise of Antichrist.

Their Identity
**These are the two olive trees and the two lampstands that stand before
the Lord of the earth.** (11:4)

The question of who the two witnesses will be has intrigued Bible schol-
ars over the years. John identifies them as "the two olive trees and the two

lampstands that stand before the Lord of the earth," a description drawn from Zechariah's vision and prophecy in 4:1–14. While it is impossible to be dogmatic about the specific identity of these two preachers, there are a number of reasons that suggest that they may be Moses and Elijah.

First, the miracles they will perform are similar to the judgments inflicted in the Old Testament by Moses and Elijah. Elijah called down fire from heaven (2 Kings 1:10, 12) and pronounced a three-and-one-half-year drought on the land (1 Kings 17:1; James 5:17), the same length as the drought brought by the two witnesses (Revelation 11:6). Moses turned the waters of the Nile into blood (Exodus 7:17–21) and announced the other plagues on Egypt recorded in Exodus 7–11.

Second, Jewish tradition expected Moses and Elijah to return in the future. Malachi 4:5 predicted the return of Elijah, and the Jews believed that God's promise to raise up a prophet like Moses (Deuteronomy 18:15, 18) necessitated his return (John 1:21; 6:14; 7:40). Third, both Moses and Elijah (perhaps representing the Law and the Prophets) appeared with Christ at the transfiguration, the preview of the second coming (Matthew 17:3).

Fourth, both left the earth in unusual ways. Elijah never died, but was transported to heaven in a fiery chariot (2 Kings 2:11–12), and God supernaturally buried Moses' body in a secret location (Deuteronomy 34:5–6; Jude 9). The statement of Hebrews 9:27 that "it is appointed for men to die once and after this comes judgment" does not rule out Moses' return, since there are other rare exceptions to that general statement (such as Lazarus; John 11:14, 38–44).

Their Power
And if anyone wants to harm them, fire flows out of their mouth and devours their enemies; so if anyone wants to harm them, he must be killed in this way. These have the power to shut up the sky, so that rain will not fall during the days of their prophesying; and they have power over the waters to turn them into blood, and to strike the earth with every plague, as often as they desire. (11:5–6)

Whether or not the two witnesses are Moses and Elijah, they will have miraculous power similar to them. Like Noah before the flood and Moses before the plagues on Egypt, the two witnesses will fearlessly proclaim God's judgment and the need for repentance. Because of that, they will be universally hated (verses 9–10) and many will desire to harm them during the days of their preaching. When that harm is attempted, fire will flow out of their mouth and devour their enemies. There is no reason to assume that this is not literal fire, since God has in the past used fire to incinerate His enemies (Leviticus 10:2; Numbers 11:1; 16:35; Psalm 106:17–18). Those who wish to harm the two preachers must be killed in this way because God does not want their preaching stopped until their ministry is complete and will judge with death those who try to halt it.

The extent of their great power will be revealed when they demonstrate "power to shut up the sky, so that rain will not fall during the days of their prophesying." That will greatly intensify the torment people are experiencing. The third trumpet judgment resulted in the poisoning of one-third of the earth's fresh water supply (8:10–11). Added to that, the three-and-one-half-year drought lasting throughout the 1,260 days of their preaching (verse 3) brought by the two witnesses will cause widespread devastation of crops and loss of human and animal life through thirst and starvation.

Further, like Moses, the two witnesses will "have power over the waters to turn them into blood, and to strike the earth with every plague, as often as they desire." The havoc these two miracle-working preachers will wreak all over the earth will cause them to be hated and feared. People will no doubt search desperately for a way to destroy them, but they will be unstoppable for the duration of their ministry.

Their Death

When they have finished their testimony, the beast that comes up out of the abyss will make war with them, and overcome them and kill them. And their dead bodies will lie in the street of the great city which mystically is called Sodom and Egypt, where also their Lord was crucified. Those from the peoples and tribes and tongues and nations will look at their dead bodies for three and a half days, and will not permit their dead bodies to be laid in a tomb. And those who dwell on the earth will rejoice over them and celebrate; and they will send gifts to one another, because these two prophets tormented those who dwell on the earth. (11:7–10)

Sinful men will try desperately and unsuccessfully to get rid of the two witnesses throughout their ministry in a kind of kamikaze effort that results in their own incineration. God, however, will protect them until they have finished their testimony. At the end of that time, "the beast that comes up out of the abyss will make war with them."

This is the first of thirty-six references in Revelation to the beast and anticipates the more detailed information about him to come in chapters 13 and 17. He is introduced here with emphasis on his origin. He is said to come up "out of the abyss," indicating that he is empowered by Satan. Since Satan is depicted as a dragon (12:3, 9), this figure is not Satan. The revelation about him in chapter 13 indicates that the beast is a world ruler called Antichrist who imitates the true Christ and demands to be worshiped (13:1–8). The abyss is the prison for certain demons (cf. 9:1–3). Though he is a man, the beast is energized by the demonic presence and power coming from the abyss. To the great joy and relief of the sinful world, the beast will finally overcome the two witnesses and kill them.

After their deaths, their dead bodies will be left as rotting corpses in the street of the great city where they ministered and where they were killed. In the ancient world, exposing an enemy's dead body was the ultimate way of dishonoring and desecrating him (Deuteronomy 21:22–23).

The "great city" is Jerusalem, spiritually called Sodom and Egypt due to its wickedness. Tragically, the city of Jerusalem that was once God's city will be so overrun with evil that it will be like the wicked city of Sodom and the evil nation of Egypt. The description was to show that the once holy city had become no better than places which were known for their hatred of the true God. The footnote that the two witnesses will be killed in the city where their Lord was crucified makes the identification of Jerusalem unmistakably clear. That the two witnesses will die in the same city as their Lord suggests that Jerusalem will be the focal point of their preaching. It also appears that Jerusalem will be the seat of Antichrist's rule (2 Thessalonians 2:3–4).

The use of the all-inclusive phrase "peoples and tribes and tongues and nations" indicates that people around the world will look at the dead bodies of the two witnesses. In a morbid display of contempt and hatred, for three and a half days the world will not permit their dead bodies to be laid in a tomb. The unrepentant, sin-hardened masses will want to gloat along with the Antichrist and glorify him for his victory over the two irritating preachers. The deaths of the two witnesses will touch off wild celebrations around the world. Incredibly, "those who dwell on the earth" will rejoice over them and celebrate. "They will send gifts to one another, because these two prophets tormented those who dwell on the earth."

Ironically, this is the only mention in Revelation of rejoicing. Sinners will be happy because those who declared God's judgments are dead. This emotional response graphically reflects the finality of their rejection.

Their Resurrection

But after the three and a half days, the breath of life from God came into them, and they stood on their feet; and great fear fell upon those who were watching them. And they heard a loud voice from heaven saying to them, "Come up here." Then they went up into heaven in the cloud, and their enemies watched them. (11:11–12)

The partying and gift giving of "Dead Witnesses Day" will be suddenly and dramatically halted by a most shocking event. "After three and a half days, the breath of life from God came into [the two witnesses] and they stood on their feet; and great fear fell upon those who were watching them." Panic will seize the world as their hated and reviled tormentors suddenly spring to life. If this is viewed on television, it will be replayed repeatedly. The phrase "Come up here" is likely the voice of the Lord, who summoned John to heaven in 4:1. The two preachers went up into heaven in the cloud, as their enemies watched them in awe. This two-man rapture will no doubt also be replayed endlessly for the entire world to see. It is reminiscent of the ascension of Elijah (2 Kings 2:11) and the mysterious death and burial of Moses (Deuteronomy 34:5–6).

At this point, the hearts of those watching do not change. That should not be surpising. Jesus Christ said, "If [unbelievers] do not listen to Moses and the Prophets, they will not be persuaded even if someone rises from the dead" (Luke 16:31). Indeed, after hearing the teaching and observing the miraculous ministry of the Son of God, unbelievers rejected and killed Him.

Their Impact
And in that hour there was a great earthquake, and a tenth of the city fell; seven thousand people were killed in the earthquake, and the rest were terrified and gave glory to the God of heaven. The second woe is past; behold, the third woe is coming quickly. (11:13–14)

Punctuating the resurrection of the two witnesses, "in that hour there was a great earthquake, and a tenth of the city fell." Seven thousand people were killed in the earthquake. The term "people" in the Greek text is literally "names of men." That unusual phrase may indicate that the seven thousand who were killed were prominent people, perhaps leaders in Antichrist's world government.

As a result of the violent earthquake, and the astonishing resurrection of the two witnesses, "the rest were terrified and gave glory to the God of heaven." The phrase "the rest" must refer to the inhabitants of Jerusalem, Jews who will come to faith in Christ. Supporting that interpretation is the fact that giving glory to the God of heaven is a mark of genuine repentance in Revelation and elsewhere in Scripture (4:9; 14:7; 16:9; 19:7; Luke 17:18–19; Romans 4:20). This passage, then, describes the reality of the salvation of Jews in Jerusalem.

On that positive, hopeful note, the interlude ends. For the unbelieving world, however, it ends with the sobering warning that "the second woe is past; behold, the third woe is coming quickly." The seventh trumpet (the third woe, 9:12) will soon sound, bringing with it the final, violent bowl judgments and the return of Christ in glory to set up His kingdom. "Quickly" expresses the nearness of the last woe, which is the seven bowl judgments ushered in by the sounding of the seventh trumpet.

I3

The Seventh TRUMPET

(11:15–19)

The sounding of the seventh trumpet marks a significant milestone in the book of Revelation. It sets in motion the final events leading up to the return of the Lord Jesus Christ and the establishment of His earthly millennial kingdom. During its tenure will come the final fury of the day of the Lord judgments (16:1–21), the final harvest of judgment on earth (11:18; 16:19), and the Lamb's defeat of the kings of the earth (17:12–18), culminating in the final triumph of Christ at Armageddon (19:11–21).

It should be noted that although the seventh trumpet is the last in the sequence of the seven trumpet judgments, it is not to be equated with the "last trumpet" in 1 Corinthians 15:52. The seventh trumpet covers an extended period of time, distinguishing it from the instantaneous ("in a moment, in the twinkling of an eye") event of the "last trumpet." Instead of calling for the moment of the rapture of the church, the seventh trumpet calls for prolonged waves of judgment on the ungodly.

The seventh trumpet not only announces consuming judgment on unbelievers, but also the coronation of the Lord Jesus Christ. In the Old Testament trumpets were frequently sounded at the coronation of a king

(2 Samuel 15:10; 1 Kings 1:39; 2 Kings 9:13; 11:12, 14). The sounding of the seventh trumpet also marks the end of the interlude that follows the sixth trumpet (10:1–11:14). Each of the three series of judgments (the seals, trumpets, and bowls) contains an interlude between the sixth and seventh events. Between the sixth and seventh seals came the interlude of chapter 7; between the sixth and seventh bowls will come the brief interlude of 16:15. These respites serve to comfort and encourage believers amid the terrors of God's judgments, reassuring them that He has not forgotten them (Malachi 3:16–4:2).

Although the seventh trumpet sounds in 11:15, the judgments associated with it are not described until chapter 15. Chapters 12–14 are a digression, taking readers back through the tribulation to the point of the seventh trumpet by a different path. They describe the tribulation not from God's perspective, but from Satan's. Chapters 4–11 focused on Christ's taking back what is rightfully His by means of the seal and trumpet judgments. Chapters 12–14 focus on the ultimate human usurper, the final Antichrist, whose career spans the same time period as the seal and trumpet judgments.

PRAISE FOR SOVEREIGNTY

Then the seventh angel sounded; and there were loud voices in heaven, saying, "The kingdom of the world has become the kingdom of our Lord and of His Christ; and He will reign forever and ever." And the twenty-four elders, who sit on their thrones before God, fell on their faces and worshiped God, saying, "We give You thanks, O Lord God, the Almighty, who are and who were, because You have taken Your great power and have begun to reign. (11:15–17)

Though its effects on earth were delayed, there was an immediate response in heaven when the seventh angel sounded his trumpet. Expressing exhilaration at what was about to take place, there came loud voices in heaven saying, "The kingdom of the world has become the kingdom of our Lord and of His Christ; and He will reign forever and ever."

That dramatic proclamation is obviously connected to the effects of the seventh trumpet. There is unrestrained joy that the power of Satan is to be forever broken, and Christ is to reign supreme. The setting up of Christ's long-awaited kingdom is the apex of redemptive history.

The use of the singular term "kingdom of the world" instead of the plural "kingdoms" introduces an important truth. All of the world's diverse groups are in reality one kingdom under one king. That king is known in Scripture by many names and titles (see "Names of Satan").

NAMES OF SATAN

NAME	MEANING	CITATION
The accuser	Accuses believers before God	Revelation 12:10
Beelzebul	Lord of the flies	Matthew 12:24, 26–27
Belial	Worthless	2 Corinthians 6:15
The Devil*	Slanderer	Matthew 4:1
The dragon	Destructive creature	Revelation 12:3, 7, 9
The Evil One	Intrinsically evil	John 17:15
The god of this world	Controls the philosophy of this world	2 Corinthians 4:4
The prince of the power of the air	Controller of unbelievers	Ephesians 2:2
The roaring lion	Opponent	1 Peter 5:8
The ruler of this world	Rules the world system	John 12:31
Satan*	Adversary	Matthew 4:10
The serpent of old	Deceiver in Eden	Revelation 12:9; 20:9
The tempter	Enticer to sin	1 Thessalonians 3:5

* Most common names

Adapted from "Names of Satan," *Ryrie Study Bible*, expanded ed. (Chicago:Moody, 1995), 2029.

While God ordains human governments for the well-being of man (Romans 13:1), those same governments refuse to submit to Him or acknowledge His sovereignty (Acts 4:26). They are essentially part of Satan's kingdom.

Jesus affirmed that Satan, though a usurper and not the rightful king, is the present ruler of the world. Three times in John's gospel Jesus called Satan "the ruler of this world" (John 12:31; 14:30; 16:11). As he did at Babel, Satan will rule in the future over a united fallen humanity in one visible kingdom under Antichrist's (the Beast of 13:1–4) leadership.

The tense of the verb translated "has become" describes a future event that is so certain that it can be spoken of as if it had already taken place. Heaven rejoices as if the long-anticipated day when Christ will establish His kingdom had already arrived, although some time on earth must elapse before that actually happens. The phrase "the kingdom of our Lord and of His Christ" emphasizes two realities. "Lord" usually refers to Jesus throughout the New Testament, while in Revelation it more often refers to God the Father, emphasizing their equality of nature. This phrase also describes the kingdom in its broadest sense, looking forward to divine rule over the creation and the new creation. No differentiation is made between the earthly millennial kingdom and the eternal kingdom. At the end of the thousand years, the millennial kingdom will merge with the eternal kingdom, in which Christ will reign forever and ever.

Zeroing in on one particular group in heaven offering praise, John notes that the twenty-four elders fell on their faces (5:8, 14; 7:11; 19:4) and worshiped God. As representatives of the glorified, raptured church, these elders had been eagerly waiting for Christ to take back the earth from Satan. Their joyous cry of praise is filled with gratitude: "We give You thanks, O Lord God, the Almighty, who are and who were, because You have taken Your great power and have begun to reign" and reflects their exhilaration that their prayers for the kingdom to come have been answered.

The elders' praise focused on three of God's attributes. "Almighty" describes God's sovereign, omnipotent power. Nine of its ten New Testament uses are in Revelation (1:8; 4:8; 11:17; 15:3; 16:7, 14; 19:6, 15; 21:22). It has the sense of God exercising His all-encompassing will by means of His irresistible power. The phrase "who are and who were" expresses God's eternity. As the living God, He had no beginning and will have no end.

The elders also praised God for His sovereignty, because He had "taken His great power and . . . begun to reign." The verb translated "have taken" signifies the permanence of God's sovereign rule.

All attempts to equate this glorious reign of Christ over the whole earth with any past event or with the church is contradictory to the clear future teaching of Scripture, including especially this passage. There is no way this text can be fulfilled except by the universal reign of Jesus Christ over the whole earth, as the prophets had for so long predicted.

PAROXYSMS OF RAGE

And the nations were enraged (11:18*a*)

The seventh trumpet vision reveals that the nations were defiant and enraged at the prospect of Christ's kingdom being established over the whole earth. The verb translated "were enraged" suggests a deep-seated, ongoing hostility. This was not just a momentary emotional fit of temper but a settled burning resentment against God. Eventually, they will assemble armies to fight God (16:14, 16; 20:8–9). With no desire to repent of sin, angry resentment and hostility against heaven will drive the nations to gather for their destruction at Armageddon (cf. Psalms 2:1, 5, 12; Acts 4:24–29).

The divine judgments people will experience during the tribulation should cause them to turn from their sins and submit to God. Tragically, however, even under such frightening judgment and warnings of eternal hell, most of them will refuse to repent and will instead harden their hearts (note Romans 2:1–10, which teaches that men refuse to repent in spite of God's goodness).The unbelieving world will apparently reach that point at the final outpouring of God's wrath during the events of the seventh trumpet (16:9, 11). Their rage and hostility toward God will reach a fever pitch, and they will gather to fight against Him at the battle on the plain of Megiddo (16:14, 16). By then they will be beyond the day of grace. There will be no salvation at Armageddon. The world's desperate, last-ditch effort to keep Christ from establishing His kingdom will fail and they will be utterly destroyed.

Plan for Judgment

and Your wrath came, and the time came for the dead to be judged, and the time to reward Your bond-servants the prophets and the saints and those who fear Your name, the small and the great, and to destroy those who destroy the earth. (11:18b)

The coming of God's wrath is so certain that it can be spoken of as if it had already happened. Those who think that a loving God will not pour out His wrath on them cling to a false and dangerous hope. That God will one day judge unbelievers is a recurring theme of Scripture (Isaiah 24:17–23; 30:27–33; Ezekiel 38–39). The sounding of the seventh trumpet marks the fulfillment of the great judgment event that the prophets foresaw and saints of all ages have longed for (cf. Psalms 3:7; 7:6; 35:1–8; 44:26). It will be the time when God pours out His wrath on His enemies.

Not only will the seventh trumpet signal the outpouring of God's wrath on earth, it will also indicate that "the time has come for the dead to be judged." "Time" translates a Greek word that refers to a season, era, occasion, or event. The establishing of Christ's kingdom will be a fitting time for the dead to be judged. The great white throne judgment (20:11–15) is not in view in this passage, since that judgment explicitly involves only unbelievers. It is best to see the reference to judgment here as a general reference to all future judgments. The elders in their song make no attempt to separate the different phases of judgment as they are separated in the closing chapters of Revelation. They simply sing of future judgments as though they were one event, in the same way that other Scriptures do not distinguish future judgments from each other (John 5:25, 28–29; Acts 17:31; 24:21).

The judgment will be the time for God to reward His "bond-servants the prophets and the saints and those who fear His name, the small and the great." Though the power to serve God in a way worthy of reward is a gift of God's grace, still believers are encouraged to work in view of those promised rewards. In 22:12 Jesus declared, "Behold, I am coming quickly, and My reward is with Me, to render to every man according to what he has done." To the Corinthians Paul wrote, "Now he who plants and he who waters are one; but each will receive his own reward according to his own labor" (1 Corinthians 3:8). The reward promised believers is that they will inherit the kingdom, in both its millennial (Matthew 25:34–40; Mark 10:29–31) and eternal (Revelation 21:7) phases. Believers are also promised crowns, including the crown of righteousness (2 Timothy 4:8), the crown of life (James 1:12; Revelation 2:10), and the crown of glory (1 Peter 5:4).

The phrase "Your bond-servants the prophets" encompasses all who have proclaimed God's truth throughout redemptive history, from Moses to the two witnesses (11:3–13). Scripture frequently designates prophets as the Lord's servants (e.g., 2 Kings 9:7; Ezra 9:11; Jeremiah 7:25; Ezekiel 38:17). The time has come for them to receive "a prophet's reward" (Matthew 10:41). All those faithful men who stood for God in dark days and against opposition will then find their work revealed and rewarded.

Another group to be rewarded is the saints, further defined as those "who fear Your name" (cf. Psalm 34:9; Luke 1:50). "Saints" is a common biblical description for the redeemed in both the Old and New Testaments (5:8; 8:3–4; Psalm 16:3; Daniel 7:18; Matthew 27:52; Acts 9:13; 26:10; Romans 1:7; 8:27). All of God's saints, "the small and the great," will receive rewards.

The judgment will also "destroy those who destroy the earth." That is not a reference to those who pollute the environment, but to those who pollute the earth with their sin. That includes all unbelievers, especially in the context of Revelation of the false economic and religious system called Babylon (18:2), Antichrist and his followers, and Satan himself. The apostle Paul wrote that the "mystery of lawlessness" (2 Thessalonians 2:7) is already at work in the church age, but during the tribulation period it will reach its pinnacle of destructive activity, shredding the very fabric of society in every evil way.

Given stewardship and dominion over the earth (Genesis 1:28), humans instead fell into sin and throughout their history have continually corrupted the earth (Romans 8:19–21). When that corrupting reaches its apex, God will destroy the earth and create a new one (21:1).

PROMISE OF COMMUNION

And the temple of God which is in heaven was opened; and the ark of
His covenant appeared in His temple, and there were flashes of lightning
and sounds and peals of thunder and an earthquake and a great hail-
storm. (11:19)

Bound up in the seventh trumpet is the promise to believers of unbroken
fellowship with God forever. That fellowship is symbolized by the imagery
of verse 19. The opening of "the temple of God which is in heaven" (the
place where His presence dwells; chapters 4, 5) revealed the ark of His
covenant. The ark symbolizes that the covenant God has promised to
men is now available in its fullness. In the midst of the fury of His judgment on unbelievers, God throws open the Holy of Holies (where the ark
was located; Exodus 26:33–34; 2 Chronicles 5:7) and draws believers into
His presence. That would have been unthinkable in the Old Testament
temple, when only the high priest entered the Holy of Holies once a year
(Hebrews 9:7).

The ark symbolizes God's communion with the redeemed because it
was there that blood sacrifices were offered to atone for men's sins
(Leviticus 16:2–16; Hebrews 9:3–7). Also, it was from above the ark that
God spoke to Moses (Numbers 7:89). The ark of the covenant is called in
Scripture the ark of testimony (Exodus 25:22), the ark of God (1 Samuel
3:3), and the ark of God's strength (Psalm 132:8). Inside it was "a golden
jar holding the manna, and Aaron's rod which budded, and the tables of
the covenant" (Hebrews 9:4). All that symbolized that God would supply
His people, was sovereign over His people, gave His law to His people,
and entered into an eternal, saving covenant with His people.

Along with the ark in the heavenly temple there were "flashes of
lightning and sounds and peals of thunder and an earthquake and a great
hailstorm." Similar events are associated with God's majestic, glorious
heavenly throne in 4:5. In 8:5 and 16:17–18 they are associated with
judgment. Heaven is the source of vengeance on unbelievers, as well as
covenant blessings for the redeemed.

The message of the seventh trumpet is that Jesus Christ is the sovereign King. He will one day take the rule of the earth away from Satan and human rulers. When He returns, He will bring covenant blessings to the redeemed, but eternal judgment to those who reject Him.

14

The WAR

(12:1–17)

The final battles of Satan's long war against God are yet to be fought. They will take place in the future, during the last half of the seven-year tribulation period, the time Jesus called the great tribulation (Matthew 24:21). At that time Satan, aided by the absence of the raptured church and the presence of increased demon hordes (9:1–11), will mount his most desperate assaults against God's purposes and His people. But despite the savage fury with which those assaults will be carried out, they will not succeed. Jesus will effortlessly crush Satan and his forces (19:11–21) and send him to the abyss for the duration of the millennial kingdom (20:1–2). After leading a final rebellion at the close of the millennium, Satan will be consigned to eternal punishment in the lake of fire (20:3, 7–10).

In describing that final war, the inspired apostle John first introduces the main characters involved in it: the woman (Israel), the dragon (Satan), and the male child (Jesus Christ).

THE CHARACTERS OF THE WAR (12:1–6)

The Woman

A great sign appeared in heaven: a woman clothed with the sun, and the moon under her feet, and on her head a crown of twelve stars; and she was with child; and she cried out, being in labor and in pain to give birth. (12:1–2)

The first thing John saw in this vision was "a great sign," the first of seven signs in the last half of Revelation (12:3; 13:13, 14; 15:1; 16:14; 19:20). The Greek word for "great" appears repeatedly in this vision (verses 3, 9, 12, 14). Everything John saw seemed to be huge either in size or in significance. This "sign" describes a symbol that points to a reality. In this case, the description plainly shows that the woman John saw was not an actual woman. Also, the reference to "the rest of her children," those "who keep the commandments of God and hold to the testimony of Jesus" (verse 17), shows that this woman is a symbolic mother.

The woman is the second of four symbolic women identified in Revelation. The first, though an actual woman, had the symbolic name Jezebel (2:20). and represented paganism. The third, depicted as a harlot, appears in 17:1–7. She represents the apostate church. The fourth woman (19:7–8) is the bride of the Lamb and represents the true church. Some argue that the woman in this present vision represents the church also, but as the context makes clear, she represents Israel. The Old Testament also pictures Israel as a woman (Jeremiah 3:1, 20; Ezekiel 16:32–35; Hosea 2:2) whom God will ultimately restore to Himself (Isaiah 50:1). A reference to the ark of the covenant (11:19) adds further support for identifying the woman as Israel.

John saw that the woman was "clothed with the sun, and had the moon under her feet, and on her head a crown of twelve stars." That fascinating description reflects Joseph's dream (Genesis 37:9–11). That the woman was clothed with the sun reflects redeemed Israel's unique glory and exalted status as God's chosen nation. It also links her with Jacob (the sun in Joseph's dream), an heir in the Abrahamic covenant. The reference to the moon under her feet may be a further description of Israel's exalted status. It could also include the concept of God's covenantal relationship with Israel, since the moon was part of the cycle of Israel's required times of worship (Numbers 29:5–6; Nehemiah 10:33; Psalm 81:3; Isaiah 1:13–14; Colossians 2:16). The crown of twelve stars on the woman's head refers to the twelve tribes of Israel.

Having described the woman's attire, John noted that she was with child. That also is familiar imagery describing Israel (Isaiah 26:17–18; 66:7–9; Jeremiah 4:31). Being pregnant, the woman cried out, being in labor and in pain to give birth. Just like a pregnant woman in labor feels pain, so the nation of Israel was in pain, waiting for Messiah to come forth. The cause of some of the pain is the persecution by Satan, who attempts to destroy the mother.

The Dragon

Then another sign appeared in heaven: and behold, a great red dragon having seven heads and ten horns, and on his heads were seven diadems. And his tail swept away a third of the stars of heaven and threw them to the earth. And the dragon stood before the woman who was about to give birth, so that when she gave birth he might devour her child. (12:3–4)

With the second sign, a new character emerges. Verse 9 clearly identifies the great red dragon as Satan (cf. 20:2). Satan is not an actual dragon, but a fallen angel. The symbolic language used to describe him pictures the reality of his person and character. Only in Revelation is Satan referred to as a dragon. Red, the color of fiery destruction and blood, further stresses Satan's vicious, deadly nature. Red is a fitting color for the dragon, since he attacks both the woman and her child.

The dragon is further described as having "seven heads and ten horns, and on his heads were seven diadems." He is depicted as a seven-headed monster that rules the world. These represent seven consecutive world empires running their course under Satan's dominion: Egypt, Assyria, Babylon, Medo-Persia, Greece, Rome, and Antichrist's future empire

(17:9–10). The final kingdom, ruled by Antichrist, will be a ten-nation confederacy. The ten horns represent the kings who will rule under Antichrist (17:12). The shifting of the diadems from the dragon's heads to the beast's horns (13:1) reveals the shift in power from the seven consecutive world empires to the ten kings under the final Antichrist.

Satan's pervasive, evil influence is not limited to the human realm but extends first into the angelic realm. In the picturesque language of John's vision, the dragon's tail "swept away a third of the stars of heaven and threw them to the earth." The references to the dragon's angels in verses 7 and 9 indicate that the stars of heaven are angels.

When Satan fell (Isaiah 14:12–15; Ezekiel 28:12–17), he swept away a third of the angelic host with him. Along with their defeated leader, those evil angels were cast from heaven to the earth. The number of angels who joined Satan in his rebellion is not revealed but is vast. Revelation 5:11 says that the number of the angels around God's throne numbered "myriads of myriads, and thousands of thousands." Since one-third of the angels fell, and Revelation 9:16 reveals that two hundred million demons will be released from captivity near the Euphrates River, there must be at least four hundred million holy angels.

As the next event in his dramatic vision unfolded, John noted that "the dragon stood before the woman who was about to give birth, so that when she gave birth he might devour her child." Throughout history, Satan has bent all of his efforts toward persecuting the people of God. Having failed to wipe out the people of God and the messianic line, Satan desperately attempted to murder the Messiah Himself before He could do His saving work. Yet Satan could not defeat the Son of God.

The Male Child

And she gave birth to a son, a male child, who is to rule all the nations with a rod of iron; and her child was caught up to God and to His throne. Then the woman fled into the wilderness where she had a place prepared by God, so that there she would be nourished for one thousand two hundred and sixty days. (12:5–6)

In spite of Satan's relentless efforts to prevent it, the woman (Israel) gave birth to a son. The incarnation of the male child, the Lord Jesus Christ, "who was born of a descendant of David according to the flesh" (Romans 1:3), was the fulfillment of prophecy (e.g., Genesis 3:15; Isaiah 7:14; 9:6; Micah 5:2). Israel brought forth the Messiah. Satan could not stop Christ from accomplishing redemption and therefore being exalted to the right hand of the Father as a perfect Savior.

But though he is a defeated foe, Satan will not give up. Unable to stop Christ, Satan still assaults His people. During the tribulation, Satan will increase his efforts to destroy the Jewish people, so that the nation cannot be saved as the Bible promises (Zechariah 12:10–13:1; Romans 11:25–27). So that none might be left alive to enter the millennial kingdom, he will seek to kill believing Jews. In a brief glimpse of what will be described more fully in verses 13–17, John noted that "the woman fled into the wilderness where she had a place prepared by God, so that there she would be nourished for one thousand two hundred and sixty days." God will frustrate Satan's attempt to destroy Israel during the tribulation by hiding His people, just as the Lord Jesus Christ predicted (Matthew 24:15–21).

THE WAR IN HEAVEN (12:7–12)

Having introduced the combatants in 12:1–6, John describes the first phase of Satan's final assault on God before Christ's return.

The Battle

And there was war in heaven, Michael and his angels waging war with the dragon. The dragon and his angels waged war, and they were not strong enough, and there was no longer a place found for them in heaven. (12:7–8)

There has been war in heaven since the fall of Satan (Isaiah 14:12–14; Ezekiel 28:11–18). Satan and his evil angels have actively opposed both the holy angels and God's people since Satan's fall (Daniel 10:12–13;

1 Peter 5:8).). Believers are to be aware of his schemes (2 Corinthians 2:11), give him no opportunity (Ephesians 4:27), and resist him (James 4:7).

The war raging between supernatural beings in the heavenly sphere will reach its peak during the tribulation. That future conflict will find Michael and his angels waging war with the dragon. The grammatical construction of that phrase in the Greek text indicates that Satan will start this battle. It could be translated "Michael and his angels had to fight the dragon." The Bible does not reveal how angels fight, nor does our limited knowledge of the heavenly realm permit us to speculate.

The key interpretive question is not how the battle will be fought, but what will cause it. While it is impossible to be certain, this ultimate battle may be triggered by the rapture of the church (see 1 Thessalonians 4:16–17). Possibly, as the raptured believers pass through their realm, the prince of the power of the air and his demon hosts will try to hinder their passage. That may trigger the battle with Michael and the holy angels.

Michael and Satan have known each other since they were created, and the battle during the tribulation will not be the first time they have opposed each other. In Daniel 10:13, "Michael, one of the chief princes, came to help" a holy angel against a powerful demon. Daniel 12:1 also speaks of Michael's defense of God's people: "Now at that time [the tribulation] Michael, the great prince who stands guard over the sons of your people, will arise. And there will be a time of distress such as never occurred since there was a nation until that time; and at that time your people, everyone who is found written in the book, will be rescued." The New Testament also reveals Michael to be the defender of God's people (Jude 9) and an archangel.

The reference to the dragon and his angels reinforces the truth that the demon hosts are under Satan's command (Matthew 25:41). The repetition of the phrase "waging war . . . waged war" emphasizes the force and fury of the battle. This will be an all-out battle. Satan will fight desperately to prevent Christ from establishing His millennial kingdom

Satan's full fury explodes on humanity when he is cast to the earth (12:12). At exactly what point in the tribulation Satan and the demons will be evicted from heaven is not revealed, nor is the duration of their battle with Michael and the holy angels. All that can be said with certainty is that Satan and the demons will be cast out of heaven, possibly at the rapture, but no later than the midpoint of the tribulation. Verse 12 says that Satan and his forces have only "a short time" after they leave heaven, supporting the view that they will have only the last three and a half years of the tribulation to operate, rather than the full seven years. They will not arrive on earth later than that, since they clearly are present during the terrible events of the last three and a half years, the great tribulation (9:1ff.). During that last period, Satan's full power will be directed at anyone belonging to God, especially Israel.

The Victory

And the great dragon was thrown down, the serpent of old who is called the devil and Satan, who deceives the whole world; he was thrown down to the earth, and his angels were thrown down with him. (12:9)

As a result of his defeat, the great dragon was thrown down from heaven to the earth. This describes Satan's second and permanent expulsion from heaven. The dragon is called great because of his formidable power to inflict harm and bring disaster. Earlier, he was described as having seven heads, seven crowns, and ten horns. That description pictures Satan as the ruler of the world.

The fourfold description of the dragon leaves no doubt regarding his identity. First, he is called "the serpent of old" (cf. 20:2), identifying him as the serpent in the garden of Eden (Genesis 3:1ff), emphasizing his subtlety and treachery.

The dragon is also called "the devil." "Devil" means "slanderer," or "false accuser," a fitting title for Satan. Satan is a malicious prosecutor of God's people, constantly trying to arraign them before the bar of God's holy justice.

Then the text plainly identifies the dragon as Satan. "Satan" is a Hebrew word that means "adversary," and is a fitting name for the enemy of God and His people. Tragically, the most glorious created being, the "star of the morning" (Isaiah 14:12), is now and forever branded "the adversary." He assaulted God in his original rebellion when he demanded to be "like the Most High" (Isaiah 14:14), and he deceitfully led Eve into sin by manipulating her to distrust the character and word of God (Genesis 3:2–5).

Finally, the dragon is described as "the one who deceives the whole world." The use of the present tense indicates that this is Satan's habitual, continual activity. Satan lures people to their destruction by causing them to pay "attention to deceitful spirits and doctrines of demons" (1 Timothy 4:1). He seduces people to believe him and not God (Genesis 3:4).

The Celebration

Then I heard a loud voice in heaven, saying, "Now the salvation, and the power, and the kingdom of our God and the authority of His Christ have come, for the accuser of our brethren has been thrown down, he who accuses them before our God day and night. And they overcame him because of the blood of the Lamb and because of the word of their testimony, and they did not love their life even when faced with death. For this reason, rejoice, O heavens and you who dwell in them. Woe to the earth and the sea, because the devil has come down to you, having great wrath, knowing that he has only a short time." (12:10–12)

The defeat of Satan and his demon hosts, along with the cleansing of their presence from heaven, will trigger an outburst of praise. Such sudden outbursts frequently appear in Revelation (4:8–11; 5:9–10, 11–14; 7:9–12; 11:15–18; 15:3–4; 19:1–8). The identity of those whom John heard crying out with a loud voice in heaven is not stated. This collective voice cannot be angels, since angels could not refer to humans as their brethren (19:10; 22:8–9). These worshipers are most likely the glorified saints in heaven.

The saints began by rejoicing that "the salvation, and the power, and the kingdom of our God and the authority of His Christ have come." "Salvation" is to be understood in its broadest sense. It encompasses not only the redemption of individuals, but also the deliverance of all creation from sin's curse. "Power" speaks of God's omnipotence.

They rejoiced further that "the authority of . . . Christ has come." The rule of Christ is by authority from God (Psalm 2:8; Matthew 28:18; John 17:2). So certain is the establishing of the kingdom and the rule of Christ that, though yet future, they are spoken of in the past tense. The heavenly worshipers rejoice that the first step, Satan's defeat and final ejection from heaven, has already taken place.

The heavenly worshipers also offer praise because of events on earth, where their brethren overcame Satan. Ejected from heaven, Satan and his hellish hosts will vent their full fury on God's people on earth (12:6, 13–17). There too, however, they will suffer defeat. Again speaking of a future event in the past tense because of its certainty, the inspired apostle John sees the victory already won.

It is only through God's power that any believer in any age can defeat Satan. Accordingly, the tribulation believers overcame Satan first of all "because of the blood of the Lamb." Like their martyred brethren already in heaven, they "washed their robes and made them white in the blood of the Lamb" (Revelation 7:14). No accusation against the suffering saints of the great tribulation will stand, because the Lamb's blood was shed for all their sins.

A second way these tribulation saints overcame Satan's assaults was through "the word of their testimony." Despite all the persecution they suffered, they will remain faithful witnesses to Jesus Christ. Their testimony will never waver.

The suffering tribulation saints were also able to fend off Satan because they did not love their life even when faced with death. They willingly paid the ultimate price for their loyalty to Christ. A sure mark of true believers is that they continue in the faith even to death (cf. 1 John 2:19).

The passage concludes with a final note of praise: For this reason, because of the defeat of Satan and the triumph of the saints, the heavenly chorus calls on the heavens and all who dwell in them to rejoice. That joyous note is followed by the sobering warning "Woe to the earth and the sea, because the devil has come down to you, having great wrath, knowing that he has only a short time." The Greek word for "wrath" refers to a violent outburst of rage. Satan's rage is even more violent because he knows that he has only a short time: the three and a half years of the reign of Antichrist (13:5), whom Satan places in power immediately after being cast down from heaven. It is a short time because Jesus Christ will return to establish His earthly millennial kingdom.

THE WAR ON EARTH (12:13–17)

This passage describes three attacks that Satan's forces will mount against Israel during the tribulation.

The First Attack

And when the dragon saw that he was thrown down to the earth, he persecuted the woman who gave birth to the male child. But the two wings of the great eagle were given to the woman, so that she could fly into the wilderness to her place, where she was nourished for a time and times and half a time, from the presence of the serpent. (12:13–14)

Following his defeat by Michael and the holy angels, the dragon (Satan) "was thrown down to the earth." Enraged by his ejection from heaven, the dragon furiously "persecuted the woman (Israel; 12:1) who gave birth to the male child" (Christ; 12:5). The Greek verb translated "persecuted" means "to pursue" or "to hunt." It is used in the New Testament of pursuit with hostile intent (Matthew 23:34; Acts 26:11). Here it describes Satan's hostile pursuit and persecution of the Jews as they flee into the wilderness (12:6; cf. 13:4–7).

Israel's situation when the storm of Antichrist's persecution breaks upon them during the tribulation will be terrifying and tragic. The Jews will be in desperate need of any assistance they can get, and, in God's providence, there will be some people who will help them (Matthew 25:31–40).

In the Jews' time of peril and flight they will receive help from individual Gentiles. Those Gentiles will demonstrate their faith in Christ by their willingness to help the persecuted Jews at the risk of their own lives.

Not only will God providentially use believing Gentiles to aid the Jewish people, but He will also intervene directly on their behalf. John saw in his vision that "the two wings of the great eagle were given to the woman, so that she could fly into the wilderness to her place, where she was nourished for a time and times and half a time, from the presence of the serpent." This is figurative language that symbolically depicts Israel's escape from Satan. The striking imagery of the two wings of the great eagle is taken from Exodus 19:4: "You yourselves have seen what I did to the Egyptians, and how I bore you on eagles' wings, and brought you to Myself." God will bring Israel to safety, just as He delivered the nation from Egypt.

"Wings" symbolize strength (Isaiah 40:31) and speed (2 Samuel 22:11; Psalms 18:10; 104:3), but most commonly speak of protection (Deuteronomy 32:9–11; Psalms 17:8; 57:1). "Eagle" here can also refer to a vulture (Matthew 24:28; Luke 17:37). These large birds with enormous wing spans serve as a fitting symbol for God's protection for Israel.

The location of the place where the Jews will flee is not revealed. Some have suggested Petra, an ancient city carved into the rocky cliffs of Edom between the Dead Sea and the Gulf of Aqaba. Approachable only through a narrow gorge, Petra was easy to defend in ancient times. The term "wilderness" does not reveal the exact location of Israel's place of refuge, since that term is a general one. Jesus' warning to flee to the mountains (Matthew 24:15–16) suggests that the place of refuge will not be in the coastal plain to the west of Jerusalem, or the relatively flat Negev (desert region) to the south. More likely, it will be in the mountainous region east of Jerusalem. Daniel 11:41 provides further evidence: "[Antichrist] will also enter the Beautiful Land, and many countries will fall; but these will be rescued out of his hand: Edom, Moab and the foremost of the sons of Ammon." Perhaps God will spare Edom, Moab, and Ammon, ancient countries to the east of Israel, to provide a refuge for His people.

In refuge, Israel will be supernaturally fed by God. Cut off from the world system, and unable in any case to buy and sell (13:17), the Jews will need outside help to survive. In a time of devastating miraculous judgments, God will miraculously supply provisions for His people, just as he provided their ancestors with manna and quail in the wilderness (Exodus 16:12ff.).

The duration of Israel's hiding and God's provision is defined as "a time and times and half a time." That phrase, drawn from Daniel 7:25 and 12:7, refers to the second half of the tribulation. This period will mark the overtly evil career of Antichrist. During that time God will protect Israel from the presence of the serpent. Although Satan may know where the Jews are hiding, he will be unable to defeat them because of divine protection. Frustrated by this defeat of his first assault on the Jewish people, the Devil will launch a second attack.

The Second Attack

And the serpent poured water like a river out of his mouth after the woman, so that he might cause her to be swept away with the flood. But the earth helped the woman, and the earth opened its mouth and drank up the river which the dragon poured out of his mouth. (12:15–16)

Thwarted in his initial attempt to massacre the Jewish people, Satan will resort to long-range tactics. Since the serpent is not an actual snake but a symbolic representation of Satan, the water he spews like a river out of his mouth is likely symbolic as well. In the Old Testament, floods symbolize trouble in general (2 Samuel 22:17; Job 27:20) and an invading, destroying army (Jeremiah 46:8; 47:2; Daniel 11:26). Satan's attacking force will sweep toward the Jews' hiding place like a great flood.

Yet in dramatic fashion, the earth will help the woman; "it opened its mouth and drank up the river which the dragon poured out of his mouth." The imagery is reminiscent of Moses' description in Exodus 15:12: "You stretched out Your right hand, the earth swallowed them." It may be that one of the frequent earthquakes during the tribulation (6:12; 8:5; 11:13, 19; 16:18; Matthew 24:7) will cause the ground to split open and swallow Satan's forces. Whatever this symbolic language pictures, it marks the destruction of the attacking army and the end of Satan's second assault.

The Third Attack

So the dragon was enraged with the woman, and went off to make war with the rest of her children, who keep the commandments of God and hold to the testimony of Jesus (12:17).

Frustrated, the dragon (Satan) will turn his fury toward new targets. Some have identified "the rest of her children with whom Satan will make war" as the 144,000 (7:2–8; 14:1–5). Others see them as believing Gentile tribulation saints (7:9–14), who are sons of Abraham by faith (Galatians 3:7). It seems best to take this as an all-inclusive phrase, referring to all those who name the name of Jesus Christ.

They are further described as "those who keep the commandments of God and hold to the testimony of Jesus." The word translated here as "commandments" is a word used frequently in John's writings to refer to New Testament commands (14:12; John 14:15, 21; 15:10, 12; 1 John 2:3–4; 3:22–24; 5:2–3). "The testimony of Jesus" is not testimony about Him, but the truths He taught that are revealed in the New Testament. These persecuted believers will give further evidence that their salvation is real by their obedience to Scripture.

Like his first two attacks directed against Israel, Satan's third attack on God's people will also fail. All of Satan's efforts to prevent Christ's kingdom from being established are doomed. The Lord Jesus Christ will triumph.

15

The
BEAST
and His Prophet
(13:1–18)

The astounding description of the Antichrist presented in the opening verses of Revelation 13 is the most gripping, thorough, and dramatic in all of Scripture. However, the appearance of Antichrist was not new teaching to John's readers. John wrote in his first epistle that his readers had "heard that antichrist is coming" (1 John 2:18) Nor is it the first reference to Antichrist in John's visions in Revelation; Antichrist was introduced in 11:7 as the "beast" who will kill God's two witnesses. His wicked career, which began in chapter 11, is fully developed beginning here.

Chapter 12 records the beginning of Satan's long war against God and His people. Chapter 13 records that war's culmination. Satan will try to prevent Jesus Christ from setting up His earthly kingdom by setting up his own under Antichrist.

Having been cast permanently from heaven (12:9), Satan will know that the time remaining to him is brief (12:12). To lead his last, desperate onslaught against God, he will empower his final Antichrist.

SEVEN FEATURES OF THE ANTICHRIST

The opening verses of this chapter reveal seven features of this ultimate
dictator.

1. His Ancestry
*And the dragon stood on the sand of the seashore. Then I saw a beast
coming up out of the sea, having ten horns and seven heads, and on his
horns were ten diadems, and on his heads were blasphemous names.*
(13:1)

The first sentence of this chapter belongs as the last sentence of chapter
12, since it concludes the account of the dragon. While some Greek manu-
scripts read "I stood," the older and more reliable ones read "he stood."[1]
The imagery of the sand of the seashore depicts the nations of the world
(20:8). In John's vision, Satan takes his place dominantly in their midst as
if they were his rightful possession. But in reality, he is a usurper who
seeks the world's worship and adoration.

Next the dragon summons the Antichrist, described as "a beast coming up out of the sea." The word "beast" is also used to describe Antichrist
in 11:7. It refers to a wild, vicious monster, describing Antichrist as a ferocious personality. The beast must be understood as representing both a
kingdom and a person. The beast must represent a kingdom, because of
the complex description of him in the latter half of verse 1. Yet the beast
must also represent a person, since he is always described with personal
pronouns. Daniel (Daniel 7:25; 8:24–25; 11:36–45) and Paul (2 Thessalonians 2:4) also describe the Antichrist as a person.

There has been much discussion about what the sea symbolizes. Both
Revelation 11:7 and 17:8 indicate that the beast comes up out of the
abyss, so it is best to equate the sea with the abyss. That interpretation fits
the Old Testament, which also uses the metaphor of the sea to picture
satanic activity (Job 26:12; Psalms 74:13–14; 89:9–10; Isaiah 27:1). Some
of the demons are currently in the abyss (9:1–11; Luke 8:31), and Satan
will be imprisoned in that abyss during the millennial kingdom (20:1–3).

The Antichrist will be a man (2 Thessalonians 2:4), but at some point in his life, he will be indwelt by a powerful demon from the abyss. This demon-possessed man will be a gifted orator, an intellectual genius, possess great charm and charisma, and have immense leadership power. Yet no one in human history will be more completely the devil's child than the Antichrist. His "family likeness" to Satan becomes strikingly apparent from John's description of him as having ten horns and seven heads, with ten diadems on his horns. That same grotesque description was applied to Satan in 12:3. The description of Antichrist emphasizes the importance of the ten horns by mentioning them first and associating the diadems with them instead of the heads.

"Horns" in Scripture symbolize strength and power, both for attack and defense. Here they represent the power of the kings who will rule under Antichrist's authority. "Ten" fits the imagery of the fourth beast in Daniel 7:7, 24, and is a symbolic number representing all the world's political and military might. Antichrist will rise from among these ten (Daniel 7:16–24) and will not rule merely ten nations, but the entire world (Daniel 7:23). Unlike the seven heads, which represent successive world empires, all of the rulers symbolized by the ten horns will rule at the same time (cf. 17:12).

In addition to his ten horns, the beast is described by John as having seven heads. Those seven heads represent seven successive world empires: Egypt, Assyria, Babylon, Medo-Persia, Greece, Rome, and Antichrist's final world kingdom. The ten diadems indicate the horns' regal authority and victorious power. John also noted that on the beasts' heads were blasphemous names. Like many of the Roman emperors and other monarchs before them, these rulers will choose divine names and titles that dishonor the living God.

2. His Authority

And the beast which I saw was like a leopard, and his feet were like those of a bear, and his mouth like the mouth of a lion. And the dragon gave him his power and his throne and great authority. (13:2)

As John looked more closely at the beast, he saw that it incorporated the characteristics of the animals from the vision recorded in Daniel 7:3–7. The leopard, bear, and lion were well-known in Palestine. They dramatically emphasize the characteristics of the nations they represent. The lion was a fitting symbol for the fierce, consuming power of the Babylonian Empire. The ferocity, strength, and stability of the Medo-Persian Empire led to its depiction as a bear. The Greeks' swift conquests, particularly under Alexander the Great, reflect the speed and viciousness of the leopard. John lists the three animals in reverse order from Daniel, since he was looking backward in time. Daniel, looking forward in time, listed the animals and the kingdoms they represent in chronological order.

Like the indescribable fourth beast of Daniel 7:7, which represents the Roman Empire, Antichrist's final empire will be a composite of the empires that preceded it. It will incorporate all the ferocity, viciousness, swiftness, and strength of the other world empires. This powerful empire, unparalleled in human history, will be Satan's last and greatest attempt to stop the reign of Christ. But, like all Satan's other attempts to thwart God's purposes, it will ultimately fail.

3. His Acclaim

I saw one of his heads as if it had been slain, and his fatal wound was healed. And the whole earth was amazed and followed after the beast; (13:3)

A startling event will help Antichrist solidify his hold on the world. John "saw one of his heads as if it had been slain, and his fatal wound was healed." Some argue that the head, whose "fatal wound was healed" was a kingdom that will have been destroyed and restored. They see the death and resurrection miracle as the revival of the Roman Empire. Antichrist, they believe, will unite the countries occupying the territory of the ancient Roman Empire into a new empire. That revival of power will so amaze the rest of the nations that they will also submit to his rule.

The most obvious problem with this view is that while verse 3 speaks of one of the heads being slain, other passages specify that the beast himself is slain (13:12, 14; 17:8, 11). The personal pronoun in the phrase "his fatal wound" also indicates that one of the kings is in view, not the empire as a whole. Granting that it is a person who dies and is restored to life, the question remains as to the identity of that person. Yet the head whose fatal wound will be healed can only be the future Antichrist.

Whether his death is real or fake is not clear. It may be that Antichrist is really killed and God allows him to be resurrected. More likely, Antichrist's alleged death and resurrection will be a counterfeit of Christ's death and resurrection, staged, as one of the "lying wonders" perpetrated by the false prophet (13:12–15; 2 Thessalonians 2:9 NKJV).

Whatever actually happens, people will believe that Antichrist has transcended death. Since the tribulation will be a time when the world will experience death at an unequaled level, Antichrist's apparent power over death will win him widespread acclaim. As a result, the whole earth will be amazed and follow after the beast (cf. verse 14; 2 Thessalonians 2:8–12).

4. His Adoration
they worshiped the dragon because he gave his authority to the beast; and they worshiped the beast, saying, "Who is like the beast, and who is able to wage war with him?" (13:4)

The world's fascination with Antichrist will quickly become worship. He will encourage and demand that worship by "exalt[ing] himself above every so-called god or object of worship, so that he takes his seat in the temple of God, displaying himself as being God" (2 Thessalonians 2:4). Not content with acclaim, Antichrist will seek adoration. He will be aided by his associate, the false prophet, who "makes the earth and those who dwell in it to worship the first beast [Antichrist], whose fatal wound was healed" (13:12). Not only will the deceived unbelievers worship Antichrist, but they will also worship the dragon (Satan) because he gave his authority to the beast. By worshiping Antichrist, unbelievers will actually be worshiping Satan, the real power behind him.

As the people of the world worship Antichrist, they will cry out in awe, "Who is like the beast, and who is able to wage war with him?" The implied answer to both rhetorical questions is "No one!" By referring to Antichrist in language reserved for the worship of God, Antichrist's deluded worshipers will attribute deity to him (2 Thessalonians 2:4). In the political, military, and religious realms, Antichrist will reign supreme and unchallenged by earth and hell.

5. His Arrogance

There was given to him a mouth speaking arrogant words and blas-phemies, and authority to act for forty-two months was given to him. And he opened his mouth in blasphemies against God, to blaspheme His name and His tabernacle, that is, those who dwell in heaven. (13:5–6)

Like his master, Antichrist will be an arrogant blasphemer. The phrase "there was given to him" refers to God's sovereign control of events (6:4, 8; 7:2; 9:5). God will allow Antichrist to blaspheme and so give full expression to the wickedness that will cover the earth at that time. Antichrist's arrogance, predicted by the prophet Daniel (Daniel 7:8, 11, 25;11:36) will surpass that of anyone else in human history. He will be Satan's mouthpiece, voicing his master's frustrated rage against God, and the supreme blasphemer in a world filled with blasphemers. Yet neither Antichrist's blasphemies nor his reign of terror will last indefinitely. God will grant Antichrist authority to act for only forty-two months (the last three and a half years of the tribulation, the seventieth week of Daniel's prophecy (Daniel 9:24). Antichrist and Satan will be allowed to operate only within the time limit set for them by the true Ruler of the universe.

6. His Activity

It was also given to him to make war with the saints and to overcome them, and authority over every tribe and people and tongue and nation was given to him. (13:7)

Once again the text notes that Antichrist can do only what he is given permission to do by God. Because they will refuse to worship him,

Antichrist will make war with the saints and overcome them. Believers will bear the brunt of his murderous fury. The result will be a worldwide slaughter of God's people (6:9–11; 7:9–17; 11:7; 17:6; Daniel 7:25).

Daniel long before predicted this widespread martyrdom of God's people. He wrote that Antichrist "will . . . wear down the saints of the Highest One . . . and they will be given into his hand for a time, times, and half a time [three and a half years; the last half of the tribulation]" (Daniel 7:25). This persecution will begin at the midpoint of the tribulation, when Antichrist breaks his covenant with Israel (Daniel 9:27) and sets up the abomination of desolation (Daniel 9:27; 11:31; 12:11; Matthew 24:15; 2 Thessalonians 2:3–4).

7. His Admirers

All who dwell on the earth will worship him, everyone whose name has not been written from the foundation of the world in the book of life of the Lamb who has been slain. If anyone has an ear, let him hear. If anyone is destined for captivity, to captivity he goes; if anyone kills with the sword, with the sword he must be killed. Here is the perseverance and the faith of the saints. (13:8–10)

The phrase "all who dwell on the earth" is used throughout Revelation to describe unbelievers and does not include everyone who will be alive at that time. Here the limiting factor is specifically stated. It is "everyone whose name has not been written from the foundation of the world in the book of life of the Lamb who has been slain." Unbelievers, those whose names are not recorded in the Book of Life, will "perish, because they did not receive the love of the truth so as to be saved" (2 Thessalonians 2:10).

Seven times in the New Testament, believers are identified as those whose names are written in the Book of Life (3:5; 17:8; 20:12, 15; 21:27; Philippians 4:3). The Book of Life is the registry in which God inscribed the names of those chosen for salvation before the foundation of the world. Antichrist will not be able to destroy believers' saving faith, for the Lord Jesus Christ promised, "He who overcomes will thus be clothed in white garments; and I will not erase his name from the book of life, and I will confess his name before My Father and before His angels" (3:5). Believers have been in the keeping power of God since before creation, and they will be there after the destruction of this order and the establishment of the new heaven and the new earth (21:1ff.).

Believers are doubly secure, because the Book of Life belongs to the Lamb who has been slain. Not only the decree of election, but also the atoning work of Christ seals the redemption of the elect forever. Believers "were not redeemed with perishable things like silver or gold . . . but with precious blood, as of a lamb unblemished and spotless, the blood of Christ" (1 Peter 1:18–19). Antichrist may take their lives, but he cannot destroy their faith.

This astounding vision of the beast from the sea concludes with a call for spiritual understanding. The warning "If anyone has an ear, let him hear" is echoed fifteen times in the New Testament with the phrase "He who has an ear . . ." to emphasize a particularly important truth. In all its previous uses in Revelation (2:7, 11, 17, 29; 3:6, 13, 22), it is followed by the phrase "what the Spirit says to the churches." The omission of that phrase suggests that the church is not in view in this passage, having been raptured before the start of the tribulation (cf. 3:10).

Here the phrase introduces a proverb: "If anyone is destined for captivity, to captivity he goes; if anyone kills with the sword, with the sword he must be killed." This proverb contains important practical truth for those believers alive at the time of Antichrist's persecution. They are to depend on God's providence and not take matters into their own hands.

THE FALSE PROPHET

Just as the false christs who have plagued mankind will culminate in the final Antichrist, so also will the false prophets culminate in a final false prophet (cf. 16:13; 19:20; 20:10). He will be Satan's last and most powerful lying deceiver. Along with Satan, the counterfeit of the Father, and Antichrist, the counterfeit of Jesus Christ, the false prophet will form the satanic false trinity. He will be the counterfeit of the Holy Spirit. The false prophet will be Antichrist's partner in Satan's massive final deception of the world. John's vision of the false prophet reveals three key elements essential to his role.

1. His Person
Then I saw another beast coming up out of the earth; and he had two horns like a lamb and he spoke as a dragon. (13:11)

Having seen the terrifying vision of the first beast (Antichrist) in 13:1–10, John then saw another beast. Some view this second beast as an institution or a form of government. However, the use of the Greek word "other," meaning "another of the same kind," indicates that he will be a person like the Antichrist (19:20).

In contrast to the first beast, who will come up out of the sea (13:1), the second beast will come up out of the earth. Like Antichrist, the false prophet will be indwelt by a demon out of the abyss (13:1), which is pictured here as the flaming depths of the earth. In the ancient world, the earth was less mysterious and foreboding than the sea. That the false prophet arises from the earth suggests that he will be less overpowering and terrifying than the Antichrist. He will be winsome and persuasive, similar to the wolves in sheep's clothing Jesus warned of (Matthew 7:15).

The description of the first beast, with its ten horns, seven heads, ten crowns, and seven blasphemous names (13:1), was grotesque and frightening. In contrast, the second beast merely had two horns. That indicates that he is not characterized by the same massive might as Antichrist. Unlike the savage, ferocious, fierce, and deadly Antichrist, who is likened to a leopard, bear, and lion (13:2), the false prophet seems as harmless as a lamb. He does not come as a conquering dictator, but appears as a subtle deceiver, with meekness and gentleness, though not without great authority.

Despite his deceptive appearance, the false prophet is no less a child of hell than the Antichrist. That is evident because he spoke as a dragon—a strange voice indeed for a lamb. The false prophet, like Antichrist (13:2, 5), will be the dragon Satan's mouthpiece, speaking his words. He will speak winsome, deceiving words of praise about the Antichrist, luring the world to worship the satanic dictator.

2. His Power

He exercises all the authority of the first beast in his presence. And he makes the earth and those who dwell in it to worship the first beast, whose fatal wound was healed. He performs great signs, so that he even makes fire come down out of heaven to the earth in the presence of men. And he deceives those who dwell on the earth because of the signs which it was given him to perform in the presence of the beast, telling those who dwell on the earth to make an image to the beast who had the wound of the sword and has come to life. (13:12–14)

Though primarily a subtle deceiver, the false prophet will still have power. John notes that "he exercises all the authority of the first beast" (Antichrist). That he exercises his authority in Antichrist's presence implies that Antichrist will have delegated that authority to him. The false prophet's mission will be to cause the earth and those who dwell in it to worship the first beast. He will lead the worldwide religion of Antichrist worship.

The false prophet's efforts will receive a tremendous boost from a startling, spectacular event: the apparent healing of the first beast's (Antichrist's) fatal wound (verse 3; 17:8). That is a satanic imitation not only of Christ's resurrection, but also that of the two witnesses (11:11). It is most likely that Antichrist's death will be staged, and hence his "resurrection" is a ruse. Whether a true resurrection or a faked return from death, the world will accept Antichrist's resurrection as genuine, thus greatly enhancing both his prestige and that of the false prophet.

The false prophet will also perform great signs of his own. Those signs mimic not only the miracles performed by Jesus Christ, but also those of the two witnesses (11:5–6). Those who reject the saving gospel of the Lord Jesus Christ will eagerly accept the damning false gospel preached by the false prophet since it appears to be verified by spectacular supernatural signs.

Amazingly, the false prophet, imitating the two witnesses (11:5), "even makes fire come down out of heaven to the earth." The present tense of "makes" suggests that he will repeatedly perform this supernatural act to impress with his power. "Deceives" is from a Greek word that means "to wander." It forms the root of the English word "planet," since the planets appear to wander through the heavens. The world will be utterly vulnerable to his deception during the tribulation. Having rejected the true gospel and blasphemed the true God (16:9, 11), the unbelieving world will be eager to believe the deceiving lies propagated by the false prophet.

John defines the people who will be deceived as "those who dwell on the earth," a technical phrase used to refer to unbelievers. Though persecuted, God's elect cannot be deceived (Mark 13:22). Because believers know the truth and are protected by their God (John 10:3–5, 14, 27–30), they will recognize the false prophet's teaching as lies. That the unbelieving world will be deceived is due not only to the wicked deception of Satan, the demons, Antichrist, and the false prophet, but also comes as God's judgment (2 Thessalonians 2:10–12).

As the power of Antichrist and false prophet grow, Satan will escalate the false world religion of Antichrist worship. Humanity will eventually obey the prophet's command to make an image to the beast. The world will engage in the most shocking, blatant idolatry ever seen. This blasphemous image will probably be set up on the temple grounds in Jerusalem (2 Thessalonians 2:4) and will be connected with the abomination of desolation (Daniel 9:27; 11:31; 12:11; Matthew 24:15). It will be a tribute to the awesome power of Antichrist, who has come to life to seemingly conquer death.

3. His Program

And it was given to him to give breath to the image of the beast, so that the image of the beast would even speak and cause as many as do not worship the image of the beast to be killed. And he causes all, the small and the great, and the rich and the poor, and the free men and the slaves, to be given a mark on their right hand or on their forehead, and he provides that no one will be able to buy or to sell, except the one who has the mark, either the name of the beast or the number of his name. Here is wisdom. Let him who has understanding calculate the number of the beast, for the number is that of a man; and his number is six hundred and sixty-six. (13:15–18)

The image of the Antichrist will be different from any other idol in human history. In another display of his power to deceive, the false prophet will "give breath to the image of the beast, so that the image of the beast would even speak." "Breath" translates as "spirit" or "wind." The false prophet will animate the image of Antichrist so that it gives the appearance of being alive. With today's amazing special effects technology, that is not out of the realm of possibility. Add to that the world's desperate need, amid the carnage of the tribulation, to believe in a death conqueror, and the deception becomes very believable.

After his immense worldwide success and after dropping his façade of gentleness, the false prophet will cause as many as do not worship the image of the beast to be killed. The death sentence will be decreed for those who refuse to worship the image of Antichrist. Many of the martyrs mentioned earlier in Revelation (6:9–11; 7:13–14) are those who will be killed during this terrible time of persecution. But though the death sentence will be decreed on all, not all believers will be killed. Some will survive until Christ returns and will enter His millennial kingdom as living people (Isaiah 65:20–23; Matthew 25:31–40), including many Jews (12:6–7, 14).

As part of his plan to enforce the worship of Antichrist, the false prophet will require all people "to be given a mark on their right hand or on their forehead." "Mark" was the term for images or names of the emperor on Roman coins. In the ancient world, such marks (tattoos or brands) were commonly given to slaves, soldiers, and devotees of religious cults. God sealed, with a mark on the forehead, the 144,000 to preserve them from His wrath against the unbelieving world (7:2–3). The false prophet marks the unsaved to preserve them from Antichrist's wrath against God's people. The mark will signify that the person bearing it is a loyal follower of the Antichrist. In much the same way, the Roman emperors required their subjects to prove their loyalty by offering sacrifices to Caesar. Those who refused, like those who refuse to take the Antichrist's mark, were subject to execution.

Besides the constant threat of death, refusing to take the mark of the beast will have dire practical consequences in daily living: no one will be able to buy or to sell without it. Antichrist's empire will maintain strict economic control over the world. Food, and the other necessities of life in demand on the devastated earth, will be unobtainable for those without the mark. Currency will probably vanish, to be replaced by controlled credit. Instead of a credit card, people will have a mark of some unspecified type in their forehead or hand.

Further describing the mark, John notes that it will consist of "either the name of the beast or the number of his name." Antichrist will have a universal designation consisting of his name within a numbering system. The exact identification of that phrase is unclear. What is clear is that everyone will be required to have the identifying mark or suffer the consequences.

The exclamation "Here is wisdom" is a warning to those alive at that time to be wise and discerning. They will need to recognize what is happening and understand the significance of the number connected with Antichrist's name. Those with understanding will be able to "calculate the number of the beast, for the number is that of a man; and his number is six hundred and sixty-six." Perhaps no detail in Revelation has intrigued people more than this number. There has been no end to the speculation as to its significance and how to calculate it. In Greek, Hebrew, and Latin, letters had numerical equivalents, and a myriad of schemes to associate the names of historical individuals with the number 666 have been put forth. All such speculation is futile. Since the Antichrist is still to come, the number 666 cannot be associated with any historical individual.

This sobering passage is not intended to be the source of fruitless speculation about its details. Rather, it stands as a warning to the unbelieving world. It challenges believers to lead careful, godly lives (1 Peter 4:7; 2 Peter 3:11) and to evangelize a world headed for destruction.

16

Tribulation
ANNOUNCEMENTS
(14:1–20)

Revelation 14 introduces the most triumphant group of men the world will ever know. They will emerge from the worst holocaust in history, the tribulation, battle weary but triumphant. The 144,000 will survive both Satan's wrath and God's judgments on the sinful world. Nothing will be able to harm them, because God will seal them (7:3–4).

These 144,000 will not be the only ones redeemed during the tribulation. A great host of others, both Jews (Zechariah 12:10–14; 13:1, 9; Romans 11:26–27) and Gentiles (6:9–11; 7:9, 13–14; Matthew 25:31–46) will be saved. Many will die as martyrs during the savage persecution unleashed by Antichrist. Those who will live through the horrors of the tribulation will enter the millennial kingdom. But the 144,000 Jewish evangelists are unique because all of them will survive. When Christ returns and stands on Mount Zion, they will stand with Him in triumph.

THE 144,000

Their Power

Then I looked, and behold, the Lamb was standing on Mount Zion, and with Him one hundred and forty-four thousand, having His name and the name of His Father written on their foreheads. (14:1)

The phrase "I looked, and behold" or its equivalent appears frequently in Revelation to introduce startling, dramatic events (verse 14; 4:1; 6:2, 5, 8; 7:9; 15:5; 19:11). What took John's attention was the awe-inspiring sight of "the Lamb . . . standing on Mount Zion." The appearance of the Lamb on Mount Zion is a monumental moment in redemptive history, foretold in Psalm 2:6–9.

The text also describes the 144,000 as having "His [the Lamb's] name and the name of His Father written on their foreheads." Unbelievers will receive the mark of the beast (13:16–17). The 144,000 will have the mark of God placed on their foreheads (7:3) for their protection. Satan will desperately seek to kill these fearless preachers, but God will not permit them to be harmed. They will enter the millennial kingdom as living men. Most likely, the 144,000 will continue their evangelistic work throughout that thousand-year period. While only redeemed people will enter the kingdom, the children born to them (Isaiah 65:23) will not all believe. In fact, there will be enough unregenerate people by the end of the millennium for Satan to lead a worldwide rebellion against Christ's rule (20:7–10). Therefore, Scripture speaks of salvation during the millennium (Isaiah 60:3; Zechariah 8:23)—a salvation the 144,000 will no doubt proclaim.

Their Praise

And I heard a voice from heaven, like the sound of many waters and like the sound of loud thunder, and the voice which I heard was like the sound of harpists playing on their harps. And they sang a new song before the throne and before the four living creatures and the elders; and no one could learn the song except the one hundred and forty-four thousand who had been purchased from the earth. (14:2–3)

Standing with the Lamb on Mount Zion, the 144,000 will join in the heavenly song of redemption. With all the the trouble they have faced, one might expect them to be too sorrowful to sing. However, they will joyously praise the Lord for their protection and triumph.

This is not the first time John heard a voice from heaven (4:1; 10:4, 8; 11:12; 12:10), nor the last (verse 13; 18:4; 19:1). The voice he heard was very loud and continuous, "like the sound of many waters and like the sound of loud thunder" (cf. Ezekiel 43:2; Revelation 1:15; 19:6).

The mighty voice was not mere noise. It had a musical quality, "like the sound of harpists playing on their harps." The reference to harpists and harps suggests that the voice expressed joy (2 Samuel 6:5; 1 Chronicles 13:8; 15:16, 28; 2 Chronicles 5:12–13; Nehemiah 12:27; Psalms 33:2; 71:22; 144:9; 150:3). Heaven will resound with loud praise when Jesus returns in triumph.

The new song sung in heaven is the song of redemption. The angels will join the Old Testament saints, the raptured church, and the redeemed tribulation martyrs in praising God for salvation. All heaven will overflow with praise because God's redemptive work culminating in the return of Christ is accomplished.

John notes that "no one could learn the song except the one hundred and forty-four thousand who had been purchased from the earth." Why the song is restricted to the one hundred and forty-four thousand is not stated. However, it is clear that the focus is upon the praise of Jesus for His redemptive work.

Their Purity
These are the ones who have not been defiled with women, for they have kept themselves chaste. (14:4a)

The worship of Antichrist during the tribulation will be unspeakably vile and perverse. In the midst of that darkness the 144,000 will shine forth like beacons of purity. Despite the rampant sexual sin that surrounds them, they will not be defiled with women, but will keep themselves chaste. That the specific sin that they will avoid involves women indicates that sexual purity is in view here, not detachment from the corrupt world system. What it means is that they will stand apart from the sin of their culture.

Their Partisanship
These are the ones who follow the Lamb wherever He goes. (14:4*b*)

The 144,000 are further characterized as the ones who "follow the Lamb wherever He goes." The Oxford English Dictionary defines a partisan as "one who takes part or sides with another . . . a devoted or zealous supporter." The triumphant 144,000 will be completely loyal to the Lamb, no matter the cost.

It is such loyal, devoted followers that Jesus seeks. In Matthew 16:24 He said, "If anyone wishes to come after Me, he must deny himself, and take up his cross and follow Me."

Their Purpose
These have been purchased from among men as first fruits to God and to the Lamb. (14:4*c*)

John explains that the 144,000 "have been purchased from among men." But while all believers have been purchased by God, the 144,000 were purchased for a special purpose. In the Old Testament the first fruits were offered to God to be used in His service (Deuteronomy 18:3–5). The 144,000, like the first fruits offering, will be set apart for divine service. The purpose of their lives will be to serve the Lord by proclaiming the gospel to the lost.

Their Precision
And no lie was found in their mouth; (14:5*a*)

The 144,000 will not propagate Satan's lies, but will speak God's truth. In all generations, triumphant Christians are characterized by "speaking the truth in love" (Ephesians 4:15). Knowing the vital importance of "accurately handling the word of truth," they will "be diligent to present [themselves] approved to God as [workmen] who [do] not need to be ashamed" (2 Timothy 2:15).

Their Perfection
they are blameless. (14:5*b*)

Because they will trust in God's power and lead lives characterized by purity, the 144,000 will be blameless. That does not, of course, mean that they will be sinless, but they will be above reproach, leading godly lives before all who see them.

THE THREE ANGELS (14:6–11)

The three angels do not appear in sequential or chronological order. Instead, they address activities that stretch across the tribulation period. Their messages anticipate the judgment of the seventh trumpet (11:15; 15; 16), which includes the final judgments at the end of the tribulation. The messages they bring are designed to produce a fear leading to saving faith. God will graciously offer sinners another opportunity to repent before unleashing the terrifying bowl judgments (16:1ff.). The first angel preaches the gospel, the second pronounces judgment, and the third promises damnation.

The First Angel: Preaching the Gospel
And I saw another angel flying in midheaven, having an eternal gospel to preach to those who live on the earth, and to every nation and tribe and tongue and people; and he said with a loud voice, "Fear God, and give Him glory, because the hour of His judgment has come; worship Him who made the heaven and the earth and sea and springs of waters." (14:6–7)

The specific angel that John saw is not revealed. While angels appear in every chapter from chapters 4 through 12, the nearest reference is to

Michael and his angels (12:7). The verses could also point back to the seventh angel (11:15). In any case, another of the countless myriads of angels (5:11) is selected for a very special purpose. Dramatically, the angel appears in the sky "flying in midheaven." "Midheaven" refers to the point in the sky where the sun reaches its high point at noon (8:13; 19:17). From that point, the angel would be most visible to those on the earth. There he will also be beyond the reach of Antichrist. This preaching angel will be unreachable and his ministry unhindered.

As he flies through the sky, the angel will have "an eternal gospel to preach." This is the only occurrence of the noun for "gospel" in John's writings, though the related verb translated "to preach" also appears in 10:7. Like a multifaceted jewel, Scripture describes the gospel in various terms, each looking at it from a different viewpoint, including the gospel of the kingdom, the gospel of God, the gospel of the grace of God, the gospel of the glory of Christ, and the gospel of salvation (Matthew 4:23; Mark 1:14; Acts 20:24; 2 Corinthians 4:4; Ephesisans 1:13). Here it is described as "eternal" because it provides the means to eternal life.

The angel's message is addressed to "those who live on the earth," a phrase always used in Revelation to refer to unbelievers. The all-inclusive phrase "every nation and tribe and tongue and people" stresses the comprehensive, worldwide nature of the angel's proclamation. The angel will call out with a loud voice to all unregenerate people everywhere. His loud voice ensures that he will be heard and emphasizes the urgency of his message. The angel's message to sinners is "Fear God, and give Him glory." He will call the people of the world to change their allegiance to the Lamb.

Unbelievers will be called to fear and glorify God immediately "because the hour of His judgment has come." This is the first occurrence of this specific Greek word for "judgment" in Revelation. It will appear again in 16:7, 18:10, and 19:2. Up to this point in Revelation, the word "wrath" has been used to describe God's judgment. God's righteous judgments are the outpouring of His wrath against the stubborn and unrepentant world.

It would seem that the angel's warnings would be superfluous. After all, by this point people will have experienced the devastating seal and trumpet judgments. The earth will have been devastated by worldwide wars, famines, and earthquakes, eventually they will realize those disasters are God's judgments (cf. 6:15–17), yet they will defiantly refuse to repent (9:20–21). Still, in His grace and mercy, God will again call sinners to repentance through the preaching of this angel. The angel gives one final reason for sinners to turn from Antichrist to God, proclaiming that people should "worship Him who made the heaven and the earth and sea and springs of waters." The created universe both offers proof of God's existence and provides grounds for worshiping Him (Psalm 19:1–4).

The Second Angel: Pronouncing Judgment
And another angel, a second one, followed, saying, "Fallen, fallen is Babylon the great, she who has made all the nations drink of the wine of the passion of her immorality." (14:8)

Unlike the first one, the second angel does not preach the good news of the gospel, but pronounces the bad news of judgment. Sadly, that implies that the first angel's message was largely rejected. The second angel's equally brief and direct message is "Fallen, fallen is Babylon the great." The repetition underscores the certainty of Babylon's judgment. Babylon's future fall is so certain that it can be spoken of as though it has already taken place. Babylon in this passage refers not just to the city, but to Antichrist's worldwide political, economic, and religious empire.

The final Babylon, personified as a harlot (17:1–5), is described as "she who has made all the nations drink of the wine of the passion of her immorality." The world will be intoxicated and seduced by the Babylonian false religion headed by Antichrist. The Greek word translated "passion" describes strong, consuming desires. As a result of their passion, sinners will engage in great rebellion. Having consumed the wine of the seductive harlot, the nations of the world will continue on their course of spiritual defection.

The Third Angel: Promising Damnation

Then another angel, a third one, followed them, saying with a loud voice, "If anyone worships the beast and his image, and receives a mark on his forehead or on his hand, he also will drink of the wine of the wrath of God, which is mixed in full strength in the cup of His anger; and he will be tormented with fire and brimstone in the presence of the holy angels and in the presence of the Lamb. And the smoke of their torment goes up forever and ever; they have no rest day and night, those who worship the beast and his image, and whoever receives the mark of his name." (14:9–11)

The three angels appear in a logical, perhaps chronological, sequence. The third angel will deliver his warning with a loud voice, so that all will hear and understand his message. God, being perfectly holy and righteous, judges people because they reject what they know to be true. That is why everyone sentenced to hell will be without excuse (Romans 1:20; 2:1).

The third angel's dire warning is addressed to anyone who "worships the beast and his image, and receives a mark on his forehead or on his hand." The angel warns that a terrible fate awaits those who persist in worshiping Antichrist. Once again, God graciously calls on sinners to repent in the final hour.

Those who drank the wine of the harlot Babylon also will drink of the wine of the wrath of God, "which is mixed in full strength in the cup of His anger." To drink of the wine of the wrath of God is to experience His wrath (Job 21:20; Psalm 75:8; Isaiah 51:17, 22; Jeremiah 25:15). The full fury of God's wrath, so long restrained, will be unleashed. John describes that terrifying reality by noting that "God's wrath will be mixed in full strength in the cup of His anger." "Mixed in full strength" refers to the ancient practice of diluting wine with water. The wine filling the cup of God's anger is strong, undiluted wine. God's wrath will be undiluted vengeance, unmixed with any trace of compassion.

The horrifying fate awaiting the person who drinks the wine of the wrath of God is to "be tormented with fire and brimstone." The verb translated "be tormented" speaks of the ceaseless infliction of unbearable pain. The noun form of that verb is used in Luke 16:23 to describe the agony of the rich man in Hades. Fire and brimstone are often associated in Scripture with divine judgment (Genesis 19:24–25; Luke 17:29). Hell, the final resting place of the unregenerate, is described as the "lake of fire which burns with brimstone" (19:20; 20:10; 21:8).

The third angel concludes his message declaring that "the smoke of their torment goes up forever and ever; they have no rest day and night." His description of hell as the place where the smoke of the torment of the wicked goes up forever and ever (20:10) is consistent with the rest of Scripture (cf. Isaiah 66:24; Daniel 12:2; Matthew 3:12; Luke 3:17; 2 Thessalonians 1:9).

So these three angels deliver God's last call to repentance before the final judgments fall and the Lord Jesus Christ returns. But God's gracious warnings will go unheeded by most of the sinful world. There is perhaps no clearer illustration in Scripture of the sad truth that "men loved the darkness rather than the Light, for their deeds were evil" (John 3:19).

THE SAINTS OF GOD (14:12–13)

The most startling pronouncement of blessing in all of Scripture is found in verse 13. Amazingly, this second of seven Revelation beatitudes (1:3; 16:15; 19:9; 20:6; 22:7, 14) pronounces blessing on the dead. Such a thought is incomprehensible to most people, who view death as something to be avoided.

Why are these dead blessed? The answer the beatitude presents is twofold: The dead in view here are blessed because of how they lived and because of how they died.

How They Lived
Here is the perseverance of the saints who keep the commandments of God and their faith in Jesus. (14:12)

The phrase "the perseverance of the saints" introduces one of the most important teachings in Scripture. All those God has elected, called, and justified will never lose their faith, but persevere until death. That reality provides assurance to every true believer in Christ. It reveals that believers' deaths are blessed because death ushers them into the glories of heaven.

The persevering character of saving faith is never more clearly and powerfully seen than in this passage. No group of believers will face stronger assaults on their faith than the tribulation saints. This large group of believers will include both Gentiles (7:9) and Jews (12:17). They will be saved through the ministries of the two witnesses (11:3–13) and the 144,000 (7:1–8; 14:1–5). The tribulation believers will endure the most intense persecution in human history. Yet God will set a limit on the tribulation so that the elect will not suffer more than they can bear (1 Corinthians 10:13). There is no stronger evidence that saving faith perseveres than the reality that the most tested believers in history will maintain their saving faith until the end.

The perseverance of the tribulation saints will be evident because they will "keep the commandments of God." They also will manifest perseverance through "their faith in Jesus." Even the threat of execution (13:15) will not cause them to abandon their faith in Christ. Like the heroes of faith listed in Hebrews 11, they will maintain their testimony until the end—even if that end includes martyrdom.

How They Died

And I heard a voice from heaven, saying, "Write, 'Blessed are the dead who die in the Lord from now on!'" "Yes," says the Spirit, "so that they may rest from their labors, for their deeds follow with them." (14:13)

Having lived with perseverance, the tribulation saints will die with promise. This is the sixth time in Revelation that John heard a voice from heaven (10:4, 8; 11:12; 12:10; 14:2). He will hear such a voice three more times (18:4; 19:5; 21:3). The voice commanded John to write. Twelve times in Revelation John is told to write. The apostle was under a divine mandate to record the visions he saw.

The heavenly voice ordered John to write, "Blessed are the dead who die in the Lord." These martyrs are blessed not only because they lived life to the fullest in obedience, trust, and purpose, but also because they died in the Lord. Even if there were no heaven, that would still be the best way to live. But there is heaven to follow this life for God's people; therefore the deaths of the tribulation saints will also be eternally blessed. The voice informed John that not only those already dead, but also those who die from now on are blessed. The martyred believers from that point until the end of the tribulation will have nothing to fear. Their deaths, too, will be blessed.

The Holy Spirit is quoted directly in Revelation only here and in 22:17. His emphatic "Yes" shows that He agrees with the heavenly voice that the dead are blessed. As their Comforter, the Holy Spirit longs to see that suffering end. He adds two further reasons for the tribulation martyrs' blessedness.

First, the Spirit declares them blessed because they may "rest from their labors." The Greek word translated "labors" describes difficult, exhausting work. Certainly the tribulation saints will experience the whole gamut of that word's meanings. They will be filled with deep sorrow as they watch those they love suffer torment and death. Their lives will be a hard, difficult, dangerous struggle for survival. Not having the mark of the beast, they will be excluded from society, unable to buy or sell, and live lives on the run as hunted fugitives. Death will come as a welcome relief.

The Holy Spirit also pronounces the tribulation martyrs blessed because "their deeds follow with them." The Greek word for "deeds" refers to their service to the Lord. When these believers go to heaven, the record of their diligent labor will follow along with them. The Bible teaches that God will reward believers in heaven for their earthly service to Him (Hebrews 6:10).

HARVEST TIME:
THE GRAIN HARVEST (14:14–16)

Joel, Isaiah, and the Lord Jesus Christ all spoke of a coming harvest of divine wrath when the Messiah will execute final judgment (Joel

3:12–13, 21; Isaiah 63:1–6; Matthew 13:30, 39–42). That final outpouring of the judgmental fury of the Lamb is the theme of the remaining text
of Revelation 14.

This passage pictures the final harvest of divine wrath in two agricul-
tural motifs: the grain harvest (verses 14–16) and the grape harvest (verses
17–20).The grain harvest symbolizes the seven bowl judgments. The grape
harvest symbolizes the judgment of Armageddon. Both harvests involve a
sickle and reaping.

1. The Reaper
*Then I looked, and behold, a white cloud, and sitting on the cloud was
one like a son of man, having a golden crown on His head and a sharp
sickle in His hand.* (14:14)

The familiar phrase "I looked, and behold" often introduces a new and
important subject in Revelation (cf. 4:1; 6:2, 5, 8; 7:9; 14:1). What caught
John's attention was "a white cloud," an image drawn from Daniel
7:13–14. John saw "sitting on the cloud . . . one like a son of man." This is
Jesus Christ, coming to establish His kingdom in fulfillment of Daniel's
prophecy. The brilliant, white cloud symbolizes His glory and majesty
(1:7; Acts 1:9). The reaper is sitting as He waits for the proper time to
stand and begin the reaping. That reaping (the seven bowl judgments)
will be followed by Christ's return to establish His kingdom.

The description of Christ as "one like a son of man" also derives from
Daniel's prophecy (Daniel 7:13). It was Christ's favorite title during His
earthly ministry. when He "emptied Himself, taking the form of a bond-
servant, and [was] made in the likeness of men . . . [and was] found in
appearance as a man" (Philippians 2:7–8).[1] This is the last time Scripture
refers to Him by that title, and it presents a marked contrast with the first
time the New Testament calls Him the Son of Man. Then He did not even
have a place to lay His head (Matthew 8:20). Now He is about to take
possession of the entire earth.

The reaper is further described as "having a golden crown on His
head." This crown is not the kind worn by a king (Greek *diadēma*) but the

type of crown (Greek *stephanos*) worn by victors in war or athletic events. It pictures the Son of Man as the triumphant conqueror over all His enemies (Matthew 24:30).

The reaper also had "a sharp sickle in His hand." A sickle was a long, curved, razor-sharp iron blade attached to a long, broomstick-like wooden handle. Sickles were used to harvest grain. They were held with both hands spread apart and swept back and forth, their sharp blades would cut off the grain stalks at ground level. The picture is of the Lord Jesus Christ mowing down His enemies like a harvester cutting grain.

2. The Ripeness
And another angel came out of the temple, crying out with a loud voice to Him who sat on the cloud, "Put in your sickle and reap, for the hour to reap has come, because the harvest of the earth is ripe." (14:15)

Another angel, the fourth one mentioned in this chapter (verses 6, 8–9), appears on the scene. The first three angels proclaimed that judgment was coming. The fourth brings the command to execute it. This angel came out of the heavenly temple before the throne of God. In a loud voice conveying the authority delegated to him from God, the angel cries out, "Put in your sickle and reap, for the hour to reap has come, because the harvest of the earth is ripe." He delivers the message from God the Father to the Son of Man that it is time for Him to move in judgment. God's anger has reached its limit, and His wrath is poured out. The verb translated "is ripe" actually means "dried up" or "withered." The grain pictured here has passed the point of any usefulness and is fit only to be "gathered up and burned with fire" (Matthew 13:40).

3. The Reaping
Then He who sat on the cloud swung His sickle over the earth, and the earth was reaped. (14:16)

Here is one of the most tragic and sobering statements in all of Scripture. Without fanfare, it announces the executing of divine judgment. The frightening details of that judgment are unfolded in Revelation 16. Those seven rapid-fire bowl judgments mark the first phase of the final reaping of the earth.

Harvest Time:
The Grape Harvest (14:17-20)

The vision of the grain harvest is followed by the vision of the grape harvest, which speaks of the judgment that takes place at the battle of Armageddon. This judgment is more dramatic because of the imagery of the winepress.

1. The Reaper

And another angel came out of the temple which is in heaven, and he also had a sharp sickle. (14:17)

The reaper in this vision is not the Son of Man, but an angel, the fifth one mentioned in chapter 14. Like the fourth angel (verse 15), he came out of the temple in heaven and "also had a sharp sickle." That an angel is pictured in this vision as the reaper is not surprising. The Son of Man will be assisted by holy angels in His final judgment (Matthew 13:39, 49; 2 Thessalonians 1:7).

2. The Ripeness

Then another angel, the one who has power over fire, came out from the altar; and he called with a loud voice to him who had the sharp sickle, saying, "Put in your sharp sickle and gather the clusters from the vine of the earth, because her grapes are ripe." (14:18)

As John watched, another angel appeared, the sixth one in the vision. That title "the one who has power over fire" is closely connected with the fact that he "came out from the altar." Unlike the angel in verse 17, this angel does not come from the throne of God, but from the altar associated with the prayers of the saints. His appearance means that the time had come for those prayers to be answered.

Leaving the altar, "he called with a loud [and urgent] voice to him who had the sharp sickle, saying, 'Put in your sharp sickle and gather the clusters from the vine of the earth, because her grapes are ripe.'" In answer to the saints' prayers, the time for the reaping of judgment comes. The word "ripe" is not the same Greek word used in verse 15. This word refers to something fully ripe and in its prime. It pictures earth's wicked people as bursting with the juice of wickedness and ready for the harvest of righteousness.

3. The Reaping

So the angel swung his sickle to the earth and gathered the clusters from the vine of the earth, and threw them into the great wine press of the wrath of God. And the wine press was trodden outside the city, and blood came out from the wine press, up to the horses' bridles, for a distance of two hundred miles. (14:19–20)

What resulted when the angel swung his sickle was catastrophic. All the enemies of God who survive the seven bowl judgments will be gathered like grape clusters from the vine of the earth and flung into the great wine press of the wrath of God. A winepress consisted of two stone basins connected by a trough. Grapes would be trampled in the upper basin, and the juice would collect in the lower one. The splattering of the juice as the grapes are stomped vividly pictures the splattered blood of those who will be destroyed (cf. Isaiah 63:3; Lamentation 1:15; Joel 3:13).

The staggering, horrifying bloodbath of the battle of Armageddon will be so widespread that blood will come out from the winepress, up to the horses' bridles, for a distance of two hundred miles. "The winepress [will be] trodden outside the city," as the Lord protects Jerusalem from the carnage of the battle of Armageddon (cf. 11:2; Daniel 11:45; Zechariah 14:1–4). There will be millions of people engaged in the battle of Armageddon, as all the nations gather together to fight against Christ.

Still, it is difficult to imagine that they could produce a flow of blood "up to the horses' bridles [about four feet deep] for a distance of two hundred miles" (literally "1,600 stadia"). A better interpretation, whether there are actual horses involved or not, sees this as hyperbole to suggest the slaughter in which blood will splatter into the air profusely along the whole length of the battle. When the slaughter reaches its peak, blood could flow deeply in troughs and streambeds.

Armageddon, as this passage indicates, will actually be a slaughter rather than a battle. When the Lord Jesus Christ returns, Antichrist, the false prophet, and all their human and demonic forces will be immediately destroyed. Those who refuse to repent, even after repeated warnings, will learn firsthand the sobering truth that "it is a terrifying thing to fall into the hands of the living God" (Hebrews 10:31). They would do well to heed admonition of Psalm 2: "Do homage to the Son, that He not become angry,and you perish in the way, for His wrath may soon be kindled. How blessed are all who take refuge in Him!" (verse 12).

17

The Bowl
JUDGMENTS

(15:1–16:21)

Revelation 15 and 16 present the specific phenomena of the final outpouring of God's wrath before Christ's return. That wrath is expressed by the effects of the seventh trumpet (11:15), which are the seven bowl judgments described in Revelation 16.

Remember, though, that God's nature encompasses not only righteousness and holiness, but also grace and mercy. Even during the devastating judgments of the tribulation, God will continue to call sinners to salvation. He will do so using the 144,000 Jewish evangelists (7:2–8; 14:1–5), the two witnesses (11:3–13), a host of redeemed Gentiles and Jews (7:9–17), even an angel flying in the sky (14:6–7). This reflects the amazing divine paradox: God is busily working to save sinners from His own wrath. And so, as the outpouring of divine wrath escalates, God's evangelistic efforts will escalate as well. The result will be the greatest harvest of souls in human history (cf. 7:9).

PREVIEW TO THE BOWL JUDGMENTS:
THE OUTPOURING OF GOD'S WRATH (15:1-8)

Chapter 15, the shortest in Revelation, forms a preview of these rapid-fire judgments. As this chapter unfolds, three motives for the final outpouring of God's wrath become evident.

1. The Vengeance of God

Then I saw another sign in heaven, great and marvelous, seven angels who had seven plagues, which are the last, because in them the wrath of God is finished. And I saw something like a sea of glass mixed with fire, and those who had been victorious over the beast and his image and the number of his name, standing on the sea of glass, holding harps of God. (15:1–2)

A scene in heaven anticipates the bowl judgments, as it did in the case of the seal (chapters 4–5) and trumpet (8:2–6) judgments. This is the third heavenly sign that John has seen in Revelation (12:1, 3). The terms "great" and "marvelous" express the enormous importance of this sign as it contains the final outpouring of God's wrath on the wicked, unrepentant sinners of the earth.

The sign itself consists of seven angels who had seven plagues. The same beings who serve God's people will bring God's wrath to the sinful world. The word translated "plague" literally means "a blow," or "a wound." Thus the seven plagues are not really diseases or epidemics, but deadly blows that will strike the world with killing impact.

These seven plagues (the seven bowl judgments) are the last and worst plagues, because in them the wrath of God is finished. It is important to note that the fact that they are called the last implies that the preceding trumpet and seal judgments were also plagues expressing the wrath of God. God's wrath extends throughout the tribulation and is not confined to a brief period at the very end, as some argue. That they are the last also indicates that the bowls come after the seals and trumpets in chronological sequence.

In verse 2, John "saw something like a sea of glass mixed with fire." The sea was not an actual ocean, because in 21:1 he "saw a new heaven and a new earth; for the first heaven and the first earth passed away, and there is no longer any sea." What John saw was a transparent crystal platform before God's throne, shimmering and glistening like a tranquil, sunlit sea (4:6; cf. Exodus 24:10; Ezekiel 1:22).

But the tranquil beauty of the sea was mixed with the fire of God's judgment, which was about to be poured out on the earth. Those who reject God's grace and mercy face "a terrifying expectation of judgment and the fury of a fire which will consume the adversaries" (Hebrews 10:27), because "our God is a consuming fire" (Hebrews 12:29). Fire is frequently associated in Scripture with God's judgment (Numbers 11:1; 16:35; Deuteronomy 9:3; Psalms 50:3; 97:3; Isaiah 66:15; 2 Thessalonians 1:7–9; 2 Peter 3:7).

John saw gathered around the throne of God those who had been victorious over the beast. These are the believers redeemed during the tribulation (6:9–11; 7:9–17; 12:11, 17; 14:1–5, 12–13). They will be victorious over the beast because of their undying faith in the Lord Jesus Christ. Revelation 20:4–6 describes their resurrection and reward. Tribulation saints will also triumph over the beast's image and the number of his name. The false prophet will perform many lying wonders to deceive people. One of them will be to set up an image of the beast, which he will order everyone to worship on pain of death. The false prophet will also require everyone to receive a mark representing either the beast's name, or the number of his name. Those without that mark will face execution and will be unable to buy or sell. But tribulation believers will, by God's power, eternally triumph over the whole enterprise of Satan, the beast, and the false prophet. Even those martyred for their triumphant faith will receive their glorious rewards (20:4).

That the tribulation saints are seen holding harps of God indicates that they are rejoicing and singing praise to God. Harps were also associated with praise earlier in Revelation (5:8; 14:2) and frequently in the Old Testament (2 Samuel 6:5; 1 Chronicles 13:8; Psalms 33:2; 71:22; 144:9; 150:3). These believers rejoice because their prayers for God to take vengeance on their persecutors (6:9–10) are about to be answered.

2. The Character of God
*And they sang the song of Moses, the bond-servant of God, and the song
of the Lamb, saying,*

> *"Great and marvelous are Your works,*
> *O Lord God, the Almighty;*
> *Righteous and true are Your ways,*
> *King of the nations!*
> *Who will not fear, O Lord, and glorify Your name?*
> *For You alone are holy;*
> *For all the nations will come and worship before You,*
> *For Your righteous acts have been revealed."* (15:3–4)

The song sung by the glorified saints before the throne is an anthem of
praise to God. The ultimate motive of God's wrath—to uphold His holy,
righteous character—demands that He judge sinners. It is God's holy
nature, soon to be revealed in judgment against their persecutors, that
elicits this song from the redeemed. The song of Moses is the first of several songs recorded in the Old Testament. It comes from the time of the
Exodus. As the bond-servant of God, Moses was called to lead the people
of Israel out of captivity in Egypt. God delivered them from Pharaoh's
pursuing army by parting the Red Sea, stacking the water on either side
of a path, thus allowing the Israelites to cross safely on dry land. After
they were safely across, the collapsing waters drowned the Egyptian army.
On the far side of the Red Sea, the Israelites sang a song of praise to God
for their deliverance.

The redeemed saints before God's throne also will sing the song of
the Lamb, who is their eternal Redeemer (5:8–14). Like the song of
Moses, the song of the Lamb expresses the themes of God's faithfulness,
deliverance of His people, and judgment of His enemies. The words of the
song recorded here do not match exactly either the song of Moses in
Exodus 15, or the song of the Lamb in Revelation 5. But the themes and
many of the key terms are similar.

The song of these redeemed saints extols God's character as the omnipotent, immutable, sovereign, perfect, and righteous Creator and Judge. Because He is all that, God must and will judge sinners; if He ignored their sin, He would not be holy, righteous, and true to His nature. The song closes with joyful anticipation of the millennial reign of Christ, when all the nations will come and worship before God. In the words of the psalmist, "All the earth will worship You, and will sing praises to You; they will sing praises to Your name" (Psalm 66:4).

3. The Plan of God

After these things I looked, and the temple of the tabernacle of testimony in heaven was opened, and the seven angels who had the seven plagues came out of the temple, clothed in linen, clean and bright, and girded around their chests with golden sashes. Then one of the four living creatures gave to the seven angels seven golden bowls full of the wrath of God, who lives forever and ever. And the temple was filled with smoke from the glory of God and from His power; and no one was able to enter the temple until the seven plagues of the seven angels were finished. (15:5–8)

Each of the angelic players in this unfolding drama will fulfill his assigned duty according to God's plan. It has always been God's purpose to judge sinners and destroy sin. The "eternal fire . . . has [already] been prepared for the devil and his angels" (Matthew 25:41) and awaits those whom God will one day sentence to eternal punishment there. Here, in a new vision, they are given the instruments of execution.

As it does throughout Revelation, the phrase "after these things I looked" introduces a startling, dramatic new vision. Something is about to draw John's attention away from the redeemed saints singing their praises before God's glorious throne. This new vision revealed to him the bowl judgments (16:1–21), but first John saw the angels who will carry out those judgments. As he watched, the "temple of the tabernacle of testimony in heaven was opened." "Temple" refers to the Holy of Holies, the inner sanctuary where God's presence dwells, emphasizing that God is the source of the plagues.

As John watched, the seven angels who had the seven plagues came out of the temple. "They were clothed in linen, clean and bright," their apparel representing their holiness and purity. As befits such glorious and holy beings, the angels were "girded around their chests with golden sashes" that ran across the torso from the shoulder to the waist.

One of the four living creatures, a high-ranking cherubim, gave the seven angels "seven golden bowls full of the wrath of God." This Greek word for "bowls" refers to shallow saucers. The imagery is not that of a stream being poured gradually out of a pitcher, but of the whole contents of the shallow saucers being hurled down in an instant flood of judgment. Bowls were part of the temple furnishings (1 Kings 7:50; Zechariah 14:20) and were associated with the sacrifices (Exodus 27:3; 38:3). Those who refuse to drink the cup of salvation (Psalm 116:13) will be drowned in the judgments poured from the bowls of wrath. Because God lives forever and ever, He has the power to put an end to sin, so that it cannot exist again forever in His holy presence.

Out of the heavenly temple came not only the angels, but also smoke symbolizing the glory of God and His power. Smoke, an emblem of majesty (Exodus 19:16–18), also symbolized God's glorious presence in the Old Testament tabernacle or temple (Exodus 40:34–35; 1 Kings 8:10–11; Isaiah 6:1–4). This smoke also symbolizes God's wrath. No one was able to enter the temple until the seven plagues were finished. The glory cloud will remain in the heavenly temple until the earth is completely purged and prepared for the King and His kingdom.

THE BOWL JUDGMENTS (16:1-21)

Some writers have seen these bowl judgments as repeating the seal and trumpet judgments. There are similarities, but many more differences, especially in the degree of devastation. The bowls are universal, more intense than the previous judgments, and are called "the last" judgments (15:1), showing they do not go back in time to repeat earlier plagues.

The First Bowl

Then I heard a loud voice from the temple, saying to the seven angels, "Go and pour out on the earth the seven bowls of the wrath of God." So the first angel went and poured out his bowl on the earth; and it became a loathsome and malignant sore on the people who had the mark of the beast and who worshiped his image. (16:1–2)

As judgments began to unfold, John "heard a loud voice from the temple." The startling impact of loud voices is heard twenty times in Revelation. The Greek word translated "loud" appears six times in this chapter (usually translated "great"), again emphasizing the magnitude of the judgments recorded here. His loud voice is heard again after the seventh bowl is poured out (verse 17).

The seven angels were given the seven bowls containing the final judgments. God commands all seven of them, "Go and pour out on the earth the seven bowls of the wrath of God." As are all the judgments, the seven bowls will be supernatural acts of God. The text does not accept a natural, scientific explanation, as some commentators propose. The judgments will hit far too rapidly for any explanation other than that they come from God Himself. In fact, there is only a brief pause, just long enough for one of the angels to affirm that the bowl judgments are just and righteous (verses 5–7).

Responding immediately to God's command, "the first angel went and poured out his bowl on the earth." As shallow saucers, their contents are not slowly, gradually poured out, but dumped all at once. The sloshing out of the first bowl results in a sore that afflicts people. "Loathsome and malignant" translate two general Greek words for evil. Used together, they stress that the sores will be festering, painful, and incurable. These sores will bring unrelieved physical torment to those who have rejected Jesus Christ.

The sores will not affect believers, whose names have been "written from the foundation of the world in the book of life of the Lamb who has been slain" (13:8). They will come only upon those who chose to follow Antichrist, received his mark to show their allegiance (13:16–17), and worshiped his image (13:12).

The Second Bowl
The second angel poured out his bowl into the sea, and it became blood like that of a dead man; and every living thing in the sea died. (16:3)

One of the reasons the bowl judgments will be so devastating is that their effects are cumulative. Before the sores of the first bowl could heal, "the second angel poured out his bowl into the sea, and it became blood like that of a dead man; and every living thing in the sea died." This judgment is similar to the first plague in Egypt (Exodus 7:20–24) and the second trumpet judgment (8:8–9), but this time the effects will be much more intense. Since the oceans cover approximately 70 percent of the earth's surface, the effects of this judgment will be worldwide.

Exactly what supernatural means God will use to destroy the oceans is not revealed, but the effects will resemble those of the phenomenon known as the red tide, concentrated, toxic species of algae kill higher forms of marine life, including shellfish, fish, and marine mammals. The stench from the dead, decaying bodies of every living thing in the sea (only partial death occurred at the second trumpet) will be unimaginable. The transforming of the world's seas into putrid pools of stinking death will be graphic testimony to the wickedness of man and a reversal to the day when God originally gave life to all sea creatures (Genesis 1:21).

The Third Bowl
Then the third angel poured out his bowl into the rivers and the springs of waters; and they became blood. And I heard the angel of the waters saying, "Righteous are You, who are and who were, O Holy One, because You judged these things; for they poured out the blood of saints and prophets, and You have given them blood to drink. They deserve it." And I heard the altar saying, "Yes, O Lord God, the Almighty, true and righteous are Your judgments." (16:4–7)

When the third angel poured out his bowl, the same appalling judgment that affected the oceans was visited on the rivers and the springs, as they too "became blood." By the time the third bowl is poured out, freshwater will be in critically short supply. The third trumpet judgment (8:10–11) will result in the poisoning of one third of the world's freshwater. Additionally, the two witnesses will "have the power to shut up the sky, so that rain will not fall during the days of their prophesying [the last three and a half years of the tribulation]; and they have power over the waters to turn them into blood" (11:6). The temporary restraining of the earth's winds (7:1) will also cause drought. With no wind to move clouds and weather systems, the hydrological cycle will be disrupted and no rain will fall.

The destruction of what is left of the earth's freshwater will cause unthinkable hardship and suffering. The scene is so unimaginably horrible that people will wonder how a God of compassion, mercy, and grace could send such a judgment. And so there is a brief interlude in the pouring out of the judgments while an angel speaks in God's defense.

Appropriately, it is the angel of the waters who defends God's righteous judgment in song in 15:3–4. In contrast to the curses and blasphemies of men (verses 9, 11), the angel declares, "Righteous are You, who are and who were, O Holy One, because You judged these things." God's judgment of sinners is unquestionably righteous because He is the Holy One. And although His wrath is terrifying and deadly, it is a just and appropriate response to sinners' rejection of Him.

Fittingly, those who have spilled so much innocent blood will be given blood to drink. In the angel's chilling words, "They deserve it." God is just and holy and will execute vengeance for His people (Romans 12:19; Hebrews 10:30). Having willfully rejected the knowledge of the truth (Hebrews 10:26), there is nothing left for the unbelieving world but to receive what they deserve, "a terrifying expectation of judgment and the fury of a fire which will consume the adversaries" (Hebrews 10:27).

Then the apostle John heard the altar saying, "Yes, O Lord God, the Almighty, true and righteous are Your judgments." The personified altar echoes the sentiments of the angel with words similar to 15:3. It may be that the very altar under which the saints were earlier seen praying for vengeance (6:9–11) now affirms that God's true and righteous judgments are the answer to those prayers.

The Fourth Bowl

The fourth angel poured out his bowl upon the sun, and it was given to it to scorch men with fire. Men were scorched with fierce heat; and they blasphemed the name of God who has the power over these plagues, and they did not repent so as to give Him glory. (16:8–9)

In contrast to the first three angels, who poured out their bowls on the earth, the fourth angel poured out his bowl upon the sun. Searing heat exceeding anything in human experience will scorch men so severely that it will seem that the atmosphere is on fire. Those who will be scorched with the sun's fierce heat are the same "people who had the mark of the beast and who worshiped his image" (verse 2).

Another serious consequence of the sun's intense heat will be the melting of the polar ice caps. The resulting rise in the oceans' water level will inundate coastal regions, flooding areas miles inland with the noxious waters of the dead oceans. Widespread damage and loss of life will accompany that flooding, adding further to the unspeakable misery of the devastated planet. Transportation by sea will become impossible.

One would think that the unparalleled disasters of the first four bowl judgments would cause people to repent. Instead "they blasphemed the name of God." Until this point, only the Antichrist has been described as blaspheming (13:1, 5–6); here the world adopts his evil character. Neither grace nor wrath will move their wicked hearts to repentance (cf. 9:20–21; 16:11). In 11:13 the earthquake brought some to repentance, but not in this series of judgments. Such blind, blasphemous hardness of heart is incredible in the face of the devastating judgments they will be undergoing. But like their evil leader, Antichrist, they will continue to hate God and refuse to repent, which would give glory to God as a just and righteous Judge of sin (cf. Joshua 7:19–25).

The Fifth Bowl

Then the fifth angel poured out his bowl on the throne of the beast, and his kingdom became darkened; and they gnawed their tongues because of pain, and they blasphemed the God of heaven because of their pains and their sores; and they did not repent of their deeds. (16:10–11)

As He did long ago in Egypt (Exodus 10:21–29), God will turn up the intense suffering of the sinful world by turning out the lights. After the fifth angel poured out his bowl on the throne of the beast, his kingdom became darkened (cf. 9:2; Exodus 10:21–23). Commentators disagree over where specifically this bowl will be dumped. Some think it will be on the actual throne that the beast sits on; others on his capital city of Babylon; still others on his entire kingdom. It is best to see the throne as a reference to his kingdom, since the bowl poured out on the throne darkens the whole kingdom. Regardless of the exact location where the bowl is dumped, the result is that darkness engulfs the whole earth, which is Antichrist's worldwide kingdom. The beast will be as helpless before the power of God as anyone else.

The cumulative effect of the painful sores, fouled oceans, lack of drinking water, intense heat, all engulfed in thick blackness, will bring unbearable misery. Yet, incredibly, the wicked, unbelieving people of the world will still refuse to repent. John notes that they gnawed their tongues because of the most intense and excruciating pain. Still "they did not repent of their deeds." This is the last reference to their unwillingness to repent. The first five plagues were God's final call to repentance. Sinners ignored that call, and are now confirmed in their unbelief. The final two bowls, containing the severest of all the judgments, will be poured out on hardened, implacable impenitents.

The Sixth Bowl

The sixth angel poured out his bowl on the great river, the Euphrates; and its water was dried up, so that the way would be prepared for the kings from the east. And I saw coming out of the mouth of the dragon and out of the mouth of the beast and out of the mouth of the false prophet, three unclean spirits like frogs; for they are spirits of demons, performing signs, which go out to the kings of the whole world, to gather them together for the war of the great day of God, the Almighty.

("Behold, I am coming like a thief. Blessed is the one who stays awake and keeps his clothes, so that he will not walk about naked and men will not see his shame.") And they gathered them together to the place which in Hebrew is called Har-Magedon. (16:12–16)

Unlike the previous five bowls, the sixth has no specific assault on humanity but prepares for what is to come. When his turn came, the sixth angel poured out his bowl on the great river, the Euphrates. The Euphrates appeared earlier in Revelation in connection with the sixth trumpet judgment (9:14), when two hundred million demons who were bound near it were released. It was considered the longest and most significant river in the Middle East and therefore called the great river. Its source is in the snowfields and ice cap high on the slopes of Mount Ararat (located in modern Turkey), from which it flows some eighteen hundred miles before emptying into the Persian Gulf. In ancient times the garden of Eden was located in the vicinity of the Euphrates (Genesis 2:10–14). The Euphrates also formed the eastern boundary of the land God gave to Israel (Genesis 15:18; Deuteronomy 1:7; 11:24; Joshua 1:4). Along with the nearby Tigris, the Euphrates is still the lifeblood of the Fertile Crescent.

By the time the sixth bowl is poured out, the Euphrates will be very different than it is today or has ever been. The blazing heat from the sun associated with the fourth bowl will melt the snow and the ice cap on Mount Ararat. That will vastly increase the volume of water in the Euphrates, causing massive damage and flooding along its course. The bridges spanning the river will surely be destroyed. Thus, the reason for the sixth bowl becomes apparent. As the angel dumped his bowl, the Euphrates's "water was dried up, so that the way would be prepared for the kings from the east." The eastern armies will need to cross the Euphrates to reach their ultimate destination of Armageddon in the land of Palestine.

God's drying up of the Euphrates is not an act of kindness toward the kings from the east, but one of judgment. They and their armies will be entering a deadly trap. The evaporation of the Euphrates will lead them to their doom, just as the parting of the Red Sea led to the destruction of the Egyptian army.

In a grotesque vision, like something out of a horror movie, John "saw coming out of the mouth of the dragon and out of the mouth of the beast and out of the mouth of the false prophet, three unclean spirits like frogs." From the mouth (symbolizing the source of influence) of each member of the unholy trinity (Satan, Antichrist, and the false prophet) came a foul, unclean spirit resembling a frog. Frogs were unclean animals (Leviticus 11:10, 41), but these are not literal frogs. John identified the froglike apparitions as spirits of demons. This graphic illustration pictures the cold-blooded vileness of these demons, who seduce the kings from the east into making the difficult journey to their doom at Armageddon under the demons' deluding influence (cf. 1 Kings 22:19–22).

Amid all the horrors of judgment, deception, and war comes a word of encouragement to believers: "Behold, I am coming like a thief. Blessed is the one who stays awake and keeps his clothes, so that he will not walk about naked and men will not see his shame." This gracious word from heaven will come before the pouring out of the seventh bowl and assure believers that they will not be forgotten. There were similar respites to encourage God's people between the sixth and seventh seals (7:1–17) and between the sixth and seventh trumpets (10:1–11:14). Because the bowl judgments take place in a short period of time, the respite between the sixth and seventh bowls is very brief.

Then the exalted Lord pronounced the third of seven beatitudes in Revelation (1:3; 14:13; 19:9; 20:6; 22:7, 14): "Blessed is the one who stays awake and keeps his clothes, so that he will not walk about naked and men will not see his shame." This describes those who will be prepared for His arrival. The imagery here is of soldiers alert and on duty. Only a soldier who stays awake and keeps his clothes on is ready for combat. Only those whom Jesus finds prepared when He returns will be blessed.

After the brief interlude of encouragement for the redeemed, the prophetic narrative returns to the events of the sixth bowl. The deceiving demon spirits will have gathered the nations "together to the place which in Hebrew is called Har-Magedon." "Har-Magedon" is a Hebrew word meaning "Mount Megiddo." Since there is no specific mountain by that name, and Har can refer to hill country, it is probably a reference to the hill country surrounding the Plain of Megiddo, some sixty miles north of Jerusalem (See Map 2 below). More than two hundred battles have been fought in that region. The Plain of Megiddo and the nearby Plain of Esdraelon will be the focal point for the Battle of Armageddon, which will rage the entire length of Israel as far south as the Edomite city of Bozrah (Isaiah 63:1). Other battles will also occur in the vicinity of Jerusalem (Zechariah 14:1–3).

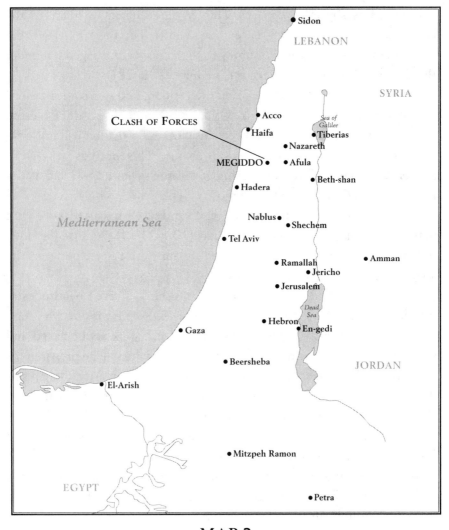

MAP 2

THE BATTLE OF ARMAGEDDON

The Seventh Bowl

Then the seventh angel poured out his bowl upon the air, and a loud voice came out of the temple from the throne, saying, "It is done." And there were flashes of lightning and sounds and peals of thunder; and there was a great earthquake, such as there had not been since man came to be upon the earth, so great an earthquake was it, and so mighty. The great city was split into three parts, and the cities of the nations fell. Babylon the great was remembered before God, to give her the cup of the wine of His fierce wrath. And every island fled away, and the mountains were not found. And huge hailstones, about one hundred pounds each, came down from heaven upon men; and men blasphemed God because of the plague of the hail, because its plague was extremely severe. (16:17–21)

The seventh bowl is the final outpouring of God's wrath on sinners in this present earth. It will be the worst calamity in the world's history. Its effects carry all the way to the establishment of the earthly kingdom of Christ. Like the fourth angel, the seventh angel did not dump his bowl on the earth, but poured it out "upon the air." Its first effects were on the earth's atmosphere, as if God were cleansing the former domain of Satan and his demon hosts (12:9). The earth (verse 2), the sea (verse 3), the waters (verse 4), the sun (verse 8), and finally the air are all the targets of judgment.

As the angel dumped his bowl, a loud voice came out of the temple from the throne. God's solemn declaration "It is done" announces the climax of the final day of the Lord that will spread doom over the entire globe. The perfect tense "it is done" describes a completed action with ongoing results. It is similar to Jesus' final words from the cross, "It is finished" (John 19:30). God's judgment of Christ on Calvary provided salvation for repentant sinners; the judgment of the seventh bowl brings doom to unrepentant sinners.

The pouring out of the seventh bowl dramatically affected the atmosphere; there were flashes of lightning and sounds and peals of thunder. Like the seventh seal (8:5) and the seventh trumpet (11:19), the seventh bowl is introduced with the imagery of a violent thunderstorm. But those earlier storms were mere previews of the mighty storm of wrath that now bursts upon the earth.

Though the seventh bowl was dumped on the earth's atmosphere, it will also have a devastating effect on the earth itself. God will punctuate this final judgment against sinners with an earthquake, just as He did His judgment of sin at Calvary (Matthew 27:51–54). This earthquake will be the most powerful one ever to strike the earth. John described it as "a great earthquake, such as there had not been since man came to be upon the earth." The shaking will be so severe that it will renovate and reconfigure the earth in preparation for the millennial kingdom, restoring it to something like its pre-flood condition (verse 20).

The first effect of this great and mighty earthquake was that "the great city was split into three parts." A comparison with 11:8 clearly identifies the great city as Jerusalem, "the great city . . . where also [the] Lord was crucified." That the great city is distinct from the cities of the nations offers further evidence that Jerusalem is in view. The massive earthquake will split Jerusalem into three parts, beginning a series of geophysical alterations to the city and its surrounding region that will conclude when the Lord Jesus Christ returns. Zechariah 14:4–10 describes these changes in detail. The Mount of Olives will split in two, and a new valley running east and west will be created (Zechariah 14:4). A spring of water will flow year-round from Jerusalem to the Mediterranean and Dead Seas (Zechariah 14:8), causing the desert to blossom like a rose (cf. Isaiah 35:1). Jerusalem will be elevated, and the surrounding region flattened into a plain (Zechariah 14:10). Thus, the purpose of the earthquake as it relates to Jerusalem is not to judge the city, but to enhance it. Jerusalem was judged earlier in the tribulation by an earthquake, which led to the salvation of those who were not killed (11:13). Thus, there is no need for further judgment on that city. The physical changes will prepare Jerusalem for the central role it will play during the millennial kingdom, when Christ will reign there as King (Psalm 110:2; Isaiah 2:3; 24:23; Micah 4:7).

Unlike Jerusalem, which was enhanced by the earthquake, the cities of the nations fell, perhaps simultaneously with the defeat of Antichrist by the Lamb (17:12–14). Specifically singled out is Babylon the great, which "was remembered before God, to give her the cup of the wine of His fierce wrath." As the capital city of Antichrist's empire, Babylon especially will be made to drink the cup of the wine of His fierce wrath (chapters 17 and 18).

The final effect of the earthquake is to prepare the earth for the millennial rule of Christ. To that end, the earth's topography will be drastically altered; "every island fled away, and the mountains were not found." Islands, which are undersea mountains, will disappear. The mountains on land will be flattened (Isaiah 40:4), completing the process that began during the sixth seal (6:12–14).

Those who somehow escape the devastation caused by the earthquake will face another catastrophe, one unprecedented in earth's history. They will be pelted with "huge hailstones, about one hundred pounds each," that will hurtle down from heaven. Unlike the seventh Egyptian plague (Exodus 9:23–24) and the first trumpet judgment (8:7), the force of these hailstones is unimaginable. The Greek term translated "about one hundred pounds" described the most weight a normal man could carry, anywhere from 90 to 135 pounds. The heaviest hailstones ever recorded weighed about two pounds. These will be fifty times heavier. No doubt many will die due to inadequate shelter or no shelter following the massive earthquake.

Still unrepentant, the survivors of the hailstorm will blaspheme God "because of the plague of the hail, because its plague was extremely severe." Incredibly, tortured humanity remains hardened against God—a truth that should give pause to those who think that signs and wonders will convince people to believe the gospel. In light of the inevitable judgment to come, the warning to all unrepentant sinners is "Today if you hear His voice, do not harden your hearts" (Hebrews 4:7).

18

The
RELIGION
of Babylon
(17:1–18)

Throughout history Babylon has been an important center of false religion. In the end times, false religion will come back to where it started. The Devil who deceived the people at Babel, and from there launched false religion over the earth, will deceive the world once again. The final world religion, depicted as a harlot, is the theme of this vision.

THE EXPOSURE OF THE HARLOT

Then one of the seven angels who had the seven bowls came and spoke with me, saying, "Come here, I will show you the judgment of the great harlot who sits on many waters, with whom the kings of the earth committed acts of immorality, and those who dwell on the earth were made drunk with the wine of her immorality." And he carried me away in the Spirit into a wilderness; and I saw a woman sitting on a scarlet beast, full of blasphemous names, having seven heads and ten horns. The woman was clothed in purple and scarlet, and adorned with gold and precious stones and pearls, having in her hand a gold cup full of abominations

and of the unclean things of her immorality, and on her forehead a name
was written, a mystery, "BABYLON THE GREAT, THE MOTHER OF
HARLOTS AND OF THE ABOMINATIONS OF THE EARTH." And I
saw the woman drunk with the blood of the saints, and with the blood of
the witnesses of Jesus. When I saw her, I wondered greatly. . . .

And he said to me, "The waters which you saw where the harlot sits,
are peoples and multitudes and nations and tongues. (17:1–6, 15)

That it was one of the seven angels who had the seven bowls who came
and spoke with John connects the judgment of the harlot with the seven
last plagues (16:1–21). Chronology halts in chapters 17 and 18 as the
scene shifts from God's judgments to Antichrist's world empire, the target of those judgments. The great harlot that will be judged is not an actual
prostitute. The term "harlot" is a metaphor for false religion, spiritual defection, idolatry, and religious apostasy. John's vision exposes several aspects
of the harlot city of Babylon.

Her Authority (17:1*b*, 15)

The harlot in John's vision sits in a position of authority and sovereignty
like a king on his throne on or beside "many waters." Cities in ancient
times were usually located near a source of water, either the ocean, a river,
lake, or spring. That was true of Babylon, which was located on the
Euphrates River. Jeremiah 51:13 addresses ancient Babylon as "you who
dwell by many waters," the same phrase applied in this passage to her
future counterpart. Just as the proud capital of the Babylonian Empire
took her seat beside many waters, so also will the Babylonian harlot city
of the future.

The phrase "many waters" does not, however, refer to the harlot's geographical location. Instead, as the angel explains to John in verse 15, "The
waters which you saw where the harlot sits, are peoples and multitudes
and nations and tongues." The metaphor is an apt one, since a city situated
in a commanding position on a great waterway would be highly influential. The harlot will not merely influence, but will dominate all the unredeemed "peoples and multitudes and nations and tongues" of the earth.

The harlot's authority will be universal; the entire world will be committed to the false worship of the Babylonian system.

Her Alliances (17:2–3)

Her association with the kings of the earth reveals that the scope of the harlot's influence will be immense. The phrase "committed acts of immorality" translates a form of the Greek verb for committing sexual immorality. It aptly describes the harlot's interaction with the kings of the earth.

The harlot will not be allied just with the rulers and influential people of the world. All those "who dwell on the earth [a technical term for unbelievers] were made drunk with the wine of her immorality." All the unredeemed will be caught up in the final false religion; they will give their hearts and souls to the abominable Babylonian harlot. The angel is not describing people who are physically drunk with literal wine committing sexual immorality with an actual prostitute (though that may be happening). Instead, he is talking about those who are intoxicated with Antichrist's false world religion.

Next, the angel with whom John had been speaking "carried [him] away in the Spirit into a wilderness" (cf. 1:10; 4:2; 21:10). "Wilderness" describes a deserted, desolate wasteland like the region where modern Babylon is located. There John saw "a woman sitting on a scarlet beast," whose description identifies him as Antichrist (13:1, 4; 14:9; 16:10). That the woman was sitting on the scarlet beast signifies that he was supporting her. The initial unifying and controlling factor of Antichrist's kingdom will be religion. With the heavens and the earth being ravaged by God's judgments, and the world's political, economic, and military might crumbling, people will turn in desperation to the supernatural. The beast and the woman will coexist for a while. Religion will be separate from the kingdom of Antichrist at first. But eventually "the beast . . . will hate the harlot and will make her desolate and naked, and will eat her flesh and will burn her up with fire" (verse 16). It will be at that point that the false prophet will make the whole world worship Antichrist (13:11–14), and everything will be unified in the beast's comprehensive rule.

Scarlet is the color associated with luxury (2 Samuel 1:24), splendor, and royalty. It is also the color associated with sin (Isaiah 1:18) and the hue of blood. Antichrist will be a splendorous, royal, sinful, bloody beast, full of blasphemous names. In his arrogant self-deification, Antichrist will take for himself the names and titles that belong to God.

This demonic scarlet beast is further described as having seven heads and ten horns, showing the extent of his alliances. The seven heads "are seven mountains on which the woman sits, and they are seven kings; five have fallen, one is, the other has not yet come; and when he comes, he must remain a little while" (verses 9–10). They represent seven mountains, seven past, present, and future governments. The ten horns represent ten kings (verse 12), who will rule as subordinates to Antichrist (verse 13).

The harlot's alliances will be comprehensive. Her deadly embrace will encompass all the unredeemed, from kings and rulers to common people; all will worship and submit to her religion. Far from being separated, church and state will be united as never before in human history.

Her Apparel (17:4a)

Prostitutes usually dress so as to attract attention to themselves, and metaphorically the harlot Babylon will be no different. John saw her clothed in purple and scarlet, the colors of royalty, nobility, and wealth. That she is adorned with gold and precious stones and pearls portrays her as a prostitute who is both attractive (Proverbs 7:10) and has become extremely wealthy.

Her Abominations (17:4b–5).

As a further indication of her wealth, the harlot had in her hand a gold cup. Like prostitutes who want to take everything their victims have, she will make her victims drunk (Jeremiah 51:7). The harlot's gold cup is "full of abominations and of the unclean things of her immorality."

As was customary for prostitutes to identify themselves in the Roman world, the harlot Babylon also had a name written on her forehead. The harlot is called mystery BABYLON to indicate that BABYLON in this context does not refer to a geographical location. This is not ancient Babylon, the Babylon of John's day, or the rebuilt city of Babylon in the end times. The details of this vision cannot be applied to any actual city. Here is a previously undisclosed Babylon, a secret reality to be revealed in the end times. Babylon will be the source of all the false, blasphemous worship in the end times. Her designation as "THE MOTHER OF HARLOTS" is appropriate, since harlotry in Scripture often symbolizes idolatry (e.g., Judges 2:17; 8:27, 33; Ezekiel 16:30–31, 36).

Her Accusation (17:6)

Like many harlots, this woman was drunk, but not from drinking alcohol. The Babylonian harlot is pictured as "drunk with the blood of the saints, and with the blood of the witnesses of Jesus." That vivid expression was commonly used in the ancient world to depict a murderous lust for violence. Some see "the saints" and "the witnesses of Jesus" as two distinct groups, the former being the Old Testament saints and the latter the New Testament saints. More likely, however, the two descriptions refer to the same group and describe God's people throughout history. The important point is that false religion, represented here by the harlot, is a murderer. While the world becomes drunk with lust for her, the harlot becomes drunk with the blood of God's people. The vision was so appalling that when John saw her, he "wondered greatly," expressing that he was confused, shocked, astonished, and frightened by the ghastly vision of such a magnificent figure of a woman with such a deadly intent.

THE EXPLANATION OF THE HARLOT

And the angel said to me, "Why do you wonder? I will tell you the mystery of the woman and of the beast that carries her, which has the seven heads and the ten horns.

"The beast that you saw was, and is not, and is about to come up out of the abyss and go to destruction. And those who dwell on the earth, whose name has not been written in the book of life from the foundation of the world, will wonder when they see the beast, that he was and is not and will come. Here is the mind which has wisdom. The seven heads are seven mountains on which the woman sits, and they are seven kings; five

have fallen, one is, the other has not yet come; and when he comes, he must remain a little while. The beast which was and is not, is himself also an eighth and is one of the seven, and he goes to destruction. The ten horns which you saw are ten kings who have not yet received a kingdom, but they receive authority as kings with the beast for one hour. These have one purpose, and they give their power and authority to the beast. These will wage war against the Lamb, and the Lamb will overcome them, because He is Lord of lords and King of kings, and those who are with Him are the called and chosen and faithful." . . .

"The woman whom you saw is the great city, which reigns over the kings of the earth." (17:7–14, 18)

In response to John's confusion and amazement, the angel asked, "Why do you wonder?" There was no need for John to remain puzzled by the relation of the beast to this beautiful yet bloody woman in the vision. The angel was about to explain the mystery of the woman (verse 18) and of the beast that carries her (verses 8–17).

Verse 18 identifies the woman John saw as "the great city, which reigns over the kings of the earth." Some commentators deny that the great city is a literal city, preferring to see it as a symbol of the religious aspect of Antichrist's empire. Some identify it as Rome, others as Jerusalem. But the angel quite clearly and repeatedly refers to Babylon on the Euphrates throughout chapters 17–18. The description of Babylon's destruction (18:10, 18, 21) also suggests that an actual city is in view. A rebuilt city of Babylon will be closely identified with Antichrist's world empire, perhaps as its capital city. That city will be the center of his kingdom, the extent of which will be the whole earth.

The Old Testament predictions of Babylon's total destruction (e.g., Isaiah 13:1–14:27; Jeremiah 50–51) also favor identifying the great city with Babylon on the Euphrates. The detailed description those passages give of Babylon's destruction was only partially fulfilled when the Medes and Persians sacked the ancient city of Babylon. As with many Old Testament prophecies, those predictions had both a near and a far fulfillment.

The site of modern Babylon is strategically located at the crossroads of Asia, Europe, and Africa and is not far from the Persian Gulf. It is also near the world's richest oil fields and has a virtually unlimited water supply from the Euphrates.

In verses 8–14 the angel gives John a lengthy description of the beast. He is explaining to John the relationship between the harlot and the beast, which had mystified the apostle (verses 6–7). However, the angel needed first to give him further details about the beast. The beast that John saw is Antichrist, the satanic ruler of the last and most powerful empire in human history, who will serve as Satan's instrument to attack Israel, persecute believers, conquer the world for Satan, and oppose Christ. He is described as one "who was, and is not, and is about to come" again. That phrase refers to Antichrist's faked death and resurrection (13:3, 12, 14). Up till that point, Antichrist's economic empire will co-exist with the false religious system headed by the false prophet. But after his staged "resurrection," Antichrist will turn on the false religious system and destroy it. He will tolerate only one religion—the worship of himself.

Antichrist's phony resurrection and swift destruction of the false religious system will shock the world. As it does throughout Revelation, the phrase "those who dwell on the earth" describes unbelievers. They are the ones whose name has not been written in the Book of Life from the foundation of the world (13:8). Amazed and deceived by Antichrist, his followers will wonder when they see the beast, that he was and is not and will come. The specific cause for their amazement will be Antichrist's seemingly miraculous return to life after receiving an apparently fatal wound (13:3–4). Only the elect will not fall for Antichrist's deception (Matthew 24:24).

The angel's statement "here is the mind which has wisdom" invites John and his readers to pay close attention to what follows. This unusual expression introduces a difficult and complex aspect of this vision. It will take much spiritual insight to understand it, and perhaps only those alive at the time will fully comprehend it.

The first aspect of the vision that needs to be understood is that the seven heads of the beast (verse 3) are "seven mountains [or hills] on which the woman sits." Some commentators associate the seven mountains with Rome, famous for being built on seven hills, and identify the woman as the Roman Catholic Church. Such an interpretation is too narrow. More than just Rome must be in view, because Antichrist's empire is worldwide. Nor can the woman be the Roman Catholic Church, since verse 18 identifies her as the city of Babylon. Also "when the woman sits on the 'many waters' (verse 1) this must be taken as metaphorical since it is interpreted in v. 15. When the woman sits upon 'a scarlet . . . beast' this again is symbolic. The seven mountains must also be figurative."[1] Finally, the angel's call for spiritual discernment would have been pointless if the seven mountains were an obvious geographical reference to Rome.

Speculation is unnecessary, because the text plainly identifies the mountains as seven kings. Mountains are sometimes used in the Old Testament to represent rule or power (Psalm 30:7; Isaiah 2:2; Jeremiah 51:25; Daniel 2:35). Here they represent seven world empires led by their rulers. The angel tells John that "five have fallen, one is, the other has not yet come." The five Gentile world empires that had fallen were Egypt, Assyria, Babylon, Medo-Persia, and Greece. The one that existed at that time was obviously Rome. The other one that has not yet come is Antichrist's final world empire.

The angel further explains that when Antichrist comes, he must "remain a little while." His empire will be short-lived; he will be given "authority to act for forty-two months" (13:5; the second half of the tribulation). Then the angel offered the comment that "the beast which was and is not, is himself an eighth [king] and is one of the seven, and he goes to destruction." How can the beast (Antichrist) be an eighth king and also one of the seven? The answer lies in the phrase "the beast . . . was and is not." Antichrist will be one of the seven kings before his supposed demise and resurrection and an eighth king afterwards during the second phase of his rule. Antichrist will go to destruction—eternal damnation in the lake of fire (19:20; 20:10). Unlike the first six empires, his empire will be destroyed by a direct act of God.

The angel further explained that the ten horns that John saw are "ten kings." They cannot be known to any earlier generation because they have not yet received a kingdom, since they are part of Antichrist's future empire. They will receive authority as kings with the beast for one hour. Perhaps Antichrist's empire will be divided into ten administrative regions, which these ten kings will rule under him. The reference to "one hour" is a figure of speech that emphasizes the shortness of their rule. During their brief reign, they will be unanimously devoted to Antichrist.

The agenda of the ten kings, like that of Satan and Antichrist, will be to wage war against the Lamb at the battle of Armageddon. John notes that the Lamb will overcome them. The battle will in reality be a slaughter. Christ will completely destroy the opposing forces gathered against Him at His second coming. The reason all the forces of hell cannot defeat the Lamb is because He is "Lord of lords and King of kings."

With Christ when He returns will be "the called and chosen and faithful," a reference that can only apply to believers (19:14; Matthew 22:14). The terms are rich in their definition of believers as the eternally elect, *chosen* in the Son before the foundation of the world (Ephesians 1:4); *the called*, summoned in time by the Father to repentance and faith that saves (John 6:44); and *faithful*, demonstrating the true saving faith—the genuine eternal life that endures by the power of the Spirit (Romans 8:9). Christ will effortlessly crush the greatest armed force ever assembled when He returns with His elect and the holy angels (Matthew 24:30–31; 2 Thessalonians 1:7).

THE EXTERMINATION OF THE HARLOT

And the ten horns which you saw, and the beast, these will hate the harlot and will make her desolate and naked, and will eat her flesh and will burn her up with fire. For God has put it in their hearts to execute His purpose by having a common purpose, and by giving their kingdom to the beast, until the words of God will be fulfilled. (17:16–17)

Antichrist's alliance with the false religious system will not last. Eventually the ten horns (the ten kings) and the beast (Antichrist) will hate the harlot. Having used the false religious system to help him gain control of the world, Antichrist will discard it. He will want the world to worship only him. He will turn on the harlot and will make her "desolate and naked, and will eat her flesh and will burn her up with fire." That graphic language of extreme violence is used to make clear that Antichrist and his henchmen will completely obliterate the false religious system.

Yet Antichrist's self-serving, satanically inspired actions are precisely in the scope of God's sovereign plan. In fact, it is God who will put it in the hearts of Antichrist's followers to execute His purpose by giving their kingdom to the beast. God's power is behind the destruction and consolidation of the evil empire. As always, Satan is the instrument of God's purposes. The one-world unification government so long sought by the humanists will have finally arrived, only to be destroyed in one great act of divine judgment. All prophecy of Christ's return and the setting up of His kingdom—will be fulfilled completely.

19

The
BUSINESS
of Babylon
(18:1–24)

Throughout history the petty kingdoms and empires built by proud, arrogant, God-rejecting rebels have come and gone. The spirit of humanism first expressed at Babel has permeated human history ever since. Unshakably optimistic despite centuries of war, slaughter, injustice, and cruelty, people still seek a utopia, to be brought about by humanity's upward scientific progress. Having taken control (so they think) of their own destiny through science, sinners have no use for God and haughtily replace Him as self-styled gods devoted to their own sovereignty.

Compared to the glorious, indescribable majesty of the omnipotent God, all of man's vaunted empires are a mere "drop from a bucket" (Isaiah 40:15), and God "has fixed a day in which He will judge the world in righteousness through a Man whom He has appointed" (Acts 17:31). Nowhere in Scripture is there a more detailed description of the coming judgment than in Revelation 6–18. With the destruction of the last and greatest human empire, the stage is set for the triumphant return of the Lord Jesus Christ. That final empire is commercial Babylon, and its pending destruction is the theme of chapter 18.

Though some view it as a symbol for Antichrist's whole godless system, the Babylon described here is most likely an actual city. It is called a city five times in the chapter (verses 10, 16, 18, 19, 21), and other features in the text imply that a literal city is in view. Since the text plainly describes Babylon as a city, it is safest to view it as a real city. Although it will be one city, its influence will be worldwide. As Antichrist's capital city, it will represent his commercial empire. The judgment and destruction of Babylon will kill the head, and the rest of Antichrist's world empire will follow in death.

Despite repeated warnings—including 144,000 Jewish evangelists, the two witnesses, and an angel flying in the heavens and proclaiming the gospel message—the people of the world will refuse to repent (cf. 9:20–21; 16:9, 11). Finally, God's judgment will fall on Babylon. Chapter 18 records seven aspects of that judgment on Antichrist's commercial empire.

JUDGMENT PRONOUNCED

After these things I saw another angel coming down from heaven, having great authority, and the earth was illumined with his glory. And he cried out with a mighty voice, saying, "Fallen, fallen is Babylon the great! She has become a dwelling place of demons and a prison of every unclean spirit, and a prison of every unclean and hateful bird. For all the nations have drunk of the wine of the passion of her immorality, and the kings of the earth have committed acts of immorality with her, and the merchants of the earth have become rich by the wealth of her sensuality." (18:1–3)

This solemn opening pronouncement of judgment gives two reasons for Babylon's impending destruction: demonic activity and sensuality. The phrase "after these things" marks the beginning of a new vision. While still discussing the general theme of Antichrist's world empire, destroyed by the seven bowl judgments of chapter 16, chapter 18 moves from its religious to its commercial aspects. John saw another angel, distinct from the one in 17:1. Some view this angel as Christ, but the use of the Greek word indicating another of the same kind explains that this is an angel of the same type as the one in 17:1. He may be the angel who had earlier predicted Babylon's downfall (14:8). Three features reveal his unusual power and importance.

First, the angel came down from heaven with "great authority." Second, when he arrived, "the earth was illumined with his glory." He will make his dramatic appearance onto a darkened stage. The fifth bowl will have plunged the world into darkness (16:10). The flashing brilliance of a glorious heavenly being against the blackness will be an awe-inspiring sight to the shocked and terrified earth dwellers.

Third, the angel "cried out with a mighty voice." No one will be able to ignore him. Everyone will hear him as well as see him.

His message will add to the terror caused by his appearance. It will be a word of woe for Antichrist and his followers: "Fallen, fallen is Babylon the great!" The judgment predicted in 14:8 will now be carried out. This will be a greater and more far-reaching judgment than the one pronounced in identical words on ancient Babylon (Isaiah 21:9). A comparison of this passage with 16:17–19 suggests that this judgment takes place when the seventh bowl is poured out.

The first cause given for Babylon's destruction is that "she has become a dwelling place of demons and a prison of every unclean spirit." It was in the vicinity of Babylon that two hundred million formerly bound demons were released at the sounding of the sixth trumpet (9:13–16). They, along with the demons released from the abyss at the sounding of the fifth trumpet (9:1–11), those cast from heaven with Satan (12:4, 9), and those previously on earth, will be confined in Babylon.

Babylon will also be "a prison of every unclean and hateful bird." That phrase symbolizes the city's total destruction. Like grotesque carrion birds, the demons will hover over the doomed city, waiting for its fall. The depiction of the demons as unclean and hateful reflects heaven's view of them.

Babylon's destruction will also come because "all the nations have drunk of the wine of the passion of her immorality, and the kings of the earth have committed acts of immorality with her, and the merchants of the earth have become rich by the wealth of her sensuality." Antichrist's evil empire will spread its influence to all the nations of the world. Having drunk of the wine of the passion of her immorality (14:8; 17:2), the people of the world will fall into a religious and materialistic daze. The all-encompassing terms "all the nations, the kings of the earth, and the merchants of the earth" reveal that Babylon will seduce the entire world.

JUDGMENT AVOIDED

I heard another voice from heaven, saying, "Come out of her, my people, so that you will not participate in her sins and receive of her plagues; for her sins have piled up as high as heaven, and God has remembered her iniquities." (18:4–5)

God's judgment on this commercially prosperous but morally bankrupt society can be avoided, as another voice from heaven makes clear. The message the angel proclaims, "Come out of her, my people," is a call for God's people to disentangle themselves from the world system. It may also be an evangelistic call to God's elect to come to faith in Christ and come out of Satan's kingdom (cf. Colosssians 1:13). In both cases, the message is to abandon the system.

First, believers are to flee Babylon so that they "will not participate in her sins." The materialistic Babylon will exert an almost irresistible influence on believers to participate in her sins. Second, God's people must also flee so they do not "receive of her plagues." It is best to see these plagues as specific judgments on Babylon, perhaps with the outpouring of the seventh bowl (16:17–19). Finally, believers must flee Babylon because "her sins have piled up as high as heaven." "Piled" is from a Greek word that literally means "to glue together" or "to join." Then the angel adds that "God has remembered her iniquities." He will take note of them as He did that earlier monument to man's sinful, prideful rebellion at the tower of Babel (Genesis 11).

JUDGMENT DEFINED

"Pay her back even as she has paid, and give back to her double accord-ing to her deeds; in the cup which she has mixed, mix twice as much for her. To the degree that she glorified herself and lived sensuously, to the same degree give her torment and mourning; for she says in her heart, 'I sit as a queen and I am not a widow, and will never see mourning.' For this reason in one day her plagues will come, pestilence and mourning and famine, and she will be burned up with fire; for the Lord God who judges her is strong." (18:6–8)

The angel now speaks to God. His call for vengeance on Babylon parallels the prayers of the martyred saints recorded in 6:9–10. Babylon has been extended enough grace and heard enough warnings. It is time for her destruction.

The angel's plea is reminiscent of the Old Testament saints' pleas for vengeance on ancient Babylon. In Psalm 137:8 the psalmist wrote, "O daughter of Babylon, you devastated one, how blessed will be the one who repays you with the recompense with which you have repaid us." Jeremiah also pleaded for vengeance on Babylon (Jeremiah 50:14–15, 29).

The angel's request that God give back to Babylon double "according to her deeds" (literally "double the double things") is a request that Babylon's punishment fit her crimes. Double has been her iniquity, double will be her punishment.

Further stating his request that God fully punish Babylon, the angel asks that "in the cup which she has mixed," God would "mix twice as much for her." Fittingly, in the very cup that Babylon used to deceive the nations (verse 3; 14:8; 17:2, 4) she is to receive a double portion of God's wrath. The imagery of the cup of God's wrath also appears in 14:10 and 16:19.

Then the angel calls on God a third time to exact complete vengeance on Babylon: "To the degree that she glorified herself and lived sensuously, to the same degree give her torment and mourning; for she says in her heart, 'I sit as a queen and I am not a widow, and will never see mourning.'" The phrase "to the degree" is a call to match the punishment to the crime, a biblical principle (Proverbs 29:23; Isaiah 3:16ff.; Luke 1:51; 14:11).

Three sins call for Babylon's judgment. First, she was proud. She glorified herself. Second, she pursued self-gratification. She lived sensuously. Third, she was guilty of self-sufficiency. She said in her heart, "I sit as a queen and I am not a widow, and will never see mourning." For those three sins Babylon will receive torment and mourning. The Greek word for "torment" literally means torture. "Mourning" refers to the grief that the torture produces. Hell will be a place of both unimaginable torment (20:10; Luke 16:23–24, 28) and crushing grief (Matthew 8:12; 13:42).

Then the angel notes that in "one day her plagues will come." Babylon's destruction will not be progressive. The wicked city will be instantly destroyed. Daniel 5 records the similar fate that befell ancient Babylon; the city fell the very night that God wrote its doom on the wall of the king's palace (Daniel 5:30). As noted, the plagues that will destroy Babylon are specific judgments on that city, possibly in connection with the seventh bowl. Three plagues will result in Babylon's complete devastation: pestilence and mourning and famine—heaven's fitting answer to her proud boast. After those three plagues have run their course, Babylon will be burned up with fire.

JUDGMENT LAMENTED

"And the kings of the earth, who committed acts of immorality and lived sensuously with her, will weep and lament over her when they see the smoke of her burning, standing at a distance because of the fear of her torment, saying, 'Woe, woe, the great city, Babylon, the strong city! For in one hour your judgment has come.'

"And the merchants of the earth weep and mourn over her, because no one buys their cargoes any more—cargoes of gold and silver and precious stones and pearls and fine linen and purple and silk and scarlet, and every kind of citron wood and every article of ivory and every article made from very costly wood and bronze and iron and marble, and cinnamon and spice and incense and perfume and frankincense and wine and olive oil and fine flour and wheat and cattle and sheep, and

cargoes of horses and chariots and slaves and human lives. The fruit you long for has gone from you, and all things that were luxurious and splendid have passed away from you and men will no longer find them. The merchants of these things, who became rich from her, will stand at a distance because of the fear of her torment, weeping and mourning, saying, 'Woe, woe, the great city, she who was clothed in fine linen and purple and scarlet, and adorned with gold and precious stones and pearls; for in one hour such great wealth has been laid waste!' And every shipmaster and every passenger and sailor, and as many as make their living by the sea, stood at a distance, and were crying out as they saw the smoke of her burning, saying, 'What city is like the great city?' And they threw dust on their heads and were crying out, weeping and mourning, saying, 'Woe, woe, the great city, in which all who had ships at sea became rich by her wealth, for in one hour she has been laid waste!'" (18:9–19)

The first mourners introduced are the leaders, the kings of the earth. This group includes the ten kings who rule Antichrist's kingdom under his authority (17:12), as well as the rest of the world's leaders under them. They will greet the news of Babylon's destruction with shock and dismay. The destruction of the seat of Antichrist's political and economic power will strike a fatal blow to his empire.

As they watch her burn, the leaders will cry out in anguish, "Woe, woe, the great city, Babylon, the strong city! For in one hour your judgment has come." As the crown jewel of Antichrist's empire, Babylon will be a great city. Since it will have survived the devastating judgments of the tribulation up to that point, the leaders will believe it to be a strong city. Babylon's swift destruction will shock and amaze them, and they will cry out to her in dismay.

The next mourners to appear on the scene are the merchants of the earth. These business leaders will weep over Babylon "because no one buys their cargoes anymore." The destruction of Antichrist's capital will end any semblance of normalcy on the devastated planet. Whatever economic activity will have been taking place on an earth will then come to a halt.

Then follows a list of twenty-eight items or categories of merchandise that comprised the merchants' cargoes, ranging from "gold and silver and precious stones and pearls" to "fine flour and wheat and cattle and sheep, and cargoes of horses and chariots and slaves." These items were common commodities in the ancient world and were the source of immense financial gain. They are only representative of the great wealth of Antichrist's future commercial empire.

Continuing their lament, the merchants now address Babylon directly: "The fruit you long for has gone from you, and all things that were luxurious and splendid have passed away from you and men will no longer find them." All of the city's luxurious possessions have passed away. The words "no longer" translate a double negative in the Greek text, the strongest negative form in the Greek language. It indicates these items will never be found again.

The merchants will stand at a distance because of the fear of her torment, weeping and mourning, saying, "Woe, woe, the great city, she who was clothed in fine linen and purple and scarlet, and adorned with gold and precious stones and pearls; for in one hour such great wealth has been laid waste!" They weep and mourn, not out of some emotional sympathy for the city, but because they have been stripped of the key source of their finances. These greedy merchants are the classic illustration of all those in all times who gain the whole world, but forfeit their souls (Mark 8:36).

Then a third and final group in the vision joins the lament for Babylon: "every shipmaster and every passenger and sailor, and as many as make their living by the sea." In addition to her political and economic importance, Babylon will also be an important distribution center. With its destruction, there will be no more goods to transport by those who make their living by the sea. Like the rulers and merchants, the sailors were careful to stand at a safe distance from the city. As they gazed on the ruined city they were crying out as they saw the smoke of her burning, saying, "What city is like the great city?" Then, in a typical ancient expression of grief, the sailors threw dust on their heads (e.g., Joshua 7:6; 1 Samuel 4:12; 2 Samuel 1:2). Like the rulers and the merchants, they too will cry out, "Woe, woe, the great city." That is an expression of pain, but not of repentance. Like the rulers and the merchants, the sailors also express amazement at the swiftness of Babylon's downfall, exclaiming, "In one hour she has been laid waste!" In an astonishingly short period of time, the city that was the source of their wealth was destroyed.

JUDGMENT ENJOYED

"Rejoice over her, O heaven, and you saints and apostles and prophets, because God has pronounced judgment for you against her." (18:20)

Heaven will have quite a different perspective than Antichrist's earthly followers. The angel who began speaking in verse 4 then addressed the redeemed in heaven: the saints and apostles and prophets. He calls on them to rejoice over Babylon's fall, "because God has pronounced judgment . . . against her." Heaven rejoices, because of the triumph of righteousness, the exaltation of Jesus Christ, and the arrival of His kingdom on the earth.

JUDGMENT COMPLETED

Then a strong angel took up a stone like a great millstone and threw it into the sea, saying, "So will Babylon, the great city, be thrown down with violence, and will not be found any longer. And the sound of harpists and musicians and flute-players and trumpeters will not be heard in you any longer; and no craftsman of any craft will be found in you any longer; and the sound of a mill will not be heard in you any longer; and the light of a lamp will not shine in you any longer; and the voice of the bridegroom and bride will not be heard in you any longer; (18:21–23a)

Another strong angel (cf. 5:2; 10:1) now appeared in the vision. In a dramatic act, He "took up a stone like a great millstone [typically four to five feet in diameter, a foot thick, and very heavy] and threw it into the sea." "So," explained the angel, "will Babylon, the great city, be thrown down with violence, and will not be found any longer." In one moment, as that stone disappeared into the sea, Babylon will disappear.

So complete will be Babylon's destruction that none of the normal activities of human life will take place. There will be no music, no working, no preparing of food, no light, and no marriage. Babylon will be so thoroughly destroyed that it will never rise again, as predicted by the Old Testament prophets (Isaiah 13:19–22; 14:22–23; Jeremiah 50:13, 39; 51:37).

JUDGMENT JUSTIFIED

"for your merchants were the great men of the earth, because all the nations were deceived by your sorcery. And in her was found the blood of prophets and of saints and of all who have been slain on the earth." (18:23b–24)

Three final reasons are given for Babylon's judgment. First, her "merchants were the great men of the earth," using their wealth to ascend to positions of power, prominence, and influence. A second reason for Babylon's judgment is that her sorcery deceived the nations. "Sorcery" is from the Greek root word from which we derive the English words "pharmacy" and "pharmaceuticals." The word is used in the New Testament to refer to magic and occult practices (9:21; Galatians 5:20). Babylon's hold on the world will not be entirely due to her military and economic power, but also to her occult influence.

The final reason for Babylon's judgment is her murderous slaughter of God's people; "in her was found the blood of prophets and of saints and of all who have been slain on the earth." The heavenly rejoicing over Babylon's downfall in chapter 19 also mentions this: "After these things I heard something like a loud voice of a great multitude in heaven, saying, 'Hallelujah! Salvation and glory and power belong to our God; because His judgments are true and righteous; for He has judged the great harlot who was corrupting the earth with her immorality, and He has avenged the blood of His bond-servants on her'" (19:1–2).

20

The Second
COMING
of the Lord Jesus Christ
(19:1–21)

As that long-awaited time of Jesus Christ's appearance approaches, the scene in Revelation shifts from earth, where it has been since chapter 6, to heaven. The praise seen in heaven throughout Revelation reaches a crescendo in this text. The heavenly rejoicing is not over those who reject God, but because Christ will soon remove sinners from the world. God will then be properly honored, Christ enthroned, and the earth restored to its lost glory. Heaven rejoices because history is finally going to reach its culmination as the true King establishes His kingdom on earth.

As the text unfolds, two major sections emerge. First, five reasons are provided in support of heaven's joy (19:1–10). Second, Christ's glorious return is revealed for John and his readers (verses 11–21).

THE REASONS FOR HEAVEN'S JOY

Five reasons for heaven's joy become evident in the first ten verses.

1. Full Salvation Has Come.

After these things I heard something like a loud voice of a great multitude in heaven, saying, "Hallelujah! Salvation and glory and power belong to our God; (19:1)

As it does throughout Revelation, the phrase "after these things" marks the beginning of a new vision. This new vision takes place after the destruction of Babylon (chapters 17–18) and before the triumphant return of Jesus Christ (19:11–21) to establish the millennial kingdom (20:1–10).

In his vision John heard "something like a loud voice of a great multitude in heaven." The text does not identify those voices John heard, but they are likely angels. This great multitude does not appear to include the redeemed saints, since they are encouraged to join in the praise later (verses 5–8). The uncounted millions of holy angels make up a majestic choir.

The angelic chorus opens with an exclamation of praise: "Hallelujah!" The Greek word is a transliteration of a Hebrew phrase combining the verb for "to praise" and the noun "God." It appears only in this chapter in the New Testament (verses 3–4, 6). In its first Old Testament appearance, *Hallelujah* also expresses praise for God's judgment on the wicked oppressors of His people (Psalm 104:35).

Heaven rejoices specifically because salvation has come for God's people, and the glory and power that belong to God have been put on display. The word "salvation" celebrates the final aspect of salvation history, the glorification of the saints in Christ's kingdom. The imminent coming of Christ prompts this praise as the angels anticipate the glory of His kingdom.

2. Justice Is Provided.

"because His judgments are true and righteous; for He has judged the great harlot who was corrupting the earth with her immorality, and He has avenged the blood of His bond-servants on her." (19:2)

Heaven also rejoices because God's judgments are "true and righteous," as evidenced by the destruction of wicked Babylon. Babylon is identified as "the great harlot" (17:1, 15–16), Satan and Antichrist's system that seduced the unbelieving world to believe Satan's lies.

A further reason for Babylon's judgment was her mistreatment of God's people (18:24). As a result, God has avenged the blood of His bond-servants on her. That God will exact vengeance for His people is clearly taught in Scripture (e.g., Deuteronomy 32:42–43).

3. Rebellion Is Ended.

And a second time they said, "Hallelujah! Her smoke rises up forever and ever." (19:3)

Babylon's judgment provoked the first outburst of heavenly rejoicing. The aftermath of her destruction prompts the heavenly chorus to again say, "Hallelujah!" At the climax of her judgment, Babylon was "burned up with fire" (18:8), and sinners mourned as they watched the pall of smoke rise into the sky (18:9, 18). That the smoke "rises up forever and ever" indicates that this judgment is final and irreversible. The language is similar to that used of God's destruction of Sodom and Gomorrah (Genesis 19:28), and Edom (Isaiah 34:10).

The destruction of the last and most powerful empire in human history marks the end of human rule. The rebellion that began in the garden of Eden is finally ended (apart from the revolt at the end of the millennium (20:7–10). There will be no more false religion or injustice.

4. God Is in Control.

And the twenty-four elders and the four living creatures fell down and worshiped God who sits on the throne saying, "Amen. Hallelujah!" And a voice came from the throne, saying, "Give praise to our God, all you His bond-servants, you who fear Him, the small and the great." Then I heard something like the voice of a great multitude and like the sound of many waters and like the sound of mighty peals of thunder, saying, "Hallelujah! For the Lord our God, the Almighty, reigns." (19:4–6)

Hallelujahs also ring out from other heavenly residents. The twenty-four elders are best seen as representatives of the church. The four living creatures are cherubim, a high-ranking order of angels. Prostrate before God's throne, the two new additions to the heavenly chorus cried out, "Amen. Hallelujah!" That phrase comes from Psalm 106:48 and indicates their solemn agreement with the heavenly rejoicing over Babylon's downfall.

The text does not identify the owner of the voice from the throne, but it is likely an angel, since he refers to God as "our God." The voice authoritatively calls another group to join in the praise, saying, "Give praise to our God, all you His bond-servants, you who fear Him, the small and the great." The redeemed believers in heaven are described as God's bond-servants (verse 2; cf. 1:1; 2:20). The all-inclusive phrase "the small and the great" transcends all human categories to embrace everyone. All the redeemed are called to praise God.

When the redeemed obeyed the command from the heavenly voice and added their voices to the heavenly chorus, John "heard something like the voice of a great multitude." The loud chorus of praise rose to a deafening level. The apostle likened it to "the sound of many waters and . . . the sound of mighty peals of thunder." The fitting finale to the heavenly oratorio of praise is a fourth "Hallelujah!" followed by the motive for it— "For the Lord our God, the Almighty, reigns." The evil world system has been destroyed. God's kingdom has come in its fullness.

5. The Marriage of the Lamb Is Completed.

"Let us rejoice and be glad and give the glory to Him, for the marriage of the Lamb has come and His bride has made herself ready." It was given to her to clothe herself in fine linen, bright and clean; for the fine linen is the righteous acts of the saints.

Then he said to me, "Write, 'Blessed are those who are invited to the marriage supper of the Lamb.'" And he said to me, "These are true words of God." Then I fell at his feet to worship him. But he said to me, "Do not do that; I am a fellow servant of yours and your brethren who hold the testimony of Jesus; worship God. For the testimony of Jesus is the spirit of prophecy." (19:7–10)

The heavenly praise continues rejoicing and giving God glory for the marriage of the Lamb. A marriage was the single greatest celebration and social event of the biblical world. Wedding preparations and celebrations in ancient times were even more elaborate and involved than those of today. They consisted of three distinct stages. First was the betrothal, or engagement. This was an arrangement by both sets of parents contracting the marriage of their children. It was legally binding and could only be broken by a divorce (Matthew 1:18–19). The second stage of a wedding was the presentation, a time of festivities just before the actual ceremony. Those festivities could last up to a week or more, depending on the economic and social status of the bride and groom. The third and most significant stage was the actual ceremony, during which the vows were exchanged. At the end of the presentation festivities, the groom and his attendants would go to the bride's house and take her and her bridesmaids to the ceremony. After the ceremony would come a final meal, followed by the consummation of the marriage.

The entire heavenly chorus is encouraged to "rejoice and be glad and give the glory to Him" because all the preparation is complete and the marriage of the Lamb has come. Betrothed in eternity past, presented in the Father's house since the rapture, the church is now ready for the wedding ceremony to begin. It will coincide with the start of the millennial kingdom and stretch throughout that thousand-year period, finally consummated in the new heavens and the new earth (21:1–2). In the new heavens and the new earth, the bride concept will be expanded to include not only the church, but also all the redeemed of all ages as the New Jerusalem becomes the bridal city (21:1–2).

In preparation for her marriage to the Lamb, "His bride has made herself ready." That was not by her own works, but rather by God's gracious working. The bride has made herself ready in the power of God, by the grace of God, through the work of the Spirit of God (Philippians 2:12–13; Colossians 1:29). Purged from all sin and impurity (1 Corinthians 3:12–15), she is a flawless, blameless virgin.

Having been presented glorified and spotless before God's throne, the church is able to "clothe herself in fine linen, bright and clean." Fine linen was expensive and beautiful cloth, like that worn by Joseph (Genesis 41:42). "Bright" in Greek means "glistening" or "radiant." Such dazzling garments were worn earlier in Revelation by angels (15:6), and will be the clothing of those in heaven when Christ returns (verse 14).

Then the angel who had been speaking with John told him, "Write, 'Blessed are those who are invited to the marriage supper of the Lamb.'" This is the fourth of seven beatitudes in Revelation (see page 23), all introduced by the word "blessed." The recipients of this blessing are "those who are invited to the marriage supper of the Lamb." That they are invited guests marks them as a distinct group from the church, since a bride would hardly be invited to her own wedding. These guests represent Old Testament believers. Matthew 8:11 and Luke 13:28 both refer to Abraham, Isaac, and Jacob as being in the kingdom. Luke 13:28 also mentions the prophets. All the heroes of the faith mentioned in Hebrews 11 will be among the invited guests, as will John the Baptist (Matthew 11:11). All the tribulation saints, glorified and still alive on earth and entering the millennial kingdom, will be guests.

Some may question why the church-age believers should be granted the honor of being the bride, while believers from other ages are merely guests. But one may equally ask why God singled out Israel to be the covenant people. The only answer to both questions is that God sovereignly purposed that it be so (cf. Deuteronomy 7:7–8). It must be remembered that the wedding imagery pictures God's intimate union with His people. There will be no second-class citizens in God's kingdom, just as all the participants in a wedding enjoy the celebration. And in the new heavens and the new earth, all believers of all ages will enjoy the full glories of eternity.

The blessed truth that God will be in personal fellowship forever with all the redeemed saints of all the ages is so significant that the angel solemnly affirmed to John, "These are true words of God." So great was John's astonishment at the angel's message that he involuntarily and thoughtlessly fell at his feet to worship him. Calling him back to his senses, the angel said, "Do not do that; I am a fellow servant of yours and your brethren who hold the testimony of Jesus; worship God." (cf. 22:8–9).

Like John, the angel was a servant of God. He reminds John that he is to worship God only.

The angel's final word to John is a reminder that "the testimony of Jesus is the spirit of prophecy."

CHRIST'S GLORIOUS RETURN (19:11–21)

The second coming must be distinguished from the rapture of the church prior to the seven-year tribulation. At the rapture, Christ comes for His saints (John 14:3; 1 Thessalonians 4:16–17). At the second coming, He comes with them. At the rapture, Christ meets His saints in the air (1 Thessalonians 4:17) to take them to heaven (John 14:2–3). At the second coming, He descends with them from heaven to the earth (Zechariah 14:4).

Some attempt to harmonize those two distinctions by arguing that believers meet Christ in the air, then descend to earth with Him. By so doing, they essentially make the rapture and the second coming the same event. But that view trivializes the rapture. There is not a hint of judgment in passages describing the rapture (John 14:1–3; 1 Thessalonians 4:13–18), but judgment plays a prominent role in the second coming (19:11, 15, 17–21). The dramatic signs accompanying the second coming, such as the darkening of the sun and moon and the disruption of the "powers of the heavens" (Matthew 24:29–30), are not mentioned in the passages describing the rapture. In its description of the second coming, Revelation 19 does not mention either a rapture of living believers (1 Corinthians 15:51–52), or a resurrection of dead believers (1 Thessalonians 4:16).

This monumental, climactic passage may be divided into four sections:

1. The Return of the Conqueror

And I saw heaven opened, and behold, a white horse, and He who sat on it is called Faithful and True, and in righteousness He judges and wages war. His eyes are a flame of fire, and on His head are many diadems; and He has a name written on Him which no one knows except Himself. He is clothed with a robe dipped in blood, and His name is called The Word of God. (19:11–13)

As in 4:1, heaven opened before John's wondering eyes. But this time heaven opens not to let John in, but to let Jesus out. The time has come at last for the full, glorious revelation of Christ. As the dramatic scene unfolds, John stands with his attention on the mighty Rider. Jesus is about to receive the kingdom that the Father promised Him.

No longer is Jesus portrayed as He was in His humiliation, riding on a donkey. Instead, He rides the traditional white horse ridden by victorious Roman generals in their triumphal processions through the streets of Rome. White also symbolizes the spotless, unblemished, absolutely holy character of the Rider. The horse, the crowns (verse 12), the sharp sword, the rod of iron, and the winepress (verse 15) are symbolic. Christ's coming is reality. The symbolic language represents various aspects of that reality.

Continuing his description of the astonishing scene before him, John notes that "He who sat on the white horse is called Faithful and True." There is no more appropriate name for Jesus Christ, who earlier in Revelation was called "the faithful and true Witness" (3:14). He is faithful to His promises (cf. 2 Corinthians 1:20) and what He speaks is always true (John 8:45–46; Titus 1:2).

Because Jesus is faithful to His word and righteous character, it follows that "in righteousness He judges." When He came the first time, wicked people judged Him. When He returns, He will judge all wicked people (Acts 17:31). Angels may gather the wicked for judgment (Matthew 13:41), but the Lord Jesus will pass sentence on them.

Here Christ is seen as the warrior King who wages war against His foes. He is the executioner of all ungodly, unbelieving sinners. The only other reference in Scripture to Jesus waging war is in 2:16, when He warned the church at Pergamum to repent or that he would wage war against them.

Describing the personal appearance of the awe-inspiring Rider, John writes that "His eyes are a flame of fire." Nothing escapes the notice of His piercing vision. The eyes that wept over the fate of unrepentant Jerusalem and over the sorrow, suffering, and death in this sin-cursed world, John sees flashing with the fire of judgment.

On His head John noted that Christ wore "many diadems," a reference to a ruler's crown (12:3; 13:1). In this case, they are worn by Jesus to indicate His royal authority. "Many" indicates His collecting of all the rulers' crowns, signifying that He alone is the ruler of the earth. Collecting the crown of a vanquished king was customary in the ancient world (2 Samuel 12:30). Christ alone will be "King of Kings, and Lord of Lords" (verse 16), and "the kingdom of the world has become the kingdom of our Lord and of His Christ; and He will reign forever and ever" (11:15). The many crowns Christ will wear are indeed a fair exchange for a crown of thorns (Philippians 2:8–11).

Further, John notes that Jesus had a "name written on Him which no one knows except Himself." The meaning of that name is unknown, since we are told that no one knows it except Jesus Himself. Even the inspired apostle John could not comprehend it. Maybe it will be made known after His return.

Describing the final element of Christ's appearance, John writes that "He is clothed with a robe dipped in blood." The blood is not representative of the cross. This is a picture of judgment. The blood is the blood of His slaughtered enemies (Isaiah 63:1–6).

Why are His garments blood spattered before the battle has begun? This is not His first battle. It is His last battle. His war clothes bear the stains of many previous slaughters. At that day, they will be stained as never before when He "treads the wine press of the fierce wrath of God, the Almighty" (verse 15).

That the Rider's name is called "The Word of God" identifies Him unmistakably as Jesus Christ (John 1:1, 14; 1 John 1:1). The second Person of the Trinity is called The Word of God because He is the revelation of God.

2. The Regiments of the Conqueror
And the armies which are in heaven, clothed in fine linen, white and clean, were following Him on white horses. (19:14)

Jesus Christ will be accompanied by "the armies which are in heaven." Four divisions make up these glorified troops. First will be the bride of the

Lamb (the church), already pictured wearing "fine linen, bright and clean" (verses 7–8). Second will be the tribulation believers, who also have been pictured in heaven wearing white robes (7:9). The third group is the Old Testament saints, who are resurrected at the end of the tribulation (Daniel 12:1–2). Finally, the holy angels will also accompany Christ (Matthew 25:31). The white horses ridden by the heavenly cavalry are not literal horses. Unlike Christ, the heavenly army is unarmed. He alone will destroy His enemies. The saints will come not to fight with Jesus, but to reign with Him (20: 4–6).

3. The Rule of the Conqueror

From His mouth comes a sharp sword, so that with it He may strike down the nations, and He will rule them with a rod of iron; and He treads the wine press of the fierce wrath of God, the Almighty. And on His robe and on His thigh He has a name written, "KING OF KINGS, AND LORD OF LORDS." (19:15–16)

The impending rule of the King is described in graphic, powerful imagery. John notes first that "from His mouth comes a sharp sword." The apostle had seen that sword in an earlier vision (1:16), where it was used to defend the church against Satan's forces. That the sword comes out of His mouth symbolizes the deadly power of Christ's words. Once He spoke words of comfort, but now He speaks words of death. Christ will wield that sword with deadly effect as He strikes down the nations. The dead will include all those gathered for battle at Armageddon. The rest of the world's unredeemed people will be judged and executed at the sheep and goat judgment (Matthew 25:31–46) that follows Christ's return. This is the final stroke of death in the day of the Lord.

The swift judgment that marks the onset of Christ's kingdom will be the pattern of His rule throughout the millennium. During His thousand-year reign, He will rule the nations with a rod of iron (12:5; Psalm 2:8–9). He will instantly put down any rebellion. Using the same imagery of ruling with a rod of iron, Jesus promised that believers would rule under Him in the kingdom (Revelation 2:26–27).

Returning to the judgment at the outset of Christ's rule, John writes that "He treads the wine press of the fierce wrath of God, the Almighty." That vivid symbol of God's wrath comes from the ancient practice of stomping on grapes as part of the wine-making process. The splattering of the grape juice pictures the pouring out of the blood of Christ's enemies (14:18–20; Isaiah 63:1–3).

In a final look, John saw that Christ wore a banner around His robe and on His thigh, on which He has a name written, "KING OF KINGS, AND LORD OF LORDS." The name expresses His sovereign, absolute rule in His soon-to-be-established kingdom.

4. The Victory of the Conqueror

Then I saw an angel standing in the sun, and he cried out with a loud voice, saying to all the birds which fly in midheaven, "Come, assemble for the great supper of God, so that you may eat the flesh of kings and the flesh of commanders and the flesh of mighty men and the flesh of horses and of those who sit on them and the flesh of all men, both free men and slaves, and small and great."

And I saw the beast and the kings of the earth and their armies assembled to make war against Him who sat on the horse and against His army. And the beast was seized, and with him the false prophet who performed the signs in his presence, by which he deceived those who had received the mark of the beast and those who worshiped his image; these two were thrown alive into the lake of fire which burns with brimstone. And the rest were killed with the sword which came from the mouth of Him who sat on the horse, and all the birds were filled with their flesh. (19:17–21)

Once again an angel plays a key role in the Apocalypse. John saw this angel "standing in the sun." This means in the proximity of the sun, possibly in front of it, partially eclipsing it. He stands in a prominent place to make this important announcement. Evidently the worldwide darkness associated with the fifth bowl (16:10) has been lifted, since the sun is again visible. The lifting of that earlier darkness would also explain how the smoke from Babylon's destruction was visible at a distance (18:9–19).

As angels have frequently done in Revelation, the angel "cried out with a loud voice." He addresses all the birds, inviting them to feed on the results of the battle that will soon begin. The angel commands the birds to "assemble for the great supper of God." The brief but catastrophic day of the Lord will result in an unprecedented slaughter, with uncounted millions of dead bodies (14:20). Even after the birds have eaten, it will still take seven months to bury the bodies (Ezekiel 39:12).

At the great supper, the birds "will eat the flesh of kings and the flesh of commanders and the flesh of mighty men and the flesh of horses and of those who sit on them and the flesh of all men, both free men and slaves, and small and great." That all-inclusive statement reveals the worldwide extent of the slaughter. To have one's unburied body left as food for birds is the ultimate indignity, especially for proud kings and mighty military commanders. That same fate awaits all the God-hating rebels everywhere in the world.

Then John saw "the beast and the kings of the earth and their armies assembled to make war against Him who sat on the horse and against His army." The beast is Antichrist (11:7; 13:1–8), leader of the last and greatest empire in human history. The kings of the earth are the ten kings (17:12–14). Their armies have assembled to make war against Christ and His army.

In an instant, "the beast was seized, and with him the false prophet who performed the signs in his presence, by which he deceived those who had received the mark of the beast and those who worshiped his image; these two were thrown alive into the lake of fire." This is the first mention in Scripture of the lake of fire, which is the final hell, the ultimate destination of Satan, his angels, and the unredeemed (Matthew 25:41). Isaiah described it as the place where "their worm will not die and their fire will not be quenched" (66:24), a description echoed by the Lord Jesus Christ (Matthew 13:42; Mark 9:48). Revelation 14:11 says of those who suffer there, "The smoke of their torment goes up forever and ever; they have no rest day and night."

"And the rest were killed with the sword which came from the mouth of Him who sat on the horse, and all the birds were filled with their flesh." Without their commanders, Antichrist's leaderless forces will be destroyed. The rest of those gathered to fight against Christ were killed with the sword which came from the mouth of Him who sat on the horse. Then, just as the angel foretold, all the birds were filled with their flesh.

21

The MILLENNIUM

(20:1–10)

The millennial kingdom is called by many names in Scripture. In Matthew 19:28 Jesus calls it "the regeneration." Acts 3:19 describes the kingdom as "times of refreshing," while verse 21 of that chapter calls it "the period of restoration of all things." The apostle Paul refers to it in Ephesians 1:10 as "an administration suitable to the fullness of the times." The Bible's teaching on the kingdom is not confined to the New Testament. The kingdom is an important theme throughout Scripture; it is the goal toward which all of redemptive history progresses.

Taking the text of Revelation 20 (and the numerous other biblical passages that speak of the earthly kingdom) at face value leads to a premillennial view of eschatology. That is, Christ will return, and then establish a literal kingdom on earth, which will last for a thousand years. There are two other major views of the millennial kingdom: postmillennialism and amillennialism. The three views are summarized on the next page. At the heart of the debate over millennial views is the issue of hermeneutics. All sides in the debate agree that interpreting Old Testament prophecy literally leads naturally to premillennialism.[1]

MAJOR VIEWS REGARDING THE MILLENIUM

INTERPRETIVE SCHOOL	BASIC UNDERSTANDING OF THE MILLENIAL KINGDOM
Postmillennialism	Through Christian influence, society will continue to improve until it reaches a utopian-like state. Thus it is believers who will bring in the millennial kingdom. Christ will return after this general period of peace and prosperity has been established.
Amillennialism	The millennial kingdom is not a future, thousand-year kingdom on earth. Rather, it is a spiritual kingdom that refers to Christ's rule in the hearts of His people during the church age. Some amillennialists believe the millennial kingdom is a literal kingdom in heaven, where Christ's saints rule with him. But they reject the notion of a future, physical kingdom on earth.
Premillennialism	The millennial kingdom refers to a future, physical kingdom that Christ will establish at His return. The kingdom, which will be centered in Jerusalem, will last for one thousand years, after which this world will be destroyed and replaced by the new earth. This view is the most natural way to understand Revelation 20–22.

Though not an exhaustive description of the earthly kingdom, Revelation 20:1–10 caps off all the biblical revelation about the millennium by revealing four essential truths about it.

1. THE REMOVAL OF SATAN

Then I saw an angel coming down from heaven, holding the key of the abyss and a great chain in his hand. And he laid hold of the dragon, the serpent of old, who is the devil and Satan, and bound him for a thousand years; and he threw him into the abyss, and shut it and sealed it over him, so that he would not deceive the nations any longer, until the thousand years were completed; after these things he must be released for a short time. (20:1–3)

The first matter for the King's attention as He sets up His kingdom is the confinement of the chief rebel. The removal of Satan will dramatically change the world. By this time, God will have destroyed all human rebels.

Those who survived the tribulation judgments will have been executed at Armageddon (19:11–21) or the goat judgment (Matthew 25:31–46). The ringleaders of the worldwide rebellion, the beast (Antichrist) and the false prophet, will have been thrown into the lake of fire (19:20). The final step in preparation for the kingdom will be the removal of Satan and his demons.

As it frequently does in Revelation, the phrase "And I saw" indicates chronological progression. The location of this passage in the chronological flow of Revelation is consistent with a premillennial view of the kingdom. After the tribulation Christ will return and set up His kingdom, followed by the new heavens and the new earth (21:1). The millennial kingdom comes after Christ's second coming but before the establishing of the new heavens and the new earth.

The identity of the angel whom John saw coming down from heaven to bind Satan is not disclosed, but he may be Michael the archangel, the great adversary of Satan (cf. 12:7). Whoever the angel is, he possesses great power. He is sent to earth with a specific agenda: to seize Satan for the thousand-year duration of the kingdom, bind him, cast him into the abyss and seal it, and then release him at the end of the thousand years.

"Abyss" appears five times in Revelation (9:11; 11:7; 17:8; 20:1, 3), always in reference to the temporary place of incarceration for certain demons. The abyss is not their final place of punishment. The lake of fire is (Matthew 25:41). The abyss is a place of torment where demons fear to be sent (Luke 8:31).

The key given to the angel by God signifies his delegated authority. He has the power to open the abyss and shut it after casting Satan inside. This chain is a great one, because of Satan's greatness and power as the highest created being (Ezekiel 28:14). The angel laid hold of Satan, who is unmistakably identified by the same four titles given him in 12:9. First, he is called "the dragon," a title given him twelve times in Revelation and a reference to his ferociousness and cruelty. The title "serpent of old" returns readers to the garden of Eden and Satan's temptation of Eve (Genesis 3:1–6). "Devil" means "slanderer" or "malicious gossip." "Satan" means "adversary," since Satan opposes God, Christ, and all believers.

The length of the period for which Satan will be bound is defined as a thousand years, the first of six precise and important references to the duration of the millennium (cf. verses 3, 4, 5, 6, 7). It is only then that he will be incarcerated in the abyss, which will be shut and sealed so he cannot deceive the nations any longer. (That does not mean that the living people in the millennium will be incapable of sinning. Amazingly, a vast part of the population, born of the believers who alone entered the kingdom, will in that perfect environment love their sin and reject the King. They will be judged with a rod of iron [2:27; 12:5; Psalm 2:9]).

2. THE REIGN OF THE SAINTS

Then I saw thrones, and they sat on them, and judgment was given to them. And I saw the souls of those who had been beheaded because of their testimony of Jesus and because of the word of God, and those who had not worshiped the beast or his image, and had not received the mark on their forehead and on their hand; and they came to life and reigned with Christ for a thousand years. The rest of the dead did not come to life until the thousand years were completed. This is the first resurrection. Blessed and holy is the one who has a part in the first resurrection; over these the second death has no power, but they will be priests of God and of Christ and will reign with Him for a thousand years. (20:4–6)

With Satan, his demons, and all God-rejecting sinners out of the way, the millennial kingdom of peace will be established. The supreme ruler in that kingdom will be Jesus Christ. He alone is "King of Kings, and Lord of Lords" (19:16). Yet He has graciously promised that His saints will reign with Him. They will rule subordinately over every aspect of life in the kingdom and will perfectly carry out His will.

In this vision, John sees the panorama of God's people resurrected, rewarded, and reigning with Christ. He saw thrones, symbolizing both judicial and regal authority, and God's people sat on them, and judgment was given to them. The glorified saints will both enforce God's will and judge disputes.

As his vision continued, John saw "the souls of those who had been beheaded because of their testimony of Jesus and because of the word of God, and those who had not worshiped the beast or his image, and had not received the mark on their forehead and on their hand." These are the martyred believers from the tribulation (6:9; 7:9–17; 12:11). Because the tribulation saints were faithful to the death, they too came to life and reigned with Christ for a thousand years.

Then John adds the parenthetical footnote that "the rest of the dead did not come to life until the thousand years were completed." These are the unbelieving dead of all ages, whose resurrection to judgment and damnation is described in verses 11–15. John calls the resurrection of the saints from all ages "the first resurrection." That resurrection is also called in Scripture the "resurrection of the righteous" (Luke 14:14; Acts 24:15), the "resurrection of life" (John 5:29), the resurrection of "those who are Christ's at His coming" (1 Corinthians 15:23), and the "better resurrection" (Hebrews 11:35).

The phrase "blessed and holy is the one who has a part in the first resurrection" introduces the fifth of seven beatitudes in Revelation (1:3; 14:13; 16:15; 19:9; 22:7, 14). Those who have a part in the first resurrection are blessed because the second death has no power over them. The second death is eternal hell. The comforting truth is that no true child of God will ever face God's eternal wrath (cf. Romans 5:9). Those who participate in the first resurrection are also blessed because they will be priests of God and of Christ. Believers are already "a royal priesthood" (1 Peter 2:9). Believers now serve as priests by worshiping God and leading others to the knowledge of Him, and will also serve in that capacity during the millennial kingdom.

A final blessing for the participants in the first resurrection is that they will reign with the Lord Jesus Christ for a thousand years, along with believers who survived the tribulation. The millennial rule of Christ and the saints will be marked by the presence of righteousness and peace (Isaiah 32:17) and joy (Isaiah 12:3–4; 61:3, 7). Physically, it will be a time when the curse is lifted (Isaiah 11:7–9; 30:23–24; 35:1–2, 7), when food will be plentiful (Joel 2:21–27), and when there will be physical health and well-being (Isaiah 33:24; 35:5–6), leading to long life (Isaiah 65:20).

3. THE RETURN OF SATAN

When the thousand years are completed, Satan will be released from his prison, (20:7)

Satan and his demon hordes remain imprisoned in the abyss for the duration of the millennium, as the Lord Jesus Christ rules with unopposed
sovereignty. They are not permitted to interfere in the affairs of the kingdom in any way. Satan's binding will end, however, when the thousand
years are completed and he is released from his prison to lead a final
rebellion of sinners.

Though the initial inhabitants of the millennial kingdom will all be
redeemed, they will still possess a sinful human nature. And as all parents
have done since the fall, they will pass that sin nature on to their offspring. Each successive generation throughout the thousand years will be
made up of sinners in need of salvation. Many will come to saving faith in
the Lord Jesus Christ. But amazingly, despite the personal rule of Christ
on earth, despite the most moral society the world will ever know, many
others will love their sin and reject Him (cf. Romans 8:7). Even the utopian
conditions of the millennium will not change the sad reality of human
depravity. As they did during His incarnational presence on earth, sinners
will refuse the grace and reject the lordship of the King of all the earth.

When Satan is loosed, he will provide the supernatural leadership
needed to bring to the surface all the sin and rebellion left in the universe.
He will pull together all the rebels, revealing the true character and intent
of those Christ-rejecting sinners, making it evident that God's judgment
of them is just.

Satan's violent hatred of God and Christ will not be altered by his
thousand years of imprisonment in the abyss. When he is released, he will
immediately set out on his final act of rebellion.

4. THE REVOLT OF SOCIETY

[Satan] will come out to deceive the nations which are in the four corners of the earth, Gog and Magog, to gather them together for the war; the number of them is like the sand of the seashore. And they came up on the broad plain of the earth and surrounded the camp of the saints and the beloved city, and fire came down from heaven and devoured them. And the devil who deceived them was thrown into the lake of fire and brimstone, where the beast and the false prophet are also; and they will be tormented day and night forever and ever. (20:8–10)

At the end of his thousand-year imprisonment, Satan "will come out to deceive the nations." He will find fertile soil in which to sow his seeds of rebellion, for many unsaved descendants of those who entered the millennial kingdom in their physical bodies (all of whom will be redeemed) will love their sin and reject Christ. They will be as unmoved by the peace, joy, and righteousness of the millennium as earlier sinners were by the devastating judgments of the tribulation (cf. 9:20–21; 16:9, 11, 21).

The actual strategy and method of Satan's deception is not revealed, but it will succeed in duping the unregenerate people of the world into revolting against the Lord Jesus Christ. His deception, however, will fit within God's purpose, which, as noted above, is to manifest His justice when He destroys the rebels. Satan's actions are always under God's sovereign control (cf. Job 1:12; 2:6), and his gathering together of these wicked rebels will be no exception.

Satan will collect the deceived nations from "the four corners of the earth" (7:1; Isaiah 11:12), an expression referring to the four main points of the compass: north, south, east, and west. In other words, the rebels will come from all over the globe.

John gives these enemies of the King of Kings the symbolic title "Gog and Magog," naming them after the invasion force that will assault Israel during the tribulation (Ezekiel 38–39). Some believe that Ezekiel 38 and 39 describe this battle at the end of the millennium. There are, however, significant differences that argue against equating the two events. Ezekiel

39:4 and 17 describe the invaders perishing on the mountains of Israel, but according to Revelation 20:9 the rebels at the end of the millennium will be destroyed on a "broad plain." Also, the language of Ezekiel 39:17–20 seems to be describing the same event depicted in Revelation 19:17–18. Third, the events of Ezekiel 38–39 fit chronologically before the description of the millennial temple given in chapters 40–48, while the battle depicted in Revelation 20:7–10 takes place after the millennium.

The name Gog appears to be used in Scripture as a general title for an enemy of God's people. Most likely, Gog is used in verse 8 to describe the human leader of Satan's forces. Some believe the people known as Magog to be the descendants of Noah's grandson of that same name (Genesis 10:2). They later became known as the Scythians and inhabited the region north of the Black and Caspian seas. Others identify them with a people who lived farther south in Asia Minor. Whoever the historical people known as Magog may have been, the term is used in this passage to describe the sinful rebels from all the nations who will gather together for the final war in human history.

Amazingly, John saw that the number of the rebels will be like the sand of the seashore—a figure of speech used in Scripture to describe a vast, uncountable multitude (Genesis 22:17). The ideal conditions of prosperity and peace that will prevail during the millennium, coupled with the long life spans of its inhabitants, will lead to a massive population explosion. Vast numbers of those people will join Satan in his final act of rebellion against God.

The rebel forces will "[come] up on the broad plain of the earth and surround the camp of the saints and the beloved city," Jerusalem—the place of Messiah's throne and the center of the millennial world. Here the saints will be enjoying the glorious presence of the Lord Jesus Christ when the attack comes.

Yet, like Armageddon a thousand years earlier (19:11–21), the "battle" will in reality be an execution. As the rebel forces move in for the attack, "fire [will come] down from heaven and [devour] them." They will be instantly exterminated. Satan's forces will be physically killed, and their souls will go into the realm of punishment, awaiting their final sentencing to eternal hell, which will take place shortly (20:11–15). Nor will their evil leader escape his fate: The Devil who deceived them will be "thrown into the lake of fire and brimstone." There he will join the beast and the false prophet, who by that time will have been in that place of torment for a thousand years (19:20).

Those sentenced to that terrible place will be "tormented day and night." There will not be a moment's relief. Scripture explicitly teaches that hell is eternal. The same Greek phrase translated "forever and ever" is used in 1:18 to speak of Christ's eternity. Jesus taught that the punishment of the wicked is as eternal as the eternal life of the righteous (Matthew 25:46). Second Thessalonians 1:9 teaches that the destruction of the wicked in hell stretches throughout all eternity.

Believers are already citizens of God's kingdom (Philippians 3:20; Colossians 1:13; 1 Thessalonians 2:12), blessed to be in fellowship with the King. But a glorious future inheritance awaits them, "imperishable and undefiled [which] will not fade away" (1 Peter 1:4).

22

The Great White
THRONE
Judgment

(20:11–15)

This passage describes the final sentencing of the lost and is the most serious, sobering, and tragic passage in the entire Bible. Commonly known as the great white throne judgment, it is the last courtroom scene that will ever take place. The accused—all the unsaved who have ever lived—will be resurrected to experience a trial like no other. There will be no debate over their guilt or innocence. There will be a prosecutor, but no defender; an accuser, but no advocate. There will be an indictment, but no defense mounted by the accused; the convicting evidence will be presented with no rebuttal or cross-examination.

No one at the great white throne judgment will have the slightest grounds for complaint about his or her sentence. Those who reject God's grace and mercy in this life will inevitably face His justice in the life to come. Unrepentant sinners will experience God's justice at the great white throne judgment.

This simple but powerful text describes the terrifying reality of the final verdict and sentence on sinners under four headings.

The Scene

Then I saw a great white throne and Him who sat upon it, from whose presence earth and heaven fled away, and no place was found for them. And I saw the dead, the great and the small, standing before the throne, (20:11–12a)

In one brief statement, John describes the terrifying scene before him. The apostle observes the Judge seated on His throne of judgment and all the accused standing before Him. The familiar phrase "Then I saw" once again introduces a new vision. This vision of the great white throne judgment follows those of the millennium (20:1–10) and the second coming (19:11–21) and immediately precedes the vision of the new heaven and the new earth (21:1ff.).

The first thing John saw was "a great white throne." Revelation mentions thrones nearly fifty times. In this case it is the seat of God's sovereign rule. It is called great not only because of its size, but also because of its authority. That it is white symbolizes its purity, holiness, and justice. The verdict handed down from this throne will be absolutely just.

Even more awe inspiring than the throne was the vision of "Him who sat upon it." The judge on the throne is none other than the eternal, almighty God (4:8–11). Sharing the throne with the Father is the Lord Jesus Christ. In 3:21 Jesus promised, "He who overcomes, I will grant to him to sit down with Me on My throne, as I also overcame and sat down with My Father on His throne." In John's vision of the new heaven and the new earth, he saw "the throne of God and of the Lamb" (22:1, 3).

Though the Father and the Son share the throne, it is the Son who is uniquely in view here, since Scripture teaches that He will judge sinners (John 5:22, 26-27; Acts 10:42). It is God in the Person of the glorified Lord Jesus Christ who will sit in final judgment on unbelievers.

After describing the vision of the Judge on His throne, John noted the startling reality that "from His presence earth and heaven fled away." That incredible statement describes the "uncreation" of the universe. The earth will have been reshaped by the devastating judgments of the tribulation and restored during the millennial kingdom. Yet it will still be tainted with sin and subject to the effects of the fall; hence, it must be destroyed. In its place God will create "a new heaven and a new earth; for the first heaven and the first earth passed away" (21:1). The present earth and heaven will not merely be moved or reshaped, since John saw in his vision that "no place was found for them." They will go totally out of existence.

The details of God's uncreation of the universe are given by Peter in 2 Peter 3:10–13, which describes the final expression of the day of the Lord: "But the day of the Lord will come like a thief, in which the heavens will pass away with a roar and the elements will be destroyed with intense heat, and the earth and its works will be burned up" (verse 10). The day of the Lord will come suddenly, unexpectedly, and with disastrous consequences for the unprepared—just like the coming of a thief.

Introducing the final element in this fearful scene, John writes that he saw "the dead, the great and the small, standing before the throne." The setting is the indescribable nothingness between the end of the present universe and the creation of the new heaven and the new earth. The dead pictured standing before the throne of divine judgment are not just from the millennial rebellion, but include all the unbelievers who have ever lived. This is the "resurrection of judgment" (John 5:29), the resurrection "to disgrace and everlasting contempt" (Daniel 12:2), the "resurrection of . . . the wicked" (Acts 24:15).

To emphasize the all-encompassing scope of the judgment, John notes that the sweeping mass of unbelievers before God's throne includes both "the great and the small." All will face judgment, "for there is no partiality with God" (Romans 2:11).

THE SUMMONS

And the sea gave up the dead which were in it, and death and Hades gave up the dead which were in them; (20:13a)

As the next scene in this ultimate courtroom drama unfolds, the prisoners are summoned from their cells to appear before the Judge. Since their deaths, their souls have been tormented in a place of punishment. Now the time has come for them to be sentenced to the final, eternal hell. Before the sea was uncreated and went out of existence (21:1), it "gave up the dead which were in it." God will summon from its depths new bodies for all who perished in the sea throughout human history. "Death" symbolizes all the places on land from which God will resurrect new bodies for the unrighteous dead. The sea and death are pictured as voracious monsters that have swallowed those bodies and will be forced to return them before their uncreation.

"Hades" is the Greek word used to describe the realm of the dead. Hades is used ten times in the New Testament, always in reference to the place of punishment (Luke 16:23) where the unrighteous dead are kept pending their sentencing to hell. In this incredible scene, Hades is emptied of its captive spirits, who are reunited with resurrection bodies before the bar of God's justice. Unbelievers, fitted with resurrection bodies suited for hell, will then be ready for their sentencing to the lake of fire where their punishment will last forever.

THE STANDARD

and books were opened; and another book was opened, which is the book of life; and the dead were judged from the things which were written in the books, according to their deeds. . . . and they were judged, every one of them according to their deeds. (20:12b, 13b)

As the judgment commences, the Judge opens the books (cf. Daniel 7:10): The books contain the record of every thought, word, and deed of every unsaved person who ever lived. God has kept perfect records of every person's life, and the dead will be judged "according to their deeds." Sinners' deeds will be measured against God's perfect, holy standard, which Jesus defined in Matthew 5:48: "Therefore you are to be perfect, as your heavenly Father is perfect." No prisoner before the bar of divine justice will be able to claim the perfect obedience to God's holy standards that He requires. They "all have sinned and fall short of the glory of God" (Romans 3:23), and are "dead in [their] trespasses and sins" (Ephesians 2:1).

God's justice demands payment for every person's sins. Christ paid that penalty for believers: "He was pierced through for our transgressions, He was crushed for our iniquities; the chastening for our well-being fell upon Him, and by His scourging we are healed. All of us like sheep have gone astray, each of us has turned to his own way; but the Lord has caused the iniquity of us all to fall on Him" (Isaiah 53:5–6; cf. 2 Corinthians 5:21). Yet unbelievers will personally pay the penalty for violating God's law—eternal destruction in hell (2 Thessalonians 1:9).

The absolute accuracy of God's judgment will ensure that unbelievers' punishment in hell fits their iniquity. Each person's life will be individually evaluated, and each person's punishment will be consistent with that evaluation. Scripture teaches that there will be varying degrees of punishment in hell. When Jesus sent the Twelve out on a preaching tour, He told them, "Whoever does not receive you, nor heed your words, as you go out of that house or that city, shake the dust off your feet. Truly I say to you, it will be more tolerable for the land of Sodom and Gomorrah in the day of judgment than for that city" (Matthew 10:14–15 cf. 11:21–24). Similarly, Jesus warned that the hypocritical scribes "who like to walk around in long robes, and like respectful greetings in the market places, and chief seats in the synagogues and places of honor at banquets, who devour widows' houses, and for appearance's sake offer long prayers; these will receive greater condemnation" (Mark 12:38–40).

Yet while there are varying degrees of punishment in hell, everyone there will suffer intolerable misery and torment. All sinners in hell will be completely separated from God and all that comes from His goodness. They will be miserable, but not equally miserable.

After the books containing the prisoners' evil deeds were opened, "another book was opened, which is the book of life." This book's imagery corresponds to the registry of citizens kept by ancient cities. It contains the names of all those whose "citizenship is in heaven" (Philippians 3:20). It is referred to several times in Revelation (verse 15; 3:5; 13:8; 17:8; 21:27). The Book of Life is the record of God's elect. All whose names are not recorded in it will be eternally damned.

Since their names were not in the Book of Life, the prisoners before the great white throne were judged, "every one of them according to their deeds." Some, in shock and horror, will protest, "Lord, Lord, did we not prophesy in Your name, and in Your name cast out demons, and in Your name perform many miracles?" But they will hear in reply the most chilling, terrifying words that any human will ever hear: "I never knew you; depart from me, you who practice lawlessness" (Matthew 7:22-23).

THE SENTENCE

Then death and Hades were thrown into the lake of fire. This is the second death, the lake of fire. And if anyone's name was not found written in the book of life, he was thrown into the lake of fire. (20:14–15)

As the sentence is passed, "death and Hades [the grave and the temporary place of punishment for everyone whose name was not found written in the Book of Life] were thrown into the lake of fire," meaning that they will go out of existence, swallowed up by the final hell. Their inmates, currently suffering in their spirits only, will be united with specially designed resurrection bodies and cast into eternal hell (Matthew 10:28). That final hell, described as the lake of fire, may already exist (Matthew 25:41), but if so, it is currently unoccupied. Its first two occupants, the beast and the false prophet, will not arrive until the end of the tribulation (19:20).

The clearest and most vivid of the New Testament terms used to describe the final hell is Gehenna. Gehenna is the valley of Ben-Hinnom (also called Topheth; 2 Kings 23:10; Isaiah 30:33; Jeremiah 7:31–32; 19:6), located southwest of Jerusalem. In Old Testament times, idolatrous Israelites burned their children in the fire there as sacrifices to false gods (Jeremiah 19:2–6). In Jesus' day, it was the site of Jerusalem's garbage dump. The fires that kept constantly burning there gave off foul-smelling smoke, and the dump was infested with maggots. Sometimes the bodies of criminals were dumped there. The valley of Ben-Hinnom was a fitting picture of eternal hell, one used repeatedly by Jesus (Matthew 5:22, 29–30; 10:28; 18:9; 23:15, 33; Mark 9:43, 45, 47; Luke 12:5).

The blessed and holy participants in the first resurrection will not experience the second death (20:6; see "Resurrection" and "Judgments" in the the chart, "Views Concerning the End Times"). But the rest of the dead, who did not participate in the first resurrection (20:5), will face the second death, which is defined here as the lake of fire. Those who die in their sins in this present world of time and space will die a second death in eternity—they will be sentenced to the lake of fire forever.

Scripture vividly portrays the various aspects of the final, fiery hell. Fire is used more than twenty times in the New Testament to depict the torment of hell. Whether the fire of hell is literal, physical fire is unknown, since the lake of fire exists outside the created universe as we know it. If the fire here is symbolic, the reality it represents will be even more horrifying and painful. The Bible also depicts hell as a place of total darkness, which will isolate its inmates from each other (e.g., Matthew 22:13; 2 Peter 2:17); as a place where the worm (possibly emblematic of an accusing conscience) devouring the wicked will never die (Isaiah 66:24; Mark 9:44); as a place of banishment from God's kingdom (Matthew 8:12; 22:13), and as a place where there is "weeping and gnashing of teeth" (Matthew 13:42; 22:13; 24:51; 25:30; Luke 13:28).

There is only one way to avoid the terrifying future of hell. Those who confess their sins and ask God to forgive them on the basis of Christ's substitutionary death on their behalf will be delivered from God's eternal wrath (Romans 5:9; 1 Thessalonians 1:10; 5:9).

VIEWS CONCERNING THE END TIMES

······································

CATEGORIES	AMILLENNIALISM	POSTMILLENNIALISM	HISTORIC PREMILLENNIALISM	FUTURIST PREMILLENNIALISM
Second coming of Christ	Single event; no distinction between rapture and second coming; introduces eternal state.	Single event; no distinction between rapture and second coming; Christ returns after millennium.	Rapture and second coming simultaneous; Christ returns to reign on earth.	Second coming in two phases: rapture for church; second coming to earth seven years later.
Resurrection	General resurrection of believers and unbelievers at second coming of Christ.	General resurrection of believers and unbelievers at second coming of Christ.	Resurrection of believers at beginning of millennium; resurrection of unbelievers at end of millennium.	Distinction in resurrections: • Church at rapture • Old Testament/tribulation saints at second coming • Unbelievers at end of millennium
Judgments	General judgment of all people.	General judgment of all people.	Judgment at second coming; judgment at end of tribulation.	Distinction in judgment: • Believers' work at rapture • Jews/Gentiles at end of tribulation • Unbelievers at end of millennium
Tribulation	Tribulation is experienced in this present age.	Tribulation is experienced in this present age.	Postrib view: church goes through the future tribulation.	Pretrib view: church is raptured prior to tribulation.
Millennium	No literal millennium on earth after second coming; kingdom present in church age.	Present age blends into millennium because of progress of gospel.	Millennium is both present and future, Christ is reigning in heaven; millennium not necessarily 1,000 yrs.	At second coming, Christ inaugurates literal 1,000-year millennium on earth.
Israel and the Church	Church is the new Israel; no distinction between Israel and church.	Church is the new Israel; no distinction between Israel and church.	Some distinction between Israel and church; future for Israel, but church is spiritual Israel.	Complete distinction between Israel and church; distinct program for each.
Adherents	L. Berkhof, O. T. Allis, G. C. Berkhouwer	Charles Hodge, B. B. Warfield, W. G. T. Shedd, A. H. Strong	G. E. Ladd, A. Reese, M. J. Erickson	L. S. Chafer, J. D. Pentecost, C. C. Ryrie, J. F. Walvoord

Adapted from Paul Benware, *Understanding End Times Prophecy* (Chicago, Moody, 2006), 143

23

Everything
NEW
(21:1–22:5)

Throughout the history of the church, God's people rightly have been preoccupied with heaven. They have longed for its joys because they have been only loosely tied to this earth. They have seen themselves as "strangers and exiles on the earth" who "desire a better country, that is, a heavenly one" (Hebrews 11:13, 16).

Sadly, that is no longer true for many in today's church. Caught up in our society's mad rush for instant gratification, material comfort, and narcissistic indulgence, the church has become worldly. The Bible makes it clear that believers are to focus on heaven. In Philippians 3:20 Paul notes that "our citizenship is in heaven." And he called upon the believers at Colossae to "keep seeking the things above, where Christ is, seated at the right hand of God. Set your mind on the things above, not on the things that are on earth (Colossians 3:1*b*–2)."

Scripture refers to heaven more than five hundred times. Revelation alone mentions heaven about fifty times. The Bible delineates three heavens (2 Corinthians 12:2). The first heaven is the earth's atmosphere (Genesis 1:20; Job 12:7; Ezekiel 38:20); the second heaven is interplanetary and interstellar space (Genesis 15:5; 22:17; Deuteronomy 1:10; 4:19; Psalm 8:3; Isaiah 13:10); the third heaven is the dwelling place of God (e.g., Deuteronomy 4:39; 1 Kings 8:30; Job 22:12; Psalm 14:2; Daniel 2:28; Matthew 5:34; Acts 7:55).

Heaven is an actual place, not a state of spiritual consciousness. Though heaven is far beyond the created world in another dimension, when believers die they will be there immediately (Luke 23:43; 2 Corinthians 5:8). Those believers alive at the rapture will also be transported to heaven immediately (1 Corinthians 15:51–55; 1 Thessalonians 4:13–18).

THE NEW HEAVEN AND NEW EARTH (21:1–8)

These first eight verses unfold six features of the new heaven and the new earth:

1. Its Appearance
Then I saw a new heaven and a new earth; for the first heaven and the first earth passed away, and there is no longer any sea. (21:1)

The phrase "I saw" is used throughout Revelation to indicate chronological progression. It has introduced each of the climactic events beginning with the return of Christ in 19:11. As this chapter opens, all the sinners of all the ages, as well as Satan and his demons, have been sentenced to the lake of fire (20:10–15). With all ungodly men and angels banished forever and the present universe destroyed (20:11), God will create a new realm for the redeemed and the holy angels to dwell in forever.

The phrase "a new heaven and a new earth" derives from two passages in Isaiah. In Isaiah 65:17 God declared, "For behold, I create new heavens and a new earth; and the former things will not be remembered or come to mind." In Isaiah 66:22 He added, " 'For just as the new heavens and the new earth which I make will endure before Me,' declares the Lord, 'so your offspring and your name will endure.' " What Isaiah predicted is now a reality in John's vision.

"New" does not mean new in a chronological sense, but new in quality. The new heaven and the new earth will not merely succeed the present universe. They will be something brand-new and fresh. God must create a new heaven and a new earth because the first heaven and the first earth passed away.

The first hint of what the new heaven and new earth will be like comes in John's observation that there will no longer be any sea. That will be a startling change from the present earth, nearly three-fourths of which is covered by water. The sea is emblematic of the present water-based environment. All life on earth is dependent on water for its survival. But believers' glorified bodies will not require water (unlike our present human bodies, whose blood is 90 percent water). The new heaven and the new earth will be based on a completely different life principle. There will be a river in heaven, not of water, but of the "water of life" (22:1, 17). Without a sea, there can be no hydrological cycle, so that every feature of life and climate will be dramatically different.

2. Its Capital
And I saw the holy city, new Jerusalem, coming down out of heaven from God, made ready as a bride adorned for her husband. (21:2)

Next John moves from a description of the new heaven and the new earth in general to a description of the capital city of the eternal state. Since the text plainly identifies it as such, there is no reason to doubt that the "new Jerusalem" is an actual city. The new Jerusalem is not heaven, but heaven's capital. (It is not synonymous with heaven, because its dimensions are given in verse 16.) It will be the third city named Jerusalem in redemptive history. The first is the historic Jerusalem, the City of David, which currently exists in Palestine. The second Jerusalem will be the restored Jerusalem where Christ will rule during the millennial kingdom.

But the new Jerusalem does not belong to the first creation, so it is neither the historic city nor the millennial city. It is the altogether new eternal city. The old Jerusalem, in ruins for twenty-five years when John received this vision, is too stained with sin to survive into the eternal state. The new Jerusalem is called the holy city because everyone in it is holy

(20:6). The concept of a city includes relationships, activity, responsibility, unity, socialization, communion, and cooperation. Unlike the evil cities of the present earth, the people in the new Jerusalem will live together in perfect harmony.

In his vision, John saw the "new Jerusalem, coming down out of heaven from God," its "architect and builder" (Hebrews 11:10). The implication is that it already exists (Hebrews 12:22–23). All of heaven is currently contained in the new Jerusalem. It is separate from the present universe. Believers who die go to the "heavenly Jerusalem," where Jesus has gone before them to prepare a place for them (John 14:1–3). But when God creates the new heaven and the new earth, the new Jerusalem will descend into the midst of that holy new universe (21:10) and serve as the dwelling place of the redeemed for all eternity.

John then notes that it was "made ready as a bride adorned for her husband." The city is pictured as a bride because it contains the bride and takes on her character. The imagery is drawn from a Jewish wedding. John saw the bride adorned for her husband because it was time for the consummation—the eternal state for believers. By this point in Revelation, the bride concept expands to include not only the church, but also all the rest of the redeemed from all the ages who live forever in that eternal city.

3. Its Supreme Reality
And I heard a loud voice from the throne, saying, "Behold, the tabernacle of God is among men, and He will dwell among them, and they shall be His people, and God Himself will be among them, (21:3)

The supreme glory and joy of heaven is the Person of God (cf. Psalm 73:25). A loud voice (probably of an angel, as God speaks in verse 5) heralds an announcement of great importance: "Behold, the tabernacle of God is among men." The Greek word translated "tabernacle" can also mean "tent" or "dwelling place." God will pitch His tent among His people; no longer will God be far off and distant. No more will His presence be veiled in the human form of Jesus Christ, even in His millennial majesty, or in the cloud and pillar of fire, or inside the Holy of Holies.

To the mind-boggling reality that the tabernacle of God is among men he adds the statement that God will "dwell among them, and they shall be His people, and God Himself will be among them" (21:3–4). This will be a manifestation of God's glorious presence to His people like no other in redemptive history and the culmination of all divine promise and human hope.

What will it be like to live in God's glorious presence in heaven? First, believers will enjoy fellowship with Him—the sin-hindered fellowship that believers have with God in this life (1 John 1:3) will become full and unlimited. Second, believers will see God as He is (John 3:2)— an eternal and expanded vision of God manifest in His shining glory (21:11, 23; 22:5). They will see all that glorified beings are able to comprehend. Third, believers will worship God. Every glimpse of heaven in Revelation reveals the redeemed and the angels in worship (4:10; 5:14; 7:11; 11:1, 16; 19:4). Fourth, believers will serve God (22:3). It is said of the saints in heaven pictured in 7:15 that "they serve [God] day and night in His temple." Believers' capacity for heavenly service will reflect their faithfulness in this life.

4. Its Uniqueness
and He will wipe away every tear from their eyes; and there will no longer be any death; there will no longer be any mourning, or crying, or pain; the first things have passed away." And He who sits on the throne said, "Behold, I am making all things new." And He said, "Write, for these words are faithful and true." Then He said to me, "It is done. I am the Alpha and the Omega, the beginning and the end." (21:4–6a)

Life in heaven will be dramatically different from anything we have known in the present world. The first change from our earthly life is that "God will wipe away every tear from their eyes" (cf. 7:17; Isaiah 25:8). That does not mean that people who arrive in heaven will be weeping as they face the record of their sins. There is no such record, because "there is now no condemnation for those who are in Christ Jesus" (Romans 8:1). What it declares is the absence of anything to be sorry about—no sadness, no disappointment, no pain. There will be no tears of regret, tears over the death of loved ones, or tears for any other reason.

Another dramatic difference from the present world will be that in heaven "there will no longer be any death." The greatest curse of human existence will be no more. "Death is swallowed up in victory" (1 Corinthians 15:54). Nor will there be any mourning, or crying in heaven. The grief and sorrow that produce mourning will not exist in heaven.

The perfect holiness and absence of sin that will characterize heaven will also mean that there will be no more pain. The glorified sin-free bodies believers will possess in heaven will not be subject to pain of any kind.

Life in heaven will be unique. All these changes indicate that the first things have passed away. Old human experience related to the original creation is gone forever, and with it all the mourning, suffering, disease, pain, and death that has characterized life since the fall. In that forever new creation, there will be no decay, no decline, and no waste. Summarizing those changes in a positive way, He who sits on the throne said, "Behold, I am making all things new." The One who sits on the throne is the same One "from whose presence earth and heaven fled away, and no place was found for them" (20:11).

Overwhelmed by all that he had seen, John seems to have lost his concentration. The glorious, majestic One on the throne then said, "Write, for these words are faithful and true" (21:5). The words John was commanded by God to write are as faithful and true as the One revealing them to him (3:14; 19:11). The One who sits on the throne is qualified to declare the end of redemptive history, because He is the Alpha and the Omega, the first and last letters of the Greek alphabet, the beginning and the end (Isaiah 44:6; 48:12). God started history, He will end it, and all of it has unfolded according to His sovereign plan.

5. Its Residents
I will give to the one who thirsts from the spring of the water of life without cost. He who overcomes will inherit these things, and I will be his God and he will be My son. (21:6b–7)

Two descriptive phrases reveal who will live in the new heaven and new earth. First, a citizen of heaven is described as "one who thirsts." That phrase signifies those who "hunger and thirst for righteousness" (Matthew 5:6). Those who will be redeemed and enter heaven are those who are dissatisfied with their hopeless, lost condition and crave God's righteousness with every part of their being. To the soul of the psalmist who panted after God (Psalm 42:1) and to all earnest seekers, the promise is that their thirst will be satisfied. God "will give to the one who thirsts from the spring of the water of life without cost" (cf. Isaiah 55:1-2).

Second, heaven belongs to "he who overcomes." An overcomer, according to 1 John 5:4-5, is one who exercises saving faith in Christ.

The most wonderful promise to the one who overcomes and who thirsts for righteousness, is God's promise "I will be his God." Equally amazing is God's promise that the one who overcomes "will be My son." Even in this life it is the believer's privilege to be the adopted son of the God of the universe (John 1:12; Romans 8:14-17). Only in heaven will that adoption be fully realized (Romans 8:23).

6. The Outcasts

"But for the cowardly and unbelieving and abominable and murderers and immoral persons and sorcerers and idolaters and all liars, their part will be in the lake that burns with fire and brimstone, which is the second death." (21:8)

John concludes his overview of the new heaven and the new earth with a serious warning. He distinguishes those who will be excluded from participation in the blessings of heaven—all unforgiven and unredeemed sinners. The first group includes "the cowardly." They fell away when their faith was challenged or opposed, because their faith was not genuine.

Because they are unbelieving, their disloyalty excludes them from heaven. They are also abominable, murderers, immoral persons, sorcerers, idolaters, and liars. Those whose lives are characterized by such things give evidence that they are not saved and will never enter the heavenly city. "Their part will be in the lake that burns with fire and brimstone, which is the second death." In contrast to the eternal bliss of the righteous in heaven, the wicked will suffer eternal torment in hell.

THE NEW JERUSALEM (21:9–22:5)

As the vision of the New Jerusalem unfolds, history has ended, and time is no more. John and his readers are transported to the eternal state. Having described the lake of fire (verse 8; 20:14–15), the vision takes the exiled apostle to the eternal resting place of the redeemed. Because it is the capital city of heaven and the link between the new heaven and the new earth, the New Jerusalem is central to the vision and is described in far more detail than the rest of the eternal state.

1. Its General Appearance

Then one of the seven angels who had the seven bowls full of the seven last plagues came and spoke with me, saying, "Come here, I will show you the bride, the wife of the Lamb." And he carried me away in the Spirit to a great and high mountain, and showed me the holy city, Jerusalem, coming down out of heaven from God, having the glory of God. Her brilliance was like a very costly stone, as a stone of crystal-clear jasper. (21:9–11)

The angel came to call John's attention to the city. "Come here, I will show you the bride, the wife of the Lamb." The New Jerusalem is described as a bride because it draws its character from its occupants. Those occupants consist of the bride of the Lamb, a title originally given to the church (19:7) but now enlarged to encompass all the redeemed of all ages, who live there forever. The New Jerusalem is likened to a bride because the redeemed are forever united to God and the Lamb. It is further defined as the "wife of the Lamb" because the marriage has taken place (19:7).

John's incredible vision began when the angel carried him away in the Spirit. When he received the visions that comprise the book of Revelation, the aged apostle was transported from the island of Patmos (1:9) in an amazing spiritual journey to see what unaided human eyes could never see. John's visions were not dreams, but spiritual realities, like those Paul saw when he was also caught up to the third heaven (2 Corinthians 12:2–4).

The first stop was "a great and high mountain." From that spot, the angel showed John "the holy city, Jerusalem." The apostle repeats his observation from verse 2 that the New Jerusalem came "down out of heaven from God." It is interesting that what is described here is not the creation of heaven. It is merely the descent of what already existed from eternity past, now situated in the center of the new heaven and the new earth.

The most distinguishing characteristic of the capital city of eternity is that it is the throne of the eternal, almighty One, and therefore had the glory of God in it. Radiating from the New Jerusalem will be the brilliance of the full manifestation of God's glory, so much so that "the city has no need of the sun or of the moon to shine on it, for the glory of God has illumined it, and its lamp is the Lamb" (verse 23).

Describing the effect of God's glory radiating from the New Jerusalem, John notes that her brilliance was "like a very costly stone, as a stone of crystal-clear jasper." The Greek word translated "brilliance" refers to something from which light radiates. To John, the heavenly city appeared like a giant lightbulb, with the brilliant light of God's glory streaming out of it. But that light did not shine through the thin glass of a lightbulb, but through what looked to John like a very costly stone of crystal-clear jasper. The city appeared to the apostle like one gigantic precious stone. "Jasper" does not refer to the modern stone of the same name, which is opaque. It is from the Greek word referring to a translucent stone. The word "jasper" in this passage is best understood as referring to a diamond, a very costly one because it is crystal-clear and unblemished. Heaven's capital city is thus pictured as a huge, flawless diamond, refracting the brilliant, blazing glory of God throughout the new heaven and the new earth.

2. Its Exterior Design
It had a great and high wall, with twelve gates, and at the gates twelve angels; and names were written on them, which are the names of the

twelve tribes of the sons of Israel. There were three gates on the east and three gates on the north and three gates on the south and three gates on the west. And the wall of the city had twelve foundation stones, and on them were the twelve names of the twelve apostles of the Lamb.

The one who spoke with me had a gold measuring rod to measure the city, and its gates and its wall. The city is laid out as a square, and its length is as great as the width; and he measured the city with the rod, fifteen hundred miles; its length and width and height are equal. And he measured its wall, seventy-two yards, according to human measurements, which are also angelic measurements. The material of the wall was jasper; and the city was pure gold, like clear glass. The foundation stones of the city wall were adorned with every kind of precious stone. The first foundation stone was jasper; the second, sapphire; the third, chalcedony; the fourth, emerald; the fifth, sardonyx; the sixth, sardius; the seventh, chrysolite; the eighth, beryl; the ninth, topaz; the tenth, chrysoprase; the eleventh, jacinth; the twelfth, amethyst. And the twelve gates were twelve pearls; each one of the gates was a single pearl. (21:12–21a)

That the city "had a great and high wall" indicates that it is not a nebulous, floating place. It has specific dimensions and limits. It can be entered and left through its twelve gates. At those gates twelve angels were stationed, to attend to God's glory and to serve His people. The gates had "names written on them, which are the names of the twelve tribes of the sons of Israel," celebrating for all eternity God's covenant relationship with Israel. They were arranged symmetrically. There were three gates each on the east, south, north, and west sides. That arrangement is reminiscent of the way the twelve tribes camped around the tabernacle (Numbers 2), and of the allotment of the tribal lands around the millennial temple (Ezekiel 48).

The massive wall of the city was anchored by "twelve foundation stones, and on them were the twelve names of the twelve apostles of the Lamb." Those stones commemorate God's covenant relationship with the church, with the apostles as the foundation (Ephesians 2:20). At the top of each gate was the name of one of the tribes of Israel. At the bottom of each gate was the name of one of the apostles. The layout of the city's gates pictures God's favor on all His redeemed people, both those under the old and new covenants.

Then a curious thing occurred. The angel who spoke with John "had a gold measuring rod to measure the city, and its gates, and its wall." This interesting event is reminiscent of the measuring of the millennial temple (Ezekiel 40:3ff.) and the measuring of the tribulation temple (11:1). The significance of all three measurements is that they mark out what belongs to God.

The results of the angel's measuring revealed that "the city is laid out as a square." The city walls are about 1,380 miles in each direction. Its length and width and height are equal. Some have suggested that the city is in the shape of a pyramid, though it is best seen as a cube.[1] The focus is that God will design the New Jerusalem with plenty of room for all the redeemed (cf. John 14:2–3).

The angel next measured the city's wall at seventy-two yards, most likely its thickness. Then, as if to emphasize that the city's dimensions are literal and not mystical, John adds the parenthetical footnote that those dimensions were given "according to human measurements, which are also angelic measurements." A yard is a yard, a foot is a foot, and a mile is a mile, whether for humans or angels.

The material that the massive city wall was made out of was jasper—the same diamond-like stone mentioned in verse 11. Not only was the wall translucent, but also the city itself "was pure gold, like clear glass." The New Jerusalem's walls and buildings must be clear for the city to radiate the glory of God.

John next turns his attention in the vision to the foundation stones of the city wall. They were adorned with every kind of precious stone, twelve of which the apostle names. The names of some of the stones have changed through the centuries, making their identification uncertain. These brightly-colored stones refract the shining brilliance of God's glory into a panoply of beautiful colors. The scene was one of breathtaking beauty, a spectrum of dazzling colors flashing from the New Jerusalem throughout the re-created universe.

The next facet of the heavenly city that caught John's eye was the twelve gates, which were twelve pearls. Pearls were highly prized and of great value in John's day. But these pearls were like no pearl ever produced by an oyster, because each one of the gates was a single gigantic pearl nearly 1,400 miles high.

3. Its Internal Character

And the street of the city was pure gold, like transparent glass. I saw no temple in it, for the Lord God the Almighty and the Lamb are its temple. And the city has no need of the sun or of the moon to shine on it, for the glory of God has illumined it, and its lamp is the Lamb. The nations will walk by its light, and the kings of the earth will bring their glory into it. In the daytime (for there will be no night there) its gates will never be closed; and they will bring the glory and the honor of the nations into it; and nothing unclean, and no one who practices abomination and lying, shall ever come into it, but only those whose names are written in the Lamb's book of life.

Then he showed me a river of the water of life, clear as crystal, coming from the throne of God and of the Lamb, in the middle of its street. On either side of the river was the tree of life, bearing twelve kinds of fruit, yielding its fruit every month; and the leaves of the tree were for the healing of the nations. (21:21b–22:2)

As if seeing the magnificent capital city of heaven from a distance was not privilege enough, John's angelic guide took him inside. As he entered the city, the apostle noted that the street of the city "was pure gold, like transparent glass." The streets in the New Jerusalem were made of the highest quality pure gold which, like everything else in the heavenly city, was transparent like glass. Translucent gold is not a material familiar to us on this earth. However, everything in heaven is transparent to let the light of God's glory blaze unrestricted.

Once inside the city, the first thing John noted was that there was "no temple in it." Up to this point, there has been a temple in heaven; but there will be no need for one now, "for the Lord God the Almighty and the Lamb are its temple." Their blazing glory will fill the new heaven and the new earth, and there will be no need for anyone to go anywhere to worship God. Believers will be constantly in His presence.

John also notes that the city has "no need of the sun or of the moon to shine on it, for the glory of God has illumined it, and its lamp is the Lamb." The new heaven and the new earth will be radically different from the present earth, which is totally dependent on the sun and moon, that is, the cycles of light and darkness and the tides of the sea. In the new heaven and the new earth, they will be unnecessary. There will be no seas (21:1), nor will the sun and moon be needed to provide light, for the glory of God will illumine the New Jerusalem and its lamp will be the Lamb. Once again in Revelation, God the Father and the Lamb, Jesus Christ, share authority (3:21).

It may be that the truth that "the kings of the earth will bring their glory into [the city]" offers further proof of the absolute equality in heaven. That phrase may indicate that there will be no social or class structure, that those who enter the city will surrender their earthly glory. Another possible interpretation is that this phrase refers to the believers living at the end of the millennium. According to that view, the statement that the kings of the earth will bring their glory into the New Jerusalem refers to the translation of those believers before the uncreation of the present universe.

Then John adds another detail to his description of the New Jerusalem. Throughout the never-ending daytime of the eternal state, "its gates will never be closed." In an ancient walled city, the gates were closed at nightfall to keep invaders and other potentially dangerous individuals from entering the city under cover of darkness. In eternity, the city will be completely secure; "there will be no night" and the gates of the New Jerusalem will never need to be closed. It will be a place of safety and refreshment, where God's people will "rest from their labors" (14:13).

The kings will not be the only ones to surrender their earthly prestige and glory when they enter heaven. The glory and the honor of the nations will also dissolve, as it were, into the eternal worship of God the Father and the Lord Jesus Christ.

All in heaven will be perfectly holy. "Nothing unclean and no one who practices abomination and lying, shall ever come into" the New Jerusalem. The only ones there will be "those whose names are written in the Lamb's book of life" (3:5; 13:8; 20:12).

The angel next showed the apostle "a river of the water of life." The water of life is not water as we know it (recall that there is no sea in the eternal state; rather, it is a symbol of eternal life; Isaiah 12:3; John 4:13–14; 7:38). Like everything else in the New Jerusalem, the river was clear as crystal so it could reflect the glory of God. It cascaded down from the throne of God and of the Lamb in a dazzling, never-ending stream. Its pure, unobstructed flow symbolizes the constant flow of everlasting life from God's throne to God's people.

The phrase "in the middle of its street" is best translated "in the middle of its path" and connected with the following phrase: "On either side of the river was the tree of life." The tree of life is the celestial counterpart to the tree of life in Eden (Genesis 2:9; 3:22–24). It provides for those who are immortal. The tree of life was a familiar Jewish concept that expressed blessing (2:7). The celestial tree symbolizes the blessing of eternal life. That the tree bears twelve kinds of fruit, "yielding its fruit every month" emphasizes the infinite variety that will fill heaven. The use of the term "month" does not refer to time, since this is the eternal state and time is no more. It is an expression of the joyous provision of eternity spoken in the familiar terms of time.

Then John makes the intriguing observation that "the leaves of the tree were for the healing of the nations." Perhaps a better way to translate it would be "life-giving" or "health-giving," since the Greek word for "healing" can also mean "therapeutic." The leaves of the tree can be likened to supernatural vitamins, since vitamins are taken not to treat illness, but to promote general health. Life in heaven will be fully energized and exciting.

The text does not say whether the saints will actually eat the leaves of the tree, though that is possible. Angels ate food with Abraham and Sarah (Genesis 18:1–8), as did Christ with His disciples after His resurrection (Luke 24:42–43; Acts 10:41). It is conceivable that the saints in heaven will eat, not out of necessity, but for enjoyment.

4. The Privileges of Its Inhabitants

There will no longer be any curse; and the throne of God and of the
Lamb will be in it, and His bond-servants will serve Him; they will see
His face, and His name will be on their foreheads. And there will no
longer be any night; and they will not have need of the light of a lamp
nor the light of the sun, because the Lord God will illumine them; and
they will reign forever and ever. (22:3–5)

As John toured the New Jerusalem, he couldn't help but notice that life
was very different for its inhabitants. The most dramatic change from the
present earth is that there "will no longer be any curse." As noted earlier,
the removal of the curse will mean the end forever of sorrow, pain, and
especially death—the most terrible aspect of the curse (Genesis 2:17).
Though there will be no temple in the New Jerusalem, "the throne of
God and of the Lamb will be in it." God the Father and the Lamb, Jesus
Christ, will reign throughout eternity. Since God will continue forever as
heaven's sovereign ruler, His bond-servants will serve Him forever. They
will spend all eternity carrying out the infinite variety of tasks that the
limitless mind of God can conceive. Incredibly, as the parable in Luke
12:35–40 indicates, the Lord will also serve them.

The saints in the New Jerusalem will also see God's face. Being perfectly holy and righteous, they will be able to endure the heavenly level
of the glorious light from God's presence without being consumed—
something impossible for humans on earth (Exodus 33:20).

The redeemed will also be God's personal possession. "His name will
be on their foreheads." That identification will leave no doubt as to who
they belong to forever. John repeats the earlier description of heaven's
magnificence: "And there will no longer be any night; and they will not
have need of the light of a lamp nor the light of the sun, because the Lord
God will illumine them" (cf. 21:22–26). Then he adds a final crescendo
describing the saints' heavenly experience: it will never end, because "they
will reign forever and ever."

The eternal capital city of heaven, the New Jerusalem, will be a place
of indescribable beauty. But the most glorious reality of all will be that

formerly sinful rebels will be made righteous, enjoy intimate fellowship with God and the Lamb, serve Them, and reign with Them forever in sheer joy and incessant praise.

24

Words of COMFORT *and Warning*

(22:6–21)

Verses 6–21 of this chapter form the epilogue to the book of Revelation. Having taken the reader through the amazing sweep of future history all the way into the eternal state, all that is left for John to record is this divine postscript. Verses 6–12 describe the responses expected of every believer to John's revelation. Verses 12–21 target unbelievers, warning them to change now while the opportunity is still available.

THE RESPONSES OF EVERY BELIEVER (22:6–12)

In a series of rapid-fire, staccato statements that move breathlessly from theme to theme, verses 6–12 outline the responses every believer should have to the imminent coming of the Lord Jesus Christ. The reality of our Lord's imminent return calls for four responses on the part of every believer:

1. Immediate Obedience
And he said to me, "These words are faithful and true"; and the Lord, the God of the spirits of the prophets, sent His angel to show to His

bond-servants the things which must soon take place. And behold, I am
coming quickly. Blessed is he who heeds the words of the prophecy of
this book." (22:6–7)

As the epilogue opens, John records that the angel who had shown him
the New Jerusalem (21:9; 22:1) said, "These words are faithful and true."
The words of the Apocalypse are as faithful and true as the One who
revealed them to John. John affirmed the angel's emphatic testimony to
the truthfulness of what he had seen and heard, writing that "the Lord,
the God of the spirits of the prophets, sent His angel to show to His bond-
servants the things which must soon take place." The God who moved the
spirits of His spokesmen the prophets to inspire both the Old and New
Testaments is the same God who sent His angel to show to His bond-
servants "the things which must soon take place." That is nothing short of
a claim by John for the full and complete inspiration of Revelation. The
prophecies recorded by those earlier biblical prophets were literally fulfilled, and those in Revelation will be as well.

"And" beginning verse 7 marks a change in speakers. The speaker is no
longer the angel who spoke in verse 6, but Jesus Christ, the One who is
coming quickly. He pronounces the sixth of seven beatitudes in Revelation
(the seven are shown in "The Seven Beatitudes of Revelation," chapter 1);
"Blessed is he who heeds the words of the prophecy of this book." Three
other times the words of Revelation are called prophecy (verses 10, 18,
19). Believers are called to guard or protect the book of Revelation. It must
be defended against those who deny its relevance, against critics who deny
its authority, and against interpreters who obscure its meaning. In fact, all
of Scripture is to be so guarded. Paul commanded Timothy, "Guard what
has been entrusted to you. . . . Retain the standard of sound words which
you have heard from me, in the faith and love which are in Christ Jesus.
"Guard, through the Holy Spirit who dwells in us, the treasure which has
been entrusted to you" (1 Timothy 6:20; 2 Timothy 1:13–14).

What does it mean, then, to "heed" the book of Revelation? It is a general command to long for Christ's return and our eternal fellowship with
Him. After reading Revelation, Christians should love Christ more, seek

to be more like Christ, hope for their resurrection bodies, and anticipate their eternal rewards. They should also understand the fearful judgment that awaits non-Christians, and call them to repentance and saving faith in the Lord Jesus.

2. Immediate Worship

I, John, am the one who heard and saw these things. And when I heard and saw, I fell down to worship at the feet of the angel who showed me these things. But he said to me, "Do not do that. I am a fellow servant of yours and of your brethren the prophets and of those who heed the words of this book. Worship God." (22:8–9)

Though not expressed in this translation, a form of "and" begins verse 8. As it did in verse 7, it marks a change of speakers. The speaker is no longer Christ, but John, who names himself for the first time since 1:9. The inspired apostle adds his testimony of the truthfulness of Revelation to that of the angel (verse 6), declaring "I, John, am the one who heard and saw these things." Then, overcome by what he heard and saw, John "fell down to worship at the feet of the angel who showed [him] these things." He had the proper response, worship, but inadvertently directed it to the wrong object. John simply collapsed in wonder and worship.

Because God alone is to be worshiped (Exodus 34:14; Matthew 4:10), the angel said to John, "Do not do that." He reminded the apostle that he, too, was a created being, declaring himself a fellow servant rather than an object of worship.

3. Immediate Proclamation

And he said to me, "Do not seal up the words of the prophecy of this book, for the time is near. Let the one who does wrong, still do wrong; and the one who is filthy, still be filthy; and let the one who is righteous, still practice righteousness; and the one who is holy, still keep himself holy." (22:10–11)

The message of the Apocalypse is not to be hidden. It is a message to be proclaimed to produce obedience and worship. John was instructed not to seal up the words of Revelation. Immediate proclamation of this book is called for because the end is near. Indeed, the coming of Christ has been imminent for every generation from John's day until the present.

That the specific words of Revelation are not to be sealed up stresses again that there is no hidden, secret meaning apart from the normal sense of the text. If the truth is not clear in those words, then this command is nonsense. If the plain, normal understanding of the words of Revelation does not convey the meaning God intended its readers to grasp, then those words *are* sealed.

The angel's next statement seems strangely out of place in this context: "Let the one who does wrong, still do wrong; and the one who is filthy, still be filthy; and let the one who is righteous, still practice righteousness; and the one who is holy, still keep himself holy." The truth it dramatically conveys is that a person's response to the proclamation of the truth will fix their eternal destinies. Those who hear the truth but continue to do wrong and be filthy will by that hardened response fix their eternal destiny in hell. On the other hand, the ones who continue to practice righteousness and keep themselves holy give evidence of genuine saving faith.

4. Immediate Service
"Behold, I am coming quickly, and My reward is with Me, to render to every man according to what he has done." (22:12)

The speaker is no longer the angel, but Christ, who repeats His declaration of verse 7, "Behold, I am coming quickly." Jesus' statement means that His coming is imminent. When He comes, Jesus will "bring His reward . . . with Him, to render to every man according to what he has done." Believers' eternal rewards will be based on their faithfulness in serving Christ in this life. The rewards believers enjoy in heaven will be capacities for serving God. The greater their faithfulness in this life, the greater will be their opportunity to serve in heaven (Matthew 25:14–30).

The knowledge that Jesus could return at any moment should not lead Christians to a life of idle waiting for His coming, but it should produce diligent, obedient, worshipful service to God and urgent proclamation of the gospel to unbelievers.

REASONS FOR RESPONDING TO GOD'S INVITATION (22:13–21)

In these its concluding verses, the Bible comes full circle. It opened with the promise of a coming Savior, who would redeem His people from their sins. That promise, which came immediately after the fall, is recorded in Genesis 3:15: "I will put enmity between you and the woman, and between your seed and her seed; he shall bruise you on the head, and you shall bruise him on the heel." Just as the Bible opens with the promise of Christ's first coming, so it ends with the promise of His second coming. God's final invitation to sinners comes in verse 17. Surrounding that invitation are several incentives designed to motivate people to respond to it.

The Invitation

The Spirit and the bride say, "Come." And let the one who hears say, "Come." And let the one who is thirsty come; let the one who wishes take the water of life without cost. (22:17)

There are two distinct invitations in this verse, separated by the two exclamations, "Come." The first part of the verse is a prayer addressed to Christ. The second part is an invitation addressed to unbelievers. The first part calls for Christ to come. The second part is the last call for unbelievers to come to faith in Christ.

To Jesus' promise of His imminent return (verses 7, 12, 20), the Holy Spirit responds, "Come." The text does not specify why the Spirit especially desires Jesus to return, but the rest of Scripture suggests both a negative and a positive reason.

Negatively, men and women throughout history have continually rejected Christ. Throughout the long, dark centuries of mankind's sin and rebellion, the Spirit has worked to bring about conviction and repentance (John 16:8–11). When the Lord Jesus Christ says He is coming, the Holy Spirit echoes, "Come." He pleads with Christ to return and end the Spirit's long battle to produce conviction in hard-hearted people. On the positive side, it is the desire and ministry of the Spirit to glorify Christ (John 16:14). The Spirit longs to see Jesus exalted in beauty, splendor, power, and majesty. That will happen when Christ returns in triumph at His second coming.

The Holy Spirit is not the only one who longs for Christ's return. Echoing His plea for Christ to come is the bride (the church). Throughout the centuries, God's people have waited for Christ's return. They long for Him to return and take them to heaven to live with Him forever (John 14:3; 1 Thessalonians 4:17). Believers are, in the words of Paul, those "who have loved His appearing" (2 Timothy 4:8). It is incongruous for someone to claim to love Jesus Christ and not long for His return.

The second use of the exclamation "Come" signals a change in perspective. The invitation is no longer for Christ to return, but for sinners to come to saving faith in Him. The phrase "let the one who hears say, 'Come'" invites those who hear the Spirit and the bride to join with them in calling for Christ's return.

The one who hears is further defined as "the one who is thirsty." Thirst is a familiar biblical concept picturing the strong sense of spiritual need that is a prerequisite for repentance. Earlier in Revelation He promised, "I will give to the one who thirsts from the spring of the water of life without cost" (21:6).

Adding another dimension to the invitation, John writes "let the one who wishes take the water of life without cost." That unlimited invitation is typical of the broad, sweeping, gracious offers of salvation made in Scripture. It also illustrates the biblical truth that salvation involves both God's sovereign choice (John 6:44) and human choice. God saves sinners, but only those who recognize their need and repent. The water of life is offered without cost to the sinner because Jesus paid the price for it through His sacrificial death on the cross.

The Incentives

"I am the Alpha and the Omega, the first and the last, the beginning and the end."

Blessed are those who wash their robes, so that they may have the right to the tree of life, and may enter by the gates into the city. Outside are the dogs and the sorcerers and the immoral persons and the murderers and the idolaters, and everyone who loves and practices lying.

"I, Jesus, have sent My angel to testify to you these things for the churches. I am the root and the descendant of David, the bright morning star." . . .

I testify to everyone who hears the words of the prophecy of this book: if anyone adds to them, God will add to him the plagues which are written in this book; and if anyone takes away from the words of the book of this prophecy, God will take away his part from the tree of life and from the holy city, which are written in this book.

He who testifies to these things says, "Yes, I am coming quickly." Amen. Come, Lord Jesus. The grace of the Lord Jesus be with all. Amen. (22:13–16, 18–21).

Surrounding the invitation in verse 17 are four incentives for sinners to accept it:

1. Because of Christ's Person (22:13, 16).

The first reason for sinners to accept God's final invitation is because it comes personally from Jesus Christ. The Lord's threefold identification of Himself repeats the same truth for emphasis. Since the original readers of Revelation spoke Greek, Jesus identifies Himself first as "the Alpha and the Omega." These words represent the symbols that form the first and last letters of the Greek alphabet. Together with the parallel phrases "the first and the last" (1:17) and "the beginning and the end," it expresses Christ's infinity, eternity, and boundless life transcending all limitations.

Christ further identifies Himself in His own words in verse 16. But before doing so, He tells John, "I, Jesus, have sent My angel to testify to you." Though angels communicated the Apocalypse to John, its source

was Jesus. The expression "I, Jesus" appears only here in the Bible. It establishes that this final invitation in Scripture is not a human invitation, but
a divine call issued personally to sinners by Jesus Christ. The Apocalypse
is addressed to the churches (1:11), though they are to proclaim it to the
entire world (22:10).

Then, in an astounding statement, Jesus declares Himself to be both
"the root and the descendant of David." That phrase sums up the biblical
teaching on Christ's two natures. Only the God-man can be both David's
ancestor and his descendant. In His deity, Christ is David's root (Mark
12:35–37). In His humanity, He is David's descendant (2 Samuel
7:12–16; Psalm 132:11–12).

Finally, Jesus describes Himself as "the bright morning star." To call
someone a star was to exalt him (Daniel 12:3). In extrabiblical Jewish
writings, the coming Messiah was called a star. As the morning star
announces the day's arrival, so Jesus' coming will announce the end of the
darkness of humanity's night and the glorious dawn of His kingdom.
Christ is the "Light of the world" (John 8:12) who calls sinners to drink
of the water of life.

2. Because of the Exclusivity of Heaven (22:14–15).

This section begins with the last of the seven beatitudes in Revelation,
each introduced by the pronouncement "blessed." This blessing is pronounced on "those who wash their robes." That phrase graphically portrays the believer's participation in the death of Christ (7:14). "Soiled
clothes" represent sinfulness in Isaiah 64:6 and Zechariah 3:3, whereas
Psalm 51:7; Isaiah 1:18; and Titus 3:5 speak of the cleansing of sin that
accompanies salvation.

Those who have experienced the washing from sin that marks salvation will forever have the right to the tree of life. The tree of life is located
in the capital city of heaven, the New Jerusalem. This will be the fulfillment of Jesus' promise, "To him who overcomes, I will grant to eat of the
tree of life which is in the Paradise of God" (2:7).

Heaven is exclusively for those who have been cleansed from their
sins by faith in the blood of Christ and whose names have been "written

from the foundation of the world in the book of life of the Lamb who has been slain" (13:8). In contrast, everyone else will remain forever outside the New Jerusalem in the lake of fire (20:15; 21:8). As in 21:8, a representative list of the type of sins that exclude people from heaven is given to John.

The inclusion of dogs on the list seems puzzling at first glance. But in ancient times dogs were not the domesticated household pets they are today. They were despised scavengers that milled about cities' garbage dumps. To call a person a dog was to describe that person as someone of low character (1 Samuel 17:43; 24:14). "Sorcerers" (from the root of the English word "pharmacy") refers to those engaged in occult practices and the drug abuse that often accompanies those practices. "Immoral persons" are those who engage in illicit sexual activities. "Murderers" are also excluded from heaven in the list given in 21:8. "Idolaters" are those who worship false gods, or who worship the true God in an unacceptable manner (21:8).

The final group excluded from heaven also includes "everyone who loves and practices lying." It is not all who have ever committed any of these sins who are excluded from heaven (1 Corinthians 6:11). Rather, it is those who love and habitually practice any such sin and refuse Christ's invitation to salvation who will be cast into the lake of fire.

3. *Because of the Truthfulness of Scripture* (22:18–19).

It is of great significance that the Bible closes with an affirmation of its truthfulness. The speaker who testifies to the authority and finality of the words of the prophecy of this book is none other than Jesus Christ. His solemn warning against tampering with Scripture applies first of all to the prophecy of the book of Revelation (1:3). The prohibition against altering the Apocalypse by implication extends to all of Scripture. Because Revelation describes the entire sweep of history from the close of the apostolic age to the eternal state, any alteration of it would be an alteration of Scripture.

4. Because of the Certainty of Christ's Return (22:20–21).

The book of Revelation and the Bible close with one final reminder and a benediction. In His last recorded words in Scripture, the Lord Jesus Christ, He who testifies to these things, affirms, "Yes, I am coming quickly." His coming is imminent, just as Revelation and the rest of the New Testament teaches. John speaks for all true believers when he responds, "Amen. Come, Lord Jesus."

The glorious, comforting truth is that those who humble themselves and accept God's offer of salvation will find Him gracious. Fittingly, the last words of the Bible, "the grace of the Lord Jesus be with all. Amen," are an expression of God's grace toward fallen humanity. The Lord of glory, as He promised in Scripture, offers heaven to those who, in light of His certain return, accept His gracious invitation and return to Him.

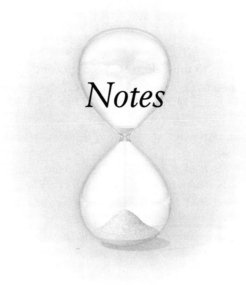

Notes

Introduction

1. Dialogue with Trypho, chapter 81.
2. Robert H. Mounce, *The Book of Revelation*, The New International Commentary on the New Testament (Grand Rapids: Eerdmans, 1977), 28.
3. Irenaeus, *Against Heresies*, 4.20.11.
4. Clement of Alexandria, *The One Who Knows God*, ed. and trans. David W. Bercot (Tyler, Tex.: Scroll Publishing, 1990), 48.
5. Irenaeus, *Against Heresies*, 5.30.3.

Chapter 2: The Preview of Christ's Return

1. Cited in Henry Bettenson, ed., *Documents of the Christian Church* (London: Oxford Univ. Press, 1967), 4.
2. Ibid, 2.
3. M. A. Smith, *From Christ to Constantine* (Downers Grove, Ill.: InterVarsity, 1973), 86.
4. F. F. Bruce, *New Testament History* (Garden City, N.Y.: Doubleday, 1972), 413.
5. R. J. Bauckham, "The Lord's Day," in D. A. Carson, ed., *From Sabbath to Lord's Day* (Grand Rapids: Zondervan, 1982), 221ff.
6. Robert Thomas, *Revelation 1–7: An Exegetical Commentary* (Chicago: Moody, 1992), 117.

Chapter 3: The Letter to the Believers at Ephesus

1. Francis Schaeffer, *The Mark of the Christian* (Downers Grove, Ill.: InterVarsity, 1970), 11.
2. William Barclay, *The Revelation of John*, vol. 1 (Philadelphia: Westminster, 1976), 60.

Chapter 4: The Letters to the Believers at Smyrna and Pergamum

1. For example, see Acts 2:13; 4:2–3, 18; 5:17–18, 28, 40; 6:9ff.; 7:54–60; 8:1ff.; 9:20–23; 12:1–3; 13:6, 45; 14:2, 19; 17:5ff., 13; 18:6, 12–13; 19:9; 20:3; 21:27ff.; 23:12ff.
2. Richard C. Trench, *Synonyms of the New Testament* reprint; (Grand Rapids: Eerdmans, 1983), 128–29.
3. Robert H. Mounce, *The Book of Revelation*, The New International Commentary on the New Testament (Grand Rapids: Eerdmans, 1977), 95.
4. William Ramsay, *The Letters to the Seven Churches of Asia* (Albany, Oreg.: AGES Software; reprint of the 1904 edition), 226.
5. Edwin Yamauchi, *New Testament Cities in Western Asia Minor* (Grand Rapids: Baker, 1980), 35–36.
6. Mounce, *The Book of Revelation*, 96.

Chapter 5: The Letters to the Believers at Thyatira and Sardis

1. William Ramsay, *The Letters to the Seven Churches of Asia* (Albany, Oreg.: AGES Software; reprint of the 1904 edition), 260.
2. The reference to the "little ones who believe" in Christ in Matthew 18:6 is not to physical children, but spiritual children—believers. It is so serious to lead another believer into sin that the Lord said death by drowning was a better option. The imagery of maiming oneself (18:8) is language depicting the need for drastic action in dealing with sin.
3. Edwin M. Yamauchi, *New Testament Cities in Western Asia Minor* (Grand Rapids: Baker, 1980), 65.
4. Robert L. Thomas, *Revelation 1–7: An Exegetical Commentary* (Chicago: Moody, 1992), 241.

Chapter 9: The Tribulation's Seal Judgments

1. Two similar cries can be seen in Hosea 10:8 and Luke 23:30, both in a time of national calamity for Israel. They are, to some degree, prophetic of the time referred to in the sixth seal.

Chapter 10: The Tribulation Saints

1. Robert L. Thomas, *Revelation 1–7: An Exegetical Commentary* (Chicago: Moody, 1992), 476.

2. Revelation 7:4–8 also teaches that the so-called ten lost tribes were, in fact, never lost (cf. 21:12; Matthew 19:28; Luke 22:30; James 1:1). Instead, representatives from the ten northern tribes filtered south and intermingled with the two southern tribes (cf. 2 Chronicles 30:1–11; 34:1–9) and thus were preserved.

3. For examples of God the Shepherd, see the Psalm 23, as well as Psalm 80:1; Isaiah 40:11; and Ezekiel 34:23. The New Testament describes Jesus as the Shepherd of His people in John 10:11ff.; Hebrews 13:20; 1 Peter 2:25; 5:4.

Chapter 11: The Six Trumpet Judgments

1. For a discussion of the use of drugs for religious experiences, see John MacArthur, *Ephesians*, The MacArthur New Testament Commentary (Chicago: Moody, 1986), 229–34.

Chapter 15: The Beast and His Prophet

1. In the 1995 text of the *New American Standard Bible*, the translators inserted the phrase "the dragon" in place of "he," since the dragon is the antecedent of the verb translated "he stood."

Chapter 16: Tribulation Announcements

1. Why the text does not use the definite article and read "the son of man" is not clear. Yet the phrase also appears without a definite article in its only other appearance in Revelation (1:13). Perhaps the article was omitted to strengthen the allusion to Daniel 7:13.

Chapter 18: The Religion of Babylon

1. James Allen, *What the Bible Teaches: Revelation* (Kilmarnock Scotland: John Ritchie, 1977), 424.

Chapter 21: The Millennium

1. Both amillennialist Floyd E. Hamilton and postmillennialist Loraine Boetttner acknowledge that a literal interpretation leads to a premillenial view. In *The Basis of Millennial Faith* (Grand Rapids: Eerdmans, 1942), 38, Hamilton writes, "Now we must frankly admit that a literal interpretation of the Old Testament prophecies gives us just such a picture of an earthly reign of the Messiah as the premillennialist pictures." See also Boettner, "A Postmillennial Response to Dispensational Premillennialism," in *The Meaning of the Millennium: Four Views*, Robert G. Clouse, ed. (Downers Grove, Ill: InterVarsity, 1977), 95.

Chapter 23: Everything New

1. Henry M. Morris has noted that "the language of the passage [is] much more naturally understood to mean a cube, with the length and breadth and height all the

EST BECAUSE THE TIME IS NEAR

same." He argues the pyramidal shape typically is associated with pagan worship, "with the pyramid's apex being dedicated to the worship of the sun, or of the host of heaven"; *The Revelation Record* (Wheaton, Ill.: Tyndale, 1983), 450.

Additional
RESOURCES

Allen, James. *What the Bible Teaches: Revelation*. Kilmarnock, Scotland: John Ritchie, 1997.

Barclay, William. *The Revelation of John*. Vol. Two. Philadelphia: Westminster, 1976.

Beasley-Murray, G. R. *The Book of Revelation*. The New Century Bible. London: Oliphants, 1974.

Beckwith, Isbon T. *The Apocalypse of John*. New York: Macmillan, 1919.

Criswell, W. A. *Expository Sermons on Revelation*. Grand Rapids: Zondervan, 1969.

Erdman, Charles R. *The Revelation of John*. Reprint. Philadelphia: Westminster, 1977.

Johnson, Alan F. *Revelation*. The Expositor's Bible Commentary. Grand Rapids: Zondervan, 1996.

Lenski, R. C. H. *The Interpretation of St. John's Revelation*. Minneapolis: Augsburg, 1943.

MacArthur, John F. *Revelation 1–11*. The MacArthur New Testament Commentary. Chicago: Moody, 1999.

_____. *Revelation 12-22*. The MacArthur New Testament Commentary. Chicago: Moody, 2000.

Morris, Henry M. *The Revelation Record*. Wheaton, Ill.: Tyndale, 1983.

Morris, Leon. *The Revelation of St. John*. The Tyndale New Testament Commentaries. Grand Rapids: Eerdmans, 1969.

Mounce, Robert H. *The Book of Revelation*. The New International Commentary on the New Testament. Grand Rapids: Eerdmans, 1977.

Phillips, John. *Exploring Revelation*. Rev. ed. Chicago: Moody, 1987; reprint; Neptune, N.J.: Loizeaux, 1991.

Ryrie, Charles C. *Revelation*. Everyman's Bible Commentary. Rev. ed. Chicago: Moody, 1996.

Seiss, Joseph A. *The Apocalypse*. Reprint, Grand Rapids: Kregel, 1987.

Swete, Henry Barclay. *Commentary on Revelation*. Reprint, Grand Rapids: Kregel, 1977.

Tenney, Merrill C. *Interpreting Revelation*. Grand Rapids: Eerdmans, 1957.

Thomas, Robert L. *Revelation 1–7: An Exegetical Commentary*. Chicago: Moody, 1992.

_____. *Revelation 8–22: An Exegetical Commentary*. Chicago: Moody, 1995.

Trench, Richard C. *Synonyms of the Greek New Testament*. Reprint; Grand Rapids: Eerdmans, 1983.

Vincent, Marvin R. *Word Studies in the Greek New Testament*. Reprint; Grand Rapids: Eerdmans, 1946.

Walvoord, John F. *The Revelation of Jesus Christ*. Chicago: Moody, 1966.

Subject
INDEX

ISBN-13: 978-0-8024-8160-3

"Sinners in the Hands of a Good God *is a wonderfully clear, readable, understandable study of the sovereignty of God and the problem of evil. David Clotfelter powerfully expounds the biblical doctrines of sin and grace—something desperately needed in a generation when both concepts have become terribly vague and confused in most people's minds.*"

– John MacArthur
Pastor, Author, and Speaker

by David Clotfelter
Find it now at your favorite local or online bookstore.

www.MoodyPublishers.com

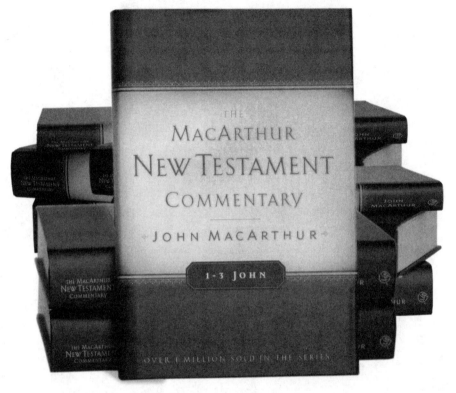